The date was

During a decade historic for change and innovation, it was an event that shook the innocence of pop music concerts into the sophistication of stadium rock. It was ground breaking and electrifying. It was a happening before the term *happening* was groovy. It survives in the memory of anyone who was there to experience the excitement, thrill, mania and love surrounding four young men who defined an image and created the soundtrack for a generation that came of age in the 1960s. For fans, associates and the innovators themselves, the echoes from a hot summer night in New York still resonate through the years.

The Beatles At Shea Stadium

The Story Behind Their
Greatest Concert

Dave Schwensen

North Shore Publishing

ALSO BY DAVE SCHWENSEN

The Beatles In Cleveland

How To Be A Working Comic

Comedy FAQs And Answers

Father's Days... And Nights

Comedy Workshop

TheClassicRocker.com

Dedication
To my family. All you need is love - and I love you guys!

In Memory
Peter Bennett and Clay Cole. It was my pleasure to connect with both during the writing of this book. They were informative, funny - and could talk your ear off, which I enjoyed immensely.

North Shore Publishing, Chicago, IL / Cleveland, OH
www.NorthShorePublishing.com

First Edition: April 2014

ISBN-13:978-0-9791030-2-5

ISBN-10:0979103029

Schwensen, Dave.
   The Beatles At Shea Stadium / Dave Schwensen
Includes Index

Cover Photo: George Orsino

Design: Arlan Frazier

Printed with love in the United States of America

"That concert in 1965 at Shea Stadium...
I saw the top of the mountain on that unforgettable night."
- John Lennon

Contents

New York, New York

The Concert

Making The Television Special

Final Words

Introduction

The Beatles' performance at New York's Shea Stadium on August 15, 1965 is one of the most exciting and important concert events in the history of popular music. Produced by Sid Bernstein and introduced on stage by television legend Ed Sullivan, John, Paul, George and Ringo played, sang, sweated and laughed for a record crowd of 55,600 fans. It was the height of Beatlemania and launched the modern era of outdoor stadium shows.

It had only been eighteen months since their U.S. television debut on *The Ed Sullivan Show*. Within that short period of time the Beatles had a continuing stream of chart-topping singles and albums, the film *A Hard Day's Night*, toured North America and other parts of the world, and kept a generation of fans waiting breathlessly for what they would accomplish next.

The album *Beatles VI* launched the second summer of Beatlemania in the U.S. on June 14th. On July 19th the title song from their next movie *Help!* was released, with the film and soundtrack album following on August 13th. Two days later they made history on a small stage in the middle of a huge stadium in New York.

In 1965 it was the largest pop-rock concert event to have ever taken place. But Shea Stadium wasn't big enough for everyone who wanted to be there. Only 55,600 seats? When compared to the number of fans that wanted to see the world's most famous foursome in person to scream themselves hoarse, stand and watch in envy, or later tell their children and grandchildren they had been an eyewitnesses to the phenomenon, Shea Stadium couldn't hold them all.

The excitement of anticipation and thrill of Beatlemania made it all seem to happen within the wink of an eye. And through it all, from one pinnacle to the next, the Beatles never gave us a chance to catch our breath and recover. Then again, if you lived through the 1960's you're probably still trying to recover.

The Beatles in the 1960s changed not only the music industry, but also the world. Their influence is still with us today and this is the story behind one of the biggest reasons why.

With A Little Help from My Friends

Authors can write firsthand accounts of their lives, experiences, thoughts and opinions. They can also create wonderful fiction based on historical and current events, or invent worlds, characters and situations that keep readers glued to every page.

When dealing with actual history, research is the key to getting it right. But to convey the *human factor*, the honest feelings, thoughts, sights, emotions, and excitement running through the words on each page, nothing speaks truer than the memories and insights from someone who actually lived it.

In putting together the facts of this historical event, the research was done. Books, articles, photos, audio recordings, and films were examined over and over. For the human factor a story this electrifying deserves, it was important to share the firsthand accounts from the following people who were there and felt the impact.

These are the eyewitnesses who lived the experience. I'm privileged as an author to be allowed to share their memories and insights in bringing this story to life.

•

Arthur Aaron has worked in the music industry for over four decades as an independent record producer, manager and music publisher. As **Sid Bernstein's** friend and official biographer, they co-authored *It's Sid Bernstein Calling...* and *Not Just The Beatles*. Arthur also gives lectures on Bernstein, the times he lived in, and his monumental contributions to the music industry.

Michael Adams is the son of **M. Clay Adams** who owned Clayco Films, Inc. and filmed the television special, *The Beatles At Shea Stadium*. Michael was on the field with the production crew during the concert.

Peter Altschuler is the son of legendary WINS New York deejay Murray Kaufman, better known as **Murray the K**. Often referred to as The Fifth Beatle, Murray was influential as the top rated deejay in New York in stoking Beatlemania in the U.S. and was an emcee at Shea Stadium. Peter curates The Murray the K Archives when he isn't recording audio books, performing in video and stage productions, or providing creative direction for ad campaigns at Wordsworth & Company. • murraythek.com • gorboduc.com.

Maxine Ascher was Personal Assistant to Sid Bernstein's good friend and financial backer, **Abe Margolies**. Maxine is still a Beatles fan and always will be.

Peter Bennett was named the World's Top Promotion Man by *Billboard Magazine* and hailed as the number one promoter in the entertainment business by *Rolling Stone*. *Performance Magazine* named him, "The world's most powerful man in the entertainment industry." *Billboard* wrote, "He made unknowns into stars and stars into superstars." Peter personally promoted over 200 Top Ten records by artists including The Beatles, and as solo artists John Lennon, Paul McCartney, George Harrison and Ringo Starr. Also Apple Records, The Rolling Stones, Elvis Presley, Michael Jackson, Aerosmith, The Who, Bobby Vinton, Bob Hope, Frank Sinatra and many others. He worked with George Harrison and Ravi Shankar in organizing the world's first fund raising rock concert, *The Concert for Bangladesh*, and promoted the album and movie. Peter along with The Beatles and The Rolling Stones changed the record and entertainment industries. Together they made history and changed the world.

Clay Cole was host of New York's top-rated pop music television program, *The Clay Cole Show*, from 1959 to 1968. Artists appearing on his show included The Rolling Stones, The Ronettes, The Four Seasons and many, many others. In June 1964 he presented *The Beatles vs. The Rolling Stones* and became the only television host to have both groups appear on the same show – The Rolling Stones live in the studio and The Beatles in a live broadcast from Chicago. He is the author of *Sh-Boom! The Explosion of Rock 'N' Roll 1953-1968*.

Ron Furmanek is a Grammy nominated producer and pioneer in remastering classic audio recordings, film and video for digital technology. Since 1988 he has produced over 200 titles for Apple, Capitol, RCA, EMI Records and others. An authority on the Beatles' recording and film history, he was a consultant and helped compile the vinyl releases of *Rarities* (1980) and *Reel Music* (1982). Based on the success of these projects, Ron was hired by Neil Aspinall and Apple to restore the Beatles' film archive. He has color corrected the film and remixed audio when needed on all of the Beatles promotional films, *The Beatles Live At The Washington Coliseum*, *Let It Be*, *Magical Mystery Tour* and as special interest to readers of this book, *The Beatles At Shea Stadium*.

Judith Kristen is an author, educator, champion for animal rights, and still a Flower Child in her 60's. But first and foremost, she is a Beatles fan – attending nine FAB concerts in total, including Shea Stadium in 1965. Her book, *A Date with a Beatle*, chronicles her days of 1964 Beatlemania with fun, excitement and adventure. Judith lives happily in The Garden State of New Jersey with her husband Andrew, two sheepdogs and five cats. • judithkristen.com • adatewithabeatle.com

Russ Lease is owner of R.W. Lease, Ltd/Beatlesuits.com specializing in tailoring detailed replications of Beatles stage apparel. Russ is the proud owner of the jacket worn by Paul McCartney at the 1965 Shea Stadium concert. • beatlesuits.com

Steve Marinucci worked over thirty seven years as a professional journalist at the *San Jose Mercury News* before moving to Examiner.com in 2006, where he is author of the *Beatles Examiner*, the best source of internet Beatles information, *Paul McCartney Examiner*, *Vintage Rock 'n 'Roll Examiner* and *TV on DVD Examiner* columns. His website, *Abbeyrd's Beatles Page* is widely regarded as the most accurate Beatle news source on the internet. • examiner.com/x-2082-Beatles-Examiner • http://abbeyrd.best.vwh.net

Ken Mansfield is the former U.S. manager of Apple Records and a Grammy Award winning producer. His association with The Beatles began in 1965 while he was with Capitol Records and continued through the legendary Apple rooftop concert and beyond. Ken is an ordained minister and in-demand public speaker. He is the author of *The Beatles, The Bible, and Bodega Bay*, *The White Book* and *Between Wyomings*. • fabwhitebook.com • aubaycom.com

Cousin Bruce Morrow is the top-rated deejay **Cousin Brucie** from New York's legendary WA-Beatle-C and member of the Radio Hall of Fame and National Association of Broadcasters Hall of Fame. Cousin

Brucie was instrumental in launching The Beatles in the U.S. by endorsing their early records, broadcasting live interviews from their hotel suites and as emcee for the 1965 concert at Shea Stadium. He went on to host the nationally syndicated *Crusin' America* and is author of *Cousin Brucie: My Life in Rock 'N' Roll Radio, Doo Wop: The Music, the Times, the Era,* and *Rock & Roll... And the Beat Goes On.* His show, *Crusin' with Cousin Brucie,* can be heard on both SIRIUS and XM radio. • sirius.com/cousinbrucie.

Joan Murray became America's first African-American female television newscaster in April 1965 when she joined CBS-TV in New York. She was host of the nationally syndicated radio program, *The Joan Murray Show,* and co-founder of The Zebra Agency, one of the first African-American advertising agencies. Among her exclusives were interviews with Dr. Martin Luther King, Walter Cronkite, and back stage with the Beatles in 1965 at both *The Ed Sullivan Show* and Shea Stadium concert. She is author of the book *The News: An Autobiography,* and proud to be a small plane pilot.

George Orsino is a retired Korean combat veteran and professional photographer from Philadelphia. His photos include the top entertainers from the city and many who passed through on tour. He was in The Beatles' dressing room and on the field during the 1965 Shea Stadium concert.

Scott Ross was assistant music director at 1010 WINS Radio in New York and popular deejay for station WBIC in Long Island. He is credited with taping one of the first interviews with The Beatles when they arrived in the U.S. and was an emcee during the 1965 concert at Shea Stadium. He has won *Billboard* and Angel Awards for excellence in radio and television, also nominated twice for ACE Awards for Best Interviewer, along with Larry King, Pat Buchanan and Dick Cavett, (King won). He is the former host of *The Scott Ross Show* on the Christian Broadcasting Network and currently an interviewer for *The 700 Club.* Scott is married to Nedra Talley-Ross of The Ronettes.

Ron Schneider was business manager for The Rolling Stones and executive producer of the concert film, *Gimme Shelter.* His financial innovations changed the way large stadium shows would be presented

---

during The Rolling Stones U.S. Tour in 1969 and the 1970 World Tour. During the late 1960's Ron also worked with his uncle Allen Klein and the Beatles in reorganizing Apple Corps. Ron attended the 1965 Shea Stadium concert with Klein, Peter Bennett, Mick Jagger and Keith Richards. • meandtherollingstones.com

Mimi Schwensen is a former Rockette at Radio City Music Hall in New York City's Rockefeller Center. On the night before the 1965 Shea Stadium concert, she had dinner with The Beatles and gave her cousin, (this author), an autograph to prove it.

Michael Sergio is the true definition of a Renaissance man living in New York City. He is an Emmy Award winning director, screenwriter, film producer, promoter, musician and actor with credits on Broadway, television and in films. He is also owner of the film distribution company, CAVU Pictures. Michael attended the 1965 concert by The Beatles and later burned his own image into the legend of Shea Stadium by parachuting onto the playing field during the sixth game of the 1986 World Series between the Mets and Red Sox. • cavupictures.com

Nedra Talley-Ross joined her cousins Veronica (Ronnie) and Estelle Bennett to form the legendary singing group, **The Ronettes**. Inducted into The Rock'n Roll Hall of Fame in 2007, the trio toured with The Beatles, recorded numerous hits and received Gold Record Awards for *Be My Baby*, *Baby, I Love You* and *Walking In The Rain*. The Ronettes first met the Beatles when they toured England in 1964 with The Rolling Stones as their opening act. Nedra is married to award-winning radio and television personality, Scott Ross.

Shaun Weiss is the son of **Nat Weiss** who was Brian Epstein's business partner, Beatles attorney, and ran The Beatles' U.S. Fan Club. Shaun's magical mystery tour took him from Beatles fan to Beatles insider. He is one of the few, (Paul and Ringo being the others), who can say he was at The Beatles first appearance on *The Ed Sullivan Show*, the 1965 Shea Stadium concert and their final public performance on the rooftop at Apple Corp.

The Fans in the Stands

As everyone knows, there could not be a book about The Beatles without mentioning their fans. The fans controlled the story. Regardless of how much talent, planning, publicity or even hype involved in building the lasting phenomenon of Beatlemania, it would not have happened if the fans hadn't fallen completely in love with the music and personalities of John, Paul, George and Ringo.

Each person in the selected group of contributors listed below has a story to tell. These are experiences, emotions and memories that inspire and drive this story. They were among the 55,600 who were at Shea Stadium on August 15, 1965 and witnessed an event no one had ever seen before. They were each a part of rock'n roll history.

Howie Altholz	Rick Andrews	Janice Bartel
Frank Branchini	Karen Bernstein	Marc Catone
Bob Eaton	Doug Fernandez	Judith Goodspeed
Diane Gunther	Eve Hoffman	Joyce Kaufman
Shirley Kellar	Arlene Levine	Rosemary McKinley
Pattie Noah	Dotty Poirier	Dan Reznicak
Ray Robinson II	Cindy Salvo	Joyce Shelfo
Debbie Stern	Mary Troumouhis	Steve Zisk

NEW YORK, NEW YORK

Pre-Fab 1963-1964

If I can make it there, I'll make it anywhere,
It's up to you, New York, New York. *

In 1963 it would be fourteen years before Liza Minnelli sang the title song for the Martin Scorsese film, *New York, New York*. Two years later Frank Sinatra made it his own with a version that has become an anthem for the city that never sleeps. But the lyrics were far from a new concept and only put into words the hopes and dreams of entertainers looking for the biggest stage, loudest applause and brightest fame.

In 1963 New York City was a magnet for musicians looking to make it. The earliest generation of rock'n roll performers, from Elvis Presley and Buddy Holly to Little Richard and Bo Diddley, had built grassroots popularity playing endless one-nighters throughout the South and Midwest, but had skyrocketed to new heights of fame with performances on *The Ed Sullivan Show* and at The Apollo Theater. An on-air stamp of approval from radio deejays Cousin Brucie and Murray the K could explode into national recognition and chart-topping hits. An appearance on New York's locally televised *The Clay Cole Show* could lead to prestigious gigs at Brooklyn's Paramount and Fox Theaters, Manhattan cabarets, and cover stories in national teen magazines.

In the early 1960's making it in New York City was the goal. But it wasn't easy. Some made it; most didn't. One review or a new trend could make or break performers overnight and often did.

By 1963 the Beatles were a chart-topping rock'n roll sensation in Europe. They had paid their dues with sweaty performances in Liverpool basement clubs and grimy bars in Hamburg, Germany. Swingin' London was now their home base from where they launched continuous tours of one-nighters in small theaters throughout the U.K.

The chaos and frenzy that followed the group at every stop was christened *Beatlemania* by the British press. Teenage girls screamed and fainted while boys stopped cutting their hair and wore Cuban-heeled boots with pointy toes to emulate the new heroes. Police protection and secretive plans worthy of a James Bond movie necessary to move The Fab Four safely from one place to another were headline news.

Arthur Aaron

In early 1963 Sid Bernstein took a course in Political Science at the New School for Social Research that was given by Max Lerner, who was a well known and respected political scientist and columnist. Lerner told his students that if they wanted to learn about democracy, they would have to learn about Great Britain. The course had a syllabus and Sid wasn't about to read the required books for Lerner's course. Because that was just Sid. He did, however, do what he thought was the next best thing and he started to read British newspapers.

He began to see small items about a music group called The Beatles. He would go every week to buy the newspapers. The articles about the Beatles began to proliferate and grow larger; from two columns... three columns... four columns...on and on. The articles would invariably speak about how this music group was selling out all their shows. And Sid remembered that the only two acts in his memory that did the same thing - sell-out - were Frank Sinatra and Elvis Presley. He intuited that this Beatles thing was a big and important happening.

Cousin Bruce Morrow

I started getting Beatles records in 1963, very early on. And we were listening to them but not really accepting it. You know; their earlier records. We didn't really love them that much. We were kind of thinking *how dare these upstarts take the American genre of rock'n roll and Anglophile it?* We didn't want to accept it for awhile, including myself.

We didn't realize that it was going to develop into a new energy for the rock'n roll genre, which was really having a tough time at that time. By 1963 it was getting very tired. And the record industry, as usual, had made a decision, *if it ain't broke, don't fix it.* So they left it alone. We didn't realize that this group was putting new energy into an American idiom, changing it a little bit and adding in an international flavor.

Clay Cole

In 1963 before the Beatles came, the music business in America was in a doldrums. There was nothing new, nothing fresh. There were answer records, the girl groups... It was just in a lull. There was nothing happening. America was ready for something new and different, because it was really at an all-time low. There was nothing new. *The Twist* had already died down by then and things were in a rut. Then bang! - came

> **"In 1963 before the Beatles came, the music business in America was in a doldrums. There was nothing new, nothing fresh." - Clay Cole**

the Beatles and it just revitalized the whole music business.

Still mostly unknown in America, Beatlemania was sweeping through England and Europe at newsworthy speed. The Beatles' first singles, *Love Me Do* and *Please Please Me*, set the stage for their debut chart-topping album, also titled *Please Please Me*, and were followed by the number one hits *From Me To You* and *She Loves You*. Britain's EMI Records was selling hundreds of thousands of copies in the U.K. alone, but couldn't convince their U.S. affiliate, Capitol Records, to follow their success in America.

In England, John Lennon, Paul McCartney, George Harrison and Ringo Starr were as recognizable as the Queen herself. But no one knew for certain how their fame would translate across the Atlantic. The key would be New York, New York. It started with a phone call from promoter Sid Bernstein to Beatles manager Brian Epstein in early 1963 proposing a concert at Carnegie Hall in February 1964. Both men were taking a chance on a group unknown to American teenagers, but made the deal hoping the Beatles would be on New York radio stations within the year. All they needed was a hit record.

Maxine Ascher

My late boss Abe Margolies was personal friends with Sid Bernstein. They grew up together. They were tremendous friends. He's the one that lent Sid the money to bring The Beatles over for Carnegie Hall.

I started working for him in 1963 and was his personal assistant. He was a jewelry manufacturer, and was the kind of man that people wanted to know. He had tickets to everything. For all of us in the office, there was nothing we didn't see if we wanted to. We did everything.

They grew up in the Bronx together and Sid was always going to Abe for money. According to what Sid told everybody, he had taken a course at The New School and they said to step out of your comfort zone and do something. He had heard of the Beatles through the show business grapevine and he found Brian Epstein and they put this deal together to bring the Beatles here.

Peter Altschuler

My father, Murray the K, was sought out by Beatles manager Brian Epstein. When the American girl groups were touring in England and would open for the Beatles, Epstein talked with them about who were the people that the Beatles needed to be in touch with in the United States in order to make that transition. A lot of them like The Ronettes, The Shirelles and all those groups that appeared on Murray's rock'n roll shows at the Brooklyn Fox Theater said if you want to make it in The United States, you've got to make it in New York. And to make it in New York, the surest person to get in the good graces of is Murray the K, because he had the biggest radio audience and the highest ratings. He was more or less king of the hill, so he didn't seek out the Beatles.

Murray played one of their early records on *The Record Review Board*, which was his nightly segment where he played five records and the listeners got to vote on which ones they liked. So it was like, "Okay, it's some group from Britain and they have a number that sounds okay. I'll put it on *The Record Review Board*." But the listeners didn't respond to it particularly. Whatever the Beatles tune was it came in third or fourth out of five.

Murray based most of his show on those listeners. What it was that worked and didn't work for them. He had *The Record Review Board* and his pick hits of the week that he'd take a chance on. So he did ongoing marketing research and that gave him a sense of what the kids liked and what they didn't like.

Peter Bennett

I was there when Murray the K played a Beatles record in New York and it bombed. I was right there in the studio and it came in fifth in his voting contest.

•

When Bernstein made the deal in March 1963 for the Beatles to play Carnegie Hall, he thought the wave of Beatlemania would hit before Epstein's deadline. But in October, the Beatles still had no airplay on U.S. radio stations and no one seemed to know who they were.

Then fate stepped in. During a stop at London's Heathrow Airport on October 31st, television host Ed Sullivan took notice of screaming fans welcoming the Beatles back from an appearance in Sweden. After learning they were a singing group and not an animal act, which were the type of performances he also presented on his Sunday evening variety show, he returned to New York and made a few calls.

Cousin Bruce Morrow

Now, Sullivan was a square. He didn't even know who the Beatles were, very honestly. At that time he was just getting an idea. He had to call Walter Cronkite to find out who the Beatles were. That's how Cronkite's daughter got the ticket to be on camera that day in the studio when The Beatles first appeared on *The Ed Sullivan Show*. And that's how Sullivan found out about The Beatles; from Walter Cronkite.

●

Sullivan contacted Brian Epstein, who told him the group had already been booked by Bernstein for two shows in Carnegie Hall on February 12th. Sullivan talked with Bernstein to confirm the date, then called Epstein and scheduled the Beatles for three headlining appearances on his show. The first would be on February 9, 1964.

For Bernstein it was like hitting the lottery. Even without radio play, an appearance on *The Ed Sullivan Show* only three days before Carnegie Hall would guarantee a sell-out.

The Beatles were poised to release their second album, *With The Beatles*, on November 22, 1963; a date memorable on both sides of the Atlantic, but for different reasons. The newest collection of songs by The Fab Four was destined to sit at the top of the British album charts for over twenty weeks, while the assassination of President John F. Kennedy in Dallas would send the U.S. into a tailspin of mourning.

Peter Bennett

The Beatles were getting big in Europe and Ed Sullivan put them on his show. They had that certain sound and when you looked at them, it was a new look. That's how the whole thing started over here. *The Ed Sullivan Show* is what did it. It was a new look on that stage.

Actually, the music industry and the country were waiting for something like this. You know, you had John F. Kennedy's assassination and the morale of the whole country was down. You needed an explosion like this.

•

The explosion began just before Christmas in 1963 when a disk jockey in Washington, D.C. played an imported copy of *I Want To Hold Your Hand*. The response from teenage listeners was overwhelming and Capitol Records, which had rejected all earlier songs by The Beatles offered by its parent company EMI Records in England, agreed to release the record.

Once again the timing could not have been better for Sid Bernstein. Just over a month before their arrival, New York disk jockeys began filling the airwaves with, "All Beatles all the time." Within weeks it had sold over a million copies and by January 17th it was the number one single in America. In New York City alone it was reportedly selling more than 10,000 copies every hour.

> **"Did we know that that era was going to be a special time that would go down in history the way it's gone down? I don't think so.."**
> **- Nedra Talley-Ross**

He knew the publicity generated by an appearance on *The Ed Sullivan Show* only three days before his bookings at Carnegie Hall would be priceless. If the Beatles were to be as popular in America as in Europe, they would never have a better opportunity than the one-two punch of Ed Sullivan and Sid Bernstein. The stars and planets seemed to be aligning in their favor. They had a hit record.

Peter Altschuler

Murray had been on vacation in Miami at the Fontainebleau Hotel when he got a call from the station that he had to come back because of the Beatles. His immediate reaction was, "Why call me? Just get an exterminator." Murray couldn't remember them.

Nedra Talley-Ross

We met the Beatles in January '64 because I remember turning eighteen in England. My birthday is January 27th and we were in England on my birthday.

The Ronettes were known for our look. With fashion in the 60's, the skirts were really tapered or you wore a flair dress. But we danced a lot and if you wore a flair dress, what could you see of your dancing? So we wore form fitting dresses with slits and a lot were with the Oriental collar that was up high. Our hair was extremely high and we wore strong eye makeup, because for someone to see your eyes from a distance, we used very high, dark eyeliner.

That was part of it; the high hair, the dark eye makeup, the slits, the dancing, the turning around, the raising of our arms and then shaking. That was our little Ronette thing and I think that made people go…

Well, from a distance on stage, you couldn't tell what we were. We had a lot people saying, "Oh they're this, they're that, they're Oriental." No…

A part of the whole thing of the Ronettes was that we were seen as this really seductive girl group. We were the bad girls of rock'n roll. But my mother and my Aunt B.B., who was mother to Ronnie and Estelle, would travel with us. We also had aunts and uncles who went on the road, so we always had someone family-wise with us. So where people thought, *oh, they're just having a ball on their own*, it wasn't really like that. You were there, but you were with your mom in the next room. You weren't doing too much.

Because we were this seductive looking girl group like they had never seen before, we really made an impact when we went to England in early '64. And with the press being the way it was over there, they were going, "The Ronettes Arrive!" We couldn't believe it. We didn't get that kind of thing in America. We were rock'n rollers.

When we were in England, whoever the people were who brought us there said there was this group called The Beatles and they would love to have a get together. They wanted to give us a party to welcome us to England. So we were like, "Okay!"

Now in reality, we're sitting in America and don't know who is doing what in England. Maybe I wasn't thinking about who was big or getting big or whatever. So we went to this party they were giving us. And you have to remember how very young we all were when we were doing this.

I'd had a recording contract by the time I was fifteen. I would do a sock hop on the weekend, go back to school on Monday and tell my music teacher and the class about it. I didn't have to sing a note to pass the class.

So at this party, we all literally acted like kids. I don't know what was wrong with us, if it was just a release from the touring schedule, or acting young or stupid. We played *Tag* with the Beatles. We literally played games and were running. I just remember running in the living room and doing all this stupid stuff. Isn't that funny?

We were also talking about America. The Beatles were totally enamored by stuff from America.

Clay Cole

Capitol Records plastered the city with something like 50,000 signs and bumper stickers. They created the mayhem and the hype that everybody bought into. There were billboards and signs and bumper stickers and radio deejays heralding the arrival. It was almost like the Martians had landed in New York City. There were these four alien boys who had this strange accent and these strange haircuts. And their music was something so totally different from the music that was currently being played in America. The girl groups and the teenage idol boys were wiped right out when The British Invasion began with The Beatles.

The 1960's were a challenging time, but a lot of the changes can be linked to the Beatles. When they first came here they were singing *Puppy Love* types of songs. They were neatly dressed in Mohair suits, velvet collars, little ties and pointy shoes. They were well groomed and scrubbed. And they were innocent and charming with songs about little teenaged puppy love. *I Want To Hold Your Hand* or lyrics like "Let me whisper in your ear" or "She loves you, yeah, yeah, yeah." But as they proved later, when they could get into the recording studio and really do some heavy work, they wrote incredible and inspiring music that again, changed the music industry.

In the beginning the buzz was all hype. The whole British Invasion was plotted by American agents and American promotion people and American record companies. It was all designed and formatted and accomplished by Americans. They created the British Invasion through a lot of hype and money. And it certainly worked.

But it wouldn't have worked if the Beatles hadn't had talent. That would've been a quick fade-out like some of the other English groups did. If they had just stuck to their novelty songs you'd never hear from them again. But the Beatles had a lot of power in their minds and were able to create music beyond anything that we had ever heard before.

Nedra Talley-Ross

The Invasion was really an *invasion*. It affected America and the American artist in a major way. And I think there's that side of people where it's easy to be followers. So there was this stampede and everybody got caught up in it. And it did take out a lot of American artists; totally. I would've hated to be a boy group at that time.

It wasn't totally where America was forsaking all that was American. There were a few who held on. The Beach Boys and The Four Seasons held the American sound, but the girls did go hysterical for the English boys and it ended the careers of a lot of American artists. I had mixed feelings because I was American. I'm glad we're all happy that the Beatles had come, but what about all the artists that they're knocking out here?

Clay Cole

I loved every British act that came on my television show and I was happy to present them. But not at the expense of American groups. I fought that bitterly. The disk jockeys turned their backs totally on all the American acts in order to exploit the British Invasion stuff on their station. And that to me was cruel and unusual punishment to a guy who had done interviews with them or free record hops, or they enhanced their credibility in each of their little towns. It just wasn't fair that all of a sudden it was "All Beatles all the time," or all British Invasion music.

Many, many, many careers were ended. They just never had another record. That's why I continued to have American artists on in equal to British artists on my show. Radio stations forgot about the American artist for awhile, but all is forgiven.

Nedra Talley-Ross

Oh yeah, the Ronettes worked with Clay Cole a lot. We were part of a review with Clay and The Capris, and some other groups. We did quite a few shows together. It was a wonderful and exciting time.

Peter Bennett

To me, it was the timing of the whole thing. That's what I would say. The guys wrote great songs and they were great musicians. They changed all the music and took over the rock field at that time. I'd been promotions manager with The Rolling Stones since 1963 and with The Animals, The Dave Clark Five, Herman's Hermits and The Kinks. Before that I was with Nat King Cole, Stevie Wonder and Sam Cooke. I'm the one who plugged their records and enhanced their careers. The Beatles changed everything radio-wise and it helped the records I was promoting.

They were different characters. You had Elvis Presley come in and change a lot. But the Beatles were something different. It was a different look. It was a different sound. There was a hook there and the hook was also their looks. It's like a hook with Madonna. Everybody wanted to dress like Madonna. Then you got a hook with Lady Gaga. But it doesn't compare to the Beatles. And not only that, you had "Beatles." You know what I mean? That was another good hook.

•

Before they ever played a note in America, *I Want To Hold Your Hand* was the number one song on both the *Billboard* and *Cash Box* list of Top 100 Singles. Sid Bernstein's two shows were completely sold-out, along with a pre-Carnegie Hall warm-up in Washington, D.C. scheduled by Brian Epstein for February 11th.

"Murray the K was as mad as a hatter, a fabulous guy, a great deejay and he knew his music. In New York there was him, and the deejay Cousin Brucie." - Ringo Starr (1)

Over a year's worth of hit songs rejected by Capitol Records were now hits for obscure labels including *Love Me Do*, (Tollie), *Please Please Me* and *From Me To You*, (Vee-Jay), and *She Loves You*, (Swan). Tracks from the albums *Introducing The Beatles* and *Meet The Beatles*, U.S. counterparts to earlier U.K. releases *Please Please Me* and *With The Beatles*, were also in heavy rotation on Top 40 radio stations throughout the country.

New York fans craving anything and everything Beatles-related knew where to tune in their radio dials. Beatles songs were spun one after another and sometimes repeatedly between fast talking banter from deejays on WINS, ("Ten Ten Wins"), the "All Americans" on WABC, (WA-Beatle-C), and WMCA with their lineup of "Good Guys." Among the most influential in growing Beatlemania from a fad into a phenomenon was Murray the K on WINS and Cousin Brucie on WABC.

Cousin Bruce Morrow

They came to New York and I remember they were aboard Pam Am Flight 101. And this is a famous story; John Lennon said to Paul McCartney as they were looking down, "Where are the streets paved with diamonds and gold?"

•

At approximately 1:30 in the afternoon on Friday, February 7, 1964, the Beatles arrived at New York's newly-named John F. Kennedy International Airport. Pop music's newest sensations waved to over three thousand screaming fans before they were ushered inside by police for a televised press conference. Waiting for them were an army of seasoned New York reporters, photographers and deejays who had yet to be convinced Beatlemania was more than a passing fad.

Start spreading the news I'm leaving today.
I want to be a part of it, New York, New York. *

Cousin Bruce Morrow

Clay Cole (center) with The Ronettes and The Capris

Murray the K with The Ronettes
Left to right - Nedra, Veronica (Ronnie) and Estelle

73 Million Viewers Can't Be Wrong

The 1960's were moving at breakneck speed. In the U.S. it began with the reins of power passing from the old guard to a charismatic and youthful president, John F. Kennedy. America in general reflected a post World War Two image of prosperity and comfort. *The Adventures of Ozzie and Harriett, Leave It to Beaver* and Sheriff Andy Taylor keeping the small TV town of Mayberry safe represented The American Dream. But for the generation that started as baby boomers and would evolve into The Flower Power Generation and The Woodstock Generation before the end of the decade, the 1960's really didn't start until JFK went to Dallas and the Beatles landed in New York.

Cousin Bruce Morrow

If you go back to the press conference they had when they landed at JFK Airport, there was a make shift press room set up with hundreds of cameras and reporters. And the reporters were kind of snide to them because at that time rock'n roll was a no-no. Rock'n roll was something that the kids wanted and that the parents were afraid of. You know, anytime something new comes in that is obviously going to take over from the preceding generation, the preceding generation gets very nervous because they don't want to pass the baton and lose the power.

By the time the Beatles came over, everyone was very aware that rock'n roll was going to become the king and mom and dad's music was going to be put under the carpet where it should have been put. At least that's my opinion, because it was kind of a mediocre decade. It was only ten years, thank God. It served as the transformation for pop music, which is necessary. Each preceding decade helps transform into the next decade of music. As it does history.

At that first press conference the reporters were not really nice to them. They were pretty rude. One of them asked, I think it was to Ringo, "Why don't you get a haircut?" And Ringo had a snide remark and it didn't go well and it made them even more nervous.

I remember after the press conference I met with them privately for a little while. That's where we really became friendly because they knew I was playing all of their music quite a bit on WABC. We became WA-Beatle-C.

They asked me why the press was so negative towards them and I explained that they're not negative; they're just doing their job. They represent mom and dad and right now mom and dad are the ones who read the newspapers. They also buy the cars and the clothes and are very nervous about this new phase of rock'n roll. After all, I said, "Look at you guys. You look different. Look at the length of your hair."

Of course their hair was nothing then. Little did mom and dad know what was going to happen a decade later when you couldn't see anybody because of their hair. So that press conference was kind of a tough one for the Beatles and it made them even more nervous.

Nedra Talley-Ross

They had the press taking every word they said and tearing it apart. And you had the people that were more from the south knocking them down and going, "Who are these people? We don't want our girls looking at them and screaming and fainting. And we don't want our boys letting their hair grow like them." And the Beatles were sitting there going, "What is this all about?" On one side they had people loving them and then another side they had people coming up against them.

Michael Sergio

It's so funny… When the Beatles first came out everybody said, "Oh, they're dangerous. They're dirty. They're bad." Then the Rolling Stones came out and all of a sudden the Beatles looked like choir boys. And if you look back at the Beatles today, they're like a church group. They're the most innocent things, even with the little Beatle haircuts that had people saying, "Oh, that's terrible. Look at them." You look at those little bowl haircuts and they look like four little guys from Catholic School or Protestant School or something.

Cousin Bruce Morrow

I remember learning sort of a good lesson. We thought maybe the Beatles would be a good six months flash in the pan and not have any sociological significance. Now when I look at something new happening, I always look at the sociological part of it too:

Is this going to have any effect on people in the way they speak, the way they wear their hair, the way they dress, the way they think?

When the Beatles came in we had no idea how things would change. I'll give you a quick little story here…

The Beatles got so involved in our lives that here's a guy we'll call Johnny. And Johnny came from 'Da Bronx. He called me on WABC one week before the Beatles came and said, "Hey Brucie! Will'ya play a record for me and my gurl. Yeah, Suzanne and I wanna hear The Falcons' *You're So Fine*." It was something like that because that's how we talked; in that kind of style.

Three weeks after The Beatles arrive, here's the same kid calling me on WA-Beatle-C: "'Ello? Sir Brucie, this is Sir Johnny of the Bronxshire. Would you mind playing a song for me and me bird?"

That really happened, by the way. So what I'm doing in a little silly way is showing you how people began to speak the King's English. It was a sociological change.

Clay Cole

The thing that really happened when they came to town is that all the radio guys really jumped on top of them. They were lined up in the halls of the hotels trying to get a sound bite or get a picture taken with them and all that. It was their duty to do it for their radio station.

Peter Altschuler

Murray the K didn't give himself the Fifth Beatle moniker. George Harrison said that on the train down to Washington. If you take a look at the Maysles film *The Beatles – The First Visit*, you can see the boys moving through the car. I don't know if they have a shot of Murray in that procession, but he was following them as they moved through the train. A conductor or security person tried to stop him and George turned around and said, "It's okay. He's the Fifth Beatle."

Murray just grabbed it and held onto it. It made sense because in any business you're going to take whatever advantage you can get. He already had Epstein coming to him. He might as well have taken whatever he could have gotten.

In the aftermath of all of this, people kept saying, "Murray the K rode to fame on the coattails of the Beatles, he had no talent, blah, blah, blah…" But by the time the Beatles came to the United States, Murray had been running shows at the Brooklyn Fox Theater for five years and before that with Clay Cole at the Brooklyn Paramount. He put on shows that people wanted to see with performers like Sammy Davis Jr., Eddie Fisher and Dean Martin and then went on into the rock'n roll business.

He brought The Rolling Stones to the attention of Sid Bernstein and in fact gave the Stones their first number one hit by suggesting they cover *It's All Over Now*. Murray co-wrote *Splish-Splash* with Bobby Darin and told Dionne Warwick that he wasn't going to play the A-side of what was considered to be her last attempt at a big hit. He was going to play the B-side which was *Walk On By*.

Shaun Weiss

Nat Weiss is my father and was Brian Epstein's partner. He was an attorney, but with the Beatles he ran the fan club. He got involved with them in late '64, but it wasn't official until '65. Before that Nat had heard of them, but never knew he was going to be involved with them. Here's what happened.

Nat was coming back from a Caribbean vacation on Friday, February 7, 1964. My sister and I went to the airport to pick them up and there was this tremendous... There were an awful lot of girls there and my sister knew some of them. And lo-and-behold it turns out to be the Beatles arriving.

So that afternoon we drove my parents back to the city and one of my sister's friends said the Beatles were at The Plaza Hotel. My sister wanted to go, but I didn't want to go see anybody called The Beatles. Nat knew nothing of the Beatles at this time.

I decided to go and we stood outside with all the fans. Then that night we were walking home. It must have been about 11:30 and we were on the side of the Plaza Hotel where the movie theater is. I heard English voices. They were in a covered area and I could hear them through the outside entrance. I went up to one of them and said, "Are you one of the Beatles?"

He said, "No, I'm their road manager. My name is Mal." That's the first time I met Mal Evans. We started talking and he asked me if I knew a place where they could have a drink. I was only seventeen, but knew there was a bar up the street.

I went back Saturday morning and Mal was walking out. He wasn't known by the fans, so I went up to him and said hi. He asked how I was and I asked if I could meet the Beatles. He said no because they were going to rehearse for *The Ed Sullivan Show*. So that afternoon we stayed at the hotel with all the girls chanting, "We want The Beatles!" and all that stuff.

On Sunday morning we went back to the hotel, but knew the Beatles were gonna be on *The Ed Sullivan Show*. So I went with my sister and a couple of her friends over to the CBS Studios.

> **"It was almost like the Martians had landed in New York City. There were these four alien boys who had this strange accent and these strange haircuts." - Clay Cole**

Cousin Bruce Morrow

That day I was not in the Sullivan Theater. WABC sent me and I was directly outside the theater. It looked like New Year's Eve that night. You couldn't see. The kids pushed to get near the Beatles and the crowds stretched from The CBS Studios, which is on 53rd Street, all the way down into the 40's. It was like celebrating New Year's Eve.

Shaun Weiss

When we got to the CBS Studios where they did *The Ed Sullivan Show*, people were waiting in line to get in. My sister befriended these two people who must have been in their fifties and they had four tickets. My sister asked them if she could have two and they said they had friends coming. But if they didn't come, they would give my sister the two tickets.

The reality was their friends did come and my sister started crying. These friends were older than the people they were meeting and when they saw all the kids they didn't want to go in. So the lady gave my sister the tickets.

When you went into the theater they would separate you. People that were dressed up and in ties would go to the front and we got shoved up into the balcony.

Mimi Schwensen

I was a Rockette at Radio City Music Hall in 1964. We were the line of high-kicking dancers and did four performances a day between showings of whatever big movie was out. While the movie was playing, we'd go to a dance class in between shows and then run back in time to dance the next show. It was a busy schedule and we were not allowed to miss a performance. If you missed a show you could lose your job.

> **"I've heard that while the show was on there were no reported crimes, or very few. When The Beatles were on *Ed Sullivan*, even the criminals had a rest."**
> **- George Harrison** (2)

Our dance studio was a few blocks away and in the same building as *The Ed Sullivan Show* on 53rd Street and Broadway. We were upstairs and the television studio was on the first floor.

I was taking a class that Sunday when the Beatles were on and because of all the fans and chaos outside, security shut down the building. They wouldn't let anyone in or out and that included me. I remember looking out the window when the Beatles arrived. I could see the tops of their heads as they went in the building.

I wasn't too happy about this because I couldn't get out. I missed our show at Radio City and almost lost my job. Because of The Beatles I almost got fired.

Shaun Weiss

When the Beatles came out there was so much screaming that I really just got caught up in the moment. I got mesmerized by these four guys with long hair. I'd heard their music because Murray the K would play it all day long, so I got caught up in the hoopla and became a fanatic. That Monday morning when I went to school my hair was down and I was talking about the Beatles and how mesmerized I was with them.

•

The Beatles' appearance on *The Ed Sullivan Show* drew a then television record with more than 73 million viewers and changed the nation's music industry almost overnight. On Tuesday their sold-out concert in Washington, D.C., where they performed in the Washington Coliseum on a boxing ring with the ropes removed and surrounded by screaming fans, was filmed and shown a month later in theaters across the country as a closed-circuit broadcast. The next evening at Carnegie Hall the demand for tickets was so overwhelming that Bernstein arranged to have three hundred additional chairs placed on stage during both shows. Every move they made was a newsworthy event and their songs dominated the airwaves and record charts. Beatlemania had a firm grip on the city and the nation, and wasn't about to let go.

Cousin Bruce Morrow

It was reported that evening when *The Ed Sullivan Show* was on there wasn't one teenage crime committed in the United States. Everybody was glued their TV sets. Including the parents who made believe they didn't like them.

•

Unfortunately for the juvenile crime rate, the Beatles' reputation as excellent babysitters between 8 and 9 pm that Sunday when they appeared on *The Ed Sullivan Show* was built on a miscommunication.

A columnist for the *Washington Post* was actually knocking the group's fans and image by saying teenagers who would normally be out stealing hubcaps on a Sunday night related more to The Beatles than law abiding, (and undoubtedly short-haired), teens who would never stay out past dark. In other words, the criminals were held captive by their assumed peers on television. This meant-to-be insult was picked up out of context and given a positive spin by *Newsweek* magazine later in the month and has lived on in Beatles legend ever since.

> **"When The Beatles came in we had no idea how things would change."**
> **- Cousin Bruce Morrow**

Peter Bennett

The Ed Sullivan Show blew it wide open and it changed into a different field. At that time you had The Beach Boys, but then this took over the trend.

Nedra Talley-Ross

I don't think any of us (performers) would've dared think that way. When you're young you live for the moment. You may have dreams, aspirations and all these things, but to the degree that it happened…

We dreamed, but we did not dream on the level, I don't think, that it all became. Did we know that that era was going to be a very special time that would go down in history the way it's gone down? I don't think so.

•

The Beatles' first visit to The United States and in particular New York City, laid the groundwork for the onslaught that would follow. The British Invasion was in full swing with chart-topping songs and *Ed Sullivan Show* appearances from The Dave Clark Five, Gerry & The Pacemakers, Peter and Gordon, The Animals, Herman's Hermits, The Rolling Stones and seemingly just about every thin, long-haired boy with an English accent and a guitar.

On April 4th, within two months of their U.S. arrival, the top five songs on *Billboard Magazine's Hot 100* were held by The Beatles (3):

1. *Can't Buy Me Love*
2. *Twist and Shout*
3. *She Loves You*
4. *I Want To Hold Your Hand*
5. *Please Please Me*

The Beatles popularity continued to surge as they moved beyond the small screen and into theaters as stars of the critically acclaimed film, *A Hard Day's Night*. John, Paul, George and Ringo became four recognizable parts of the whole that even parents of crazed teenagers could tell apart from under their shaggy heads of hair. Their 1964 late summer and early fall tour of North America established the new borderline for the generation gap as most adults continued to shake their bobbed or greased back hair in disbelief while baby boomer teens and preteens lingered under their trance and waited breathlessly for the next invasion. It came in 1965 and started in New York with a phone call from Sid Bernstein to Brian Epstein.

NEMS ENTERPRISES LTD

DIRECTORS: B. AND C. J. EPSTEIN

SUTHERLAND HOUSE, 5/6 ARGYLL STREET, LONDON, W.1

TELEPHONE: REGENT 3261

13 January, 1965

Mr. Bob Precht
CBS-TV
New York, N.Y.

Dear Bob,

Just a note to advise you that I am coming into New
York for a few days next Tuesday, January 19th, and
will be staying, as usual, at the Plaza.

I would particularly like to meet with you and Ed
while I am in New York, to discuss the possibility of
the Beatles' next appearance on your show, assuming
that you are interested.

In any event, I will look forward to seeing you
during my stay.

Best wishes.

Yours sincerely,

Brian Epstein

OFFERS CONTAINED IN THIS LETTER DO NOT CONSTITUTE CONTRACTS
LICENSED ANNUALLY BY THE LONDON COUNTY COUNCIL

Letter from Brian Epstein to *The Ed Sullivan Show* producer Bob Precht

Mania of '64
Into Phenom of '65

The Beatles debut on *The Ed Sullivan Show*, *A Hard Day's Night* and their victory tour through arenas and theaters in the U.S. and Canada during August and September were needed feel good stories of 1964. Lurking behind the scenes were troop buildups in Vietnam, racial unrest simmering to a boil in major cities, the Cold War buildup of nuclear weapons, a Space Race to claim (and possibly arm) the moon, and a younger population that wasn't going to sit back quietly and accept it as their destiny. It would be hard to find a truer lyric than when Bob Dylan sang, "The times they are a changin'."

Without waiting for fans to catch their collective breaths following their 1964 North American tour, Sid Bernstein was already planning the next onslaught of Beatlemania on New York. In the months since his two sold-out shows at Carnegie Hall, the group's popularity had soared into unforeseen heights. Still in their early twenties, John, Paul, George and Ringo were recognized individually around the world and had sold more than one hundred million records. The phenomenon continued non-stop in North America, Great Britain and spread with tours to Denmark, The Netherlands, Hong Kong, New Zealand, and Australia

As the world's newspapers reported that summer, more than 300,000 people had turned out just to watch the Beatles wave from their hotel balcony in Adelaide, Australia. Ticket requests for concerts in every city they visited in 1964 outnumbered the available seats. If they had wanted to, the Beatles could have stayed for weeks in any venue they desired and sold out every show.

The numbers told the story and influenced Bernstein's next decision. He set his sights on the newly-constructed 55,600 seat Shea Stadium in the New York City Borough of Queens.

Even though the Beatles had been breaking records for concert attendance and sales, there was no precedence or guarantee they would sell that many tickets for one show. The only other rock'n roll artist with enough star power to headline an outdoor stadium show had been Elvis Presley almost a decade earlier. In a little over a year from October 1956 until his final pre-army performances in Honolulu in November 1957, Elvis played six stadium shows. The largest was at the Cotton Bowl in Dallas during the Texas State Fair on October 11, 1956 with 26,500 fans in attendance.(4) The Beatles, who counted Elvis as one of their strongest influences, would need to draw more than twice as many paying customers to sell out Shea Stadium.

Almost a year after Ed Sullivan learned the Beatles were a singing group and not an animal act, Bernstein called Brian Epstein to inquire about promoting the Beatles in New York. And once again he suggested a venue that hadn't been built for rock'n roll.

Steve Marinucci

During an interview with Sid for *Beatles Examiner*, he told me Epstein didn't think the Beatles could fill Shea Stadium. "It's just magic what happened between us," he said. "I adlibbed and told him I'd give him ten dollars for every empty seat. I'd won his confidence and friendship during the Carnegie Hall concerts and he said, 'That's a deal.'"

•

The guarantee had been made that all 55,600 seats would be either sold or paid for by Bernstein and their manager grabbed it. Bernstein had earned his trust and respect for being the first U.S. promoter to seek him out and take a chance on the Beatles. Bernstein was either shrewd or lucky, or like many great promoters from P.T. Barnum to Ed Sullivan, a combination of both. He had called Epstein with a promise to sell out Carnegie Hall before most of New York knew *Beatles*

**"It was the power of The Beatles. It just happened and it was incredible."
- Steve Marinucci**

were different than *beetles*, and he worked to make it happen. Epstein knew if anyone could take the Beatles to the next level in America it would be Sid Bernstein.

Bernstein negotiated a deal with the City of New York and Shea Stadium to present The Beatles on August 15th. He set the ticket prices at $4.50, $5.00 and $5.65.

Clay Cole

Sid had to fight with City Hall. At first Mayor Wagner wouldn't give him permission. Then the mayor put his teenage intern, Jeffrey Katzenberg - yeah, that Jeffrey Katzenberg who years later became Chairman of Disney and CEO of DreamWorks, in charge of the show. The mayor assigned him to this concert to make sure Sid did everything he was supposed to do. And they wouldn't give him enough police protection so Sid had to pay for the extra police.

Steve Marinucci

Sid said organizing the Carnegie Hall shows were easy, but setting up the '65 Shea show was a challenge. He didn't have the money. Brian said he wanted half for the deposit. The fee was $100,000 for the date or sixty percent of the gross, which was estimated to be about $300,000. Sid didn't have the $50,000 deposit to pass him.

There was another complication. Brian said Sid couldn't advertise or do any promotions for the show until he gave him that fifty percent. "And that was $50,000 I didn't have," Bernstein said. "Nowhere near that. So I asked for a little time to get that money together." Then he asked Brian, "Can I talk about them?" And Brian said, "I can't stop you from talking."

Clay Cole

Brian Epstein wasn't sure. Hell is an empty arena. You can't book them and have empty seats. Sid was determined to sell 55,600 tickets and he did. They had 55,600 people paying five bucks for a stadium show.

•

Epstein would begin a brief stay in New York on January 19th to meet with executives from General Artists Corp (GAC), the Beatles' booking agency for North America, to discuss dates for a summer tour that would include outdoor stadium shows in Atlanta (August 18), Chicago (August 20), Bloomington (August 21) and San Diego (August 28). He would also meet with Ed Sullivan and Bob Precht, producer of *The Ed Sullivan Show*, to arrange their next appearance.

With Bernstein's concert at Shea Stadium tentatively scheduled to launch the tour on a Sunday evening, Sullivan's option would be taping the Beatles on Saturday, August 14th for later broadcast. It was agreed Bernstein would secure the August 15th date by paying the deposit while Epstein was in New York.

Steve Marinucci

Sid went into The Village and people recognized him. They asked what's next and he told them about The Beatles at Shea Stadium. He said the word went around the world without an advertisement. He took out a mailbox and waited for about two weeks to see if there was any mail in the box. There were three huge bagfuls. It was the power of the Beatles. It just happened and it was incredible.

Scott Ross

I had been assistant music director and producer at 1010 WINS in New York, but actually met the Beatles through Nedra, who was in the Ronettes. Nedra and I had been friends for years, but her mother wouldn't let her date me because she was younger and all that kind of stuff. Eventually we ended up dating and we've been married now for over forty years.

The Ronettes had quite a number of hits. *Be My Baby* was a number one song and took them to England for a tour. They were the headliners and The Rolling Stones were down on the bill somewhere. So there were a lot of ties between the groups.

When they got to England, the Beatles held a party for them. And when the Beatles came to the States they wanted to see the Ronettes. So I had an opportunity to meet them and be around them and all that. I had left WINS and was on the air as a disk jockey in Bay Shore, Long Island on a station called WBIC. It was a small station, but the signal went pretty far and could be picked up in Connecticut, New Jersey, portions of the Bronx, Brooklyn and even in New York City. I had gained a pretty good reputation as a different kind of disc jockey. It's not that I was trying to be different; it's just that I did what I wanted with my show.

I was originally from Scotland and was a Beatle long-hair. I was also younger. I used to call Murray the K at that time a fifty year old teenager. I was in the same age group and a contemporary of the Beatles, the Stones, The Dave Clark Five, The Animals, whatever. And because I was from Scotland, there was the basis of the British relationship.

The program I was doing became very popular and many people were listening because I was playing music that was not just chart stuff. I was playing album cuts and I'd have a lot of the music people on the air with me like Brian Jones from the Stones, The Dave Clark Five and others because I had befriended these guys.

When they booked Shea Stadium I started talking about it on the air. And I knew Sid, who was the promoter. I started talking about it and said if you want tickets for this thing you'd better hurry up and call Sid Bernstein's office. Evidently, I blew the circuits out. So that got Sid's attention. He called me and he said, "Boy, you've got a following."

Maxine Ascher

From what I understand, Abe Margolies gave Sid some of the money to help pay for the night. Not to pay the Beatles, but I think it was to rent Shea Stadium because it cost a lot of money to rent. And in Sid's defense it was a different time. There were no videos or t-shirts to sell. But that's how we got the tickets. Mr. Margolies said, "Here Max. Go. You'll have a good time." And where we lived in Flushing, we could walk to Shea.

•

By only "talking about it," Bernstein had sold-out Shea Stadium. In January 1965 he met with Epstein at his suite at The Plaza Hotel and paid him the full $100,000 promised for the August 15th appearance. Seven months away from the scheduled date, the Beatles had already set the record for the highest fee paid for a performance in front of what would be the largest audience for a rock'n roll concert.

Over the years there's been some controversy about the concert actually being sold-out by the time Bernstein made his full payment for the Beatles. Newspaper ads and posters with the August 15th date, ticket prices and mailing address for Sid Bernstein Enterprises advertised the concert as late as June and July.

But it's important to remember Bernstein was a promoter and knew the value of name recognition. By fulfilling his commitment he now had Epstein's permission to promote the concert and his company's

Posters and newspaper ads for August 15th concert

association with The Beatles. During the months before Shea Stadium he also produced shows by The Dave Clark Five, Herman's Hermits, The Kinks, Gerry and the Pacemakers, The Animals, The Rolling Stones and other British Invasion groups. If the name *Beatles* could draw attention, there was no reason not to mention it.

Epstein knew how to play a hot hand and kept the Beatles on an almost non-stop schedule through the first half of 1965. Beginning in February and until mid April they filmed their second movie *Help!* in England, Austria and the Bahamas, while also recording songs for the soundtrack. In May and June they finished enough songs to fill the *Help!* album for U.K. release, though the songs not featured in the film would be held back in the U.S. for later inclusion on the albums *Rubber Soul* and *Yesterday… and Today*.

Among this second batch of songs were *Yesterday* and *Act Naturally*, neither of which would be available to U.S. fans before the summer tour. *Yesterday*, famously composed by Paul McCartney in his sleep, would go on to become the most recorded song in the history of popular music. On the other hand, *Act Naturally* was a remake of a country song and sung by country music fan Ringo Starr. It's worth noting the Beatles' version would be debuted in America at Shea Stadium and kept fans wondering what song Ringo was singing.

> **"There's a dividing line: everything before The Beatles and everything after The Beatles. I refer to it as The Age of Innocence." - Clay Cole**

The group's popularity reached another pinnacle when it was announced on June 12th they would receive MBE Awards (Member of the Most Excellent Order of the British Empire). From the end of June until early July, the Beatles performed thirteen dates in France and Spain, before returning home for a month of unwinding from over a year of continuous writing, recording, performing and filming. But for Brian Epstein, the next invasion of America was firmly in his sights.

The clock was ticking and everything began falling into place. On July 23rd Capitol Records released the film's title song *Help!* backed with *I'm Down*. The single began its rise up the music charts and landed in the Beatles' accustomed number one position where it stayed for three weeks. After the premier in London on July 19th, the movie opened in New York on August 11th with fans screaming at the images of John, Paul, George and Ringo in larger than life color. The *Help!* soundtrack album was released on August 13th, the same day The Beatles departed for their North American Tour.

The total package was a press agent's dream come true. The group's popularity had roared to a level far beyond anything Brian Epstein and Sid Bernstein could have predicted less than two years earlier. The first stop was New York for their final in-studio appearance on *The Ed Sullivan Show* and the tour's opening date at Shea Stadium, where on August 15th they would perform under the brightest fame the rock'n roll world had ever seen.

NEWS FROM NEMS

SUMMER ENGAGEMENTS: THE BEATLES

Sun. 20 June : Depart London for Paris (Air France Flight AF.807 dept. 9.0 a.m.)
PARIS - Palais des Sports (2 performances)
Tue. 22 June : LYONS - Palais D'Hiver (2 performances)
Thu. 24 June : MILAN - Palais des Sports (2 performances)
Sat. 26 June : GENOA - Palais des Sports (2 performances)
Sun. 27 June :)
Mon. 28 June :) ROME - Adriana Theatro (2 performances each day)
Wed. 30 June : NICE - Palais des Fetes (1 performance)
Fri. 2 July : MADRID - Monumental Bullring (1 performance)
Sat. 3 July : BARCELONA - Barcelona Bullring (1 performance)
4 July Dept. Barcelona 10.0am 18.6?6 Arr. London 12.0 noon

* * * * * * * * * * *

Fri. 13 Aug. : Depart London for New York (TWA Flight TW.703 dept. noon)
Sat. 14 Aug. : Tape THE ED SULLIVAN SHOW (CBS Television, New York)
Sun. 15 Aug. : NEW YORK - Shea Stadium, Queens (8.0 p.m.)
Mon. 16 Aug. : "Rain Date" - held open to allow for bad-weather postponement
of Shea Stadium concert.
Tue. 17 Aug. : TORONTO, CANADA - Maple Leaf Gardens (4.0 & 8.30 p.m.)
Wed. 18 Aug. : ATLANTA, GEORGIA - Atlanta Stadium (8.30 p.m.)
Thu. 19 Aug. : HOUSTON, TEXAS - Sam Houston Coliseum (3.0 & 8.0 p.m.)
Fri. 20 Aug. : CHICAGO, ILLINOIS - Comiskey Park (4.0 & 8.0 p.m.)
Sat. 21 Aug. : MINNEAPOLIS, MINNESOTA - Metropolitan Stadium (8.0 p.m.)
Sun. 22 Aug. : PORTLAND, OREGON - Portland Coliseum (4.0 & 8.30 p.m.)
Mon/Thu
23/26 Aug. : Stay in Los Angeles
Fri. 27 Aug. :
Sat. 28 Aug. : SAN DIEGO Balboa Stadium
Sun. 29 Aug. : LOS ANGELES, CALIFORNIA - The Hollywood Bowl (8.0 p.m.)
Mon. 30 Aug. : LOS ANGELES, CALIFORNIA - The Hollywood Bowl (8.0 p.m.)
Tue. 31 Aug. : SAN FRANCISCO, CALIFORNIA - The Cow Palace (8.0 p.m.)
Wed. 1 Sep. : Scheduled return to London

* * * * * * * * * * * *

SPECIAL NOTE: Flight information included above must be treated as
tentative rather than final. The Press Division will
be unable to confirm travelling arrangements until
close to the date of each journey.

TONY BARROW / 9 JUNE 1965

With compliments from the Press Division of Nems Enterprises Limited, Sutherland House, 5-8 Argyll Street, London W1, Telephone Regent 3261

Summer 1965 Tour Schedule from Tony Barrow, Beatles Press Agent

The Fans

Pattie Noah

My older brother had introduced me to the lads the year before with *She Loves You*. I was raised in New York City, so when my brother told me he heard the Beatles were going to be doing a show at Shea, I went bananas. I begged and pleaded my mother to please let me go or I would die a slow, torturous death before her very eyes. She told my brother that if he thought it would be safe, he could take me to the show. He got tickets for us and also for our nine year old cousin, who I believe would put a death curse on him if she couldn't go with us.

Ray Robinson II

My father was boxer Sugar Ray Robinson and where the rest of the world was interested in him, I was interested in the Beatles. My father was not a Beatles fan. But I was sixteen and he didn't have too much control over where I went and what I did.

I lived in Riverdale and got on the train and bought my ticket. Those were the days when they weren't so expensive. I was astounded years ago when my eldest daughter was around thirteen and went to see Janet Jackson. The ticket cost her $120. I was like, "How can a thirteen year old be buying a ticket for $120?"

Joyce Shelfo

I was pulling babysitting duty for a neighbor who owned an ad agency in Manhattan. When he and his wife returned from a night on the town, he handed me my night's earnings and asked in a way that told me he had no idea who they were:

"Ever hear of the group The Beatles? A client gave me four tickets to their concert at Shea Stadium, but I don't want them. Do you?"

Do I want the tickets? Did I ever hear of them? Do I want to go? Are you kidding? My bedroom walls were papered with Beatles posters and cut outs from *16 Magazine* and *Beatles Book Magazine*. My tote bag had Beatles buttons all over it and Paul's was the biggest. I had a Beatles haircut. I had doubles of their albums because I played them until there were no more grooves in the vinyl. For my twelfth birthday, my sister, of the Johnny Mathis generation, presented me with a Beatles cake. I wanted to be Paul's girlfriend Jane Asher or George's Pattie Boyd. I pretended to be John in a Girl Scouts skit and even made my own guitar out of a cardboard box. My friend and I hung out at the corner drug store because the delivery boy looked a lot like Ringo. I sent Paul Kraft American Cheese slices because I read he liked them. So yes, please, I'd like to go to the concert!

Steve Zisk
It was a very significant event in my life. My father got the tickets. I was fifteen and my sister was about eight. My father took both of us.

Dotty Poirier
I was thirteen years old and won a contest on the radio station WICE in Providence, Rhode Island. I was one of sixteen teens that would go on a day trip to see the Beatles. It was very exciting and I could hardly believe it! I'll never forget the experience and the anticipation. I remember being nervous on the phone when the disc jockey announced I was one of the winners. It was like a dream.

Debbie Stern
We were only fourteen years old when the countdown and the heart thumping anticipation began. We busied ourselves as all good Beatlemaniacs did, listening to their records for hours on end, thumbing through magazines for any and all bits of information about our precious boys, and lovingly making large posters proclaiming our love for them to take with us to the big event.

Marc Catone
What I remember most is my sister Sarah, who was a really big Beatlemaniac, had *16 Magazine* and saw a listing for the North American Tour. Back in those days the communications weren't like they are now with all the radio stations and internet, so you found out the Beatles were touring through *Datebook*, *16 Magazine*, or one of those magazines. And she said, "We gotta go to this."

We were really young. I was almost fifteen and she was about twelve and we didn't know how to go about it. Somehow we found out that a local ticket agency where we lived in Danbury, Connecticut was not only selling tickets to Shea Stadium, but also were providing a bus ride for everybody who bought a block of tickets. That was pretty cool.

We bought our tickets and a funny part is that a lot of our friends thought it was outrageous that we were paying $5.65 to see the Beatles. It was unheard of to pay that much for the price of a ticket. If you look back at it now with twenty first century eyes, it seems ridiculous that anybody would think that. I remember we tried to get other people to go and except for a couple friends that did go with us, their parents said, "I'm not going to let you spend that much money!" It was too outrageous and they wouldn't let them go.

Janice Bartel

During that summer of '65 I had been hospitalized with pneumonia and my parents felt that I might be too weak to attend the Beatles concert. Are you kidding me? The Beatles were everything to me. I would crawl out of my death bed to see them, especially when I lived less than fifteen minutes from Shea Stadium.

I finally wore my parents down and they gave my sister and me the money to buy the Beatles concert tickets. I remember guarding these tickets with my life, looking at them several times a day and taking out my calendar to mark off the days until the concert. Although these were not the best seats, they were upper deck and under the lights, it really didn't matter because I was going to see The Beatles!

Some Short Notes From Sid Bernstein...

...5000 letters were received at our office the very first day after the first announcement was made about the Beatles appearance at Shea Stadium. Those 5000 letters contained orders for 16,000 tickets...easily 90% of the requests were for "first row" center seats! It is just impossible to fill requests that asked for front row seating...the Beatles stage will be placed on 2nd base. At this point, there will be no seats at all on the field ...since Shea Stadium is a hugh 55,000 seater, it might be a good idea to bring binoculars, if you own a pair.

...If these tickets reach you before June 17th, I would like to remind you that THE FIRST NEW YORK FOLK FESTIVAL will be held at Carnegie Hall for four days; June 17th, 18th, 19th and 20th. Tickets will be on sale at our office at 119 West 57th Street. Information on who is appearing can be obtained by calling 679-8281...The Folk Festival is off to a beautiful start and it includes such eminent artists as: Mose Allison, Chuck Berry, Johnny Cash, Jimmy Driftwood, Bob Gibson, Mississippi John Hurt, Phil Ochs, Dave Van Ronk, Buffy Sainte-Marie, Muddy Waters, Jesse Colin Young plus an additional 50 famous folk artists.

...NBC-TV's Hullabaloo goes back on the air September 13th...the Beatle program book that is advertised on the other side of this circular will make a valuable souvenir...next year we are planning a New York Folk Festival at Shea Stadium in July, more on that later...We have people coming in for the Beatles concert from as far as Montreal, Miami, Des Moines, Knoxville and even California...It might be a good idea for you to take a World's Fair train or bus to the Stadium, since the Stadium is almost across the street from the Fair and you won't have to fight the heavy car traffic...a note to Parents; we have very heavy security inside and outside the Stadium for the protection of all the youngsters. This means that offenders of security rules will be severely dealt with by the police authorities, for the protection of all of us...Hope you have a marvelous time.

Letter enclosed with concert tickets

HEY! Here's great news from four friends of yours about
A S P E C I A L O F F E R

"Oh... we can hardly wait to see you! But you don't have to wait to see us! Send for our all-new Autographed Beatles Picture Book – it's also the official program for the show you're going to see in August."

"It's got lots of neat photos of us – – including huge portraits we've autographed for you, so you can frame them if you like. Each costs only $1.25, autographed photos and all!"

"We never know if there will be enough books for everybody. So we've reserved copies for our friends who've ordered tickets. That's you! And – Surprise! order as many as you like now. You'll have them in July! Just fill out the coupon and mail it with your check or money order to Souvenir Pub. & Dist. Co. 19 W. 44th Street N.Y.C. 10036"

To: SOUVENIR PUBLISHING & DISTRIBUTING CO.
    19 West 44th Street, New York City 10036

Send me _____ copies of the official Beatles Autographed Picture Book
and official program at $1.25 per copy. Enclosed is a check or money order
for $_____

Name _____
                        (Please Print Clearly)

Address _____

City _____ State _____ Zip Code _____
(Please – no cash, stamps or coins – check or money order only)

DON'T MISS OUT! SUPPLY IS LIMITED! RESERVE YOUR COPIES NOW!
(Right, Ringo?)

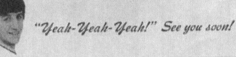

"Yeah-Yeah-Yeah!" See you soon!

New York City

The year 1965 marked the mid-point of a decade destined to be studied and analyzed for the vast and rapid changes in western culture. It was no longer surprising to see men with long hair and women in short skirts, though both could still be the subject of ridicule. But it had grown to become much more than that. The differences from a year earlier in music, fashion, attitudes and politics were stunning and many of these changes can be attributed to the influence of the Beatles. Sides were taken and the generation gap became a wider line drawn between the adults who had worked hard to maintain a comfortable lifestyle and the maturing youth that was searching for its own comfort level in the present and future.

The Beatles were instrumental in promoting these new ideals with not so subtle undertones running through their movie *Help!* On the surface it was a fun loving take-off on the popular James Bond series with the noticeably longer-haired Fab Four dodging a fanatical Eastern religious cult and a mad scientist and his assistant out to rule the world. But the deeper message could easily be transformed into the youthful rallying cry of *don't trust anyone over the age of thirty*. The Beatles toyed with the older villains and made a mockery of their established, out of date beliefs through sarcastic and deadpan humor; making the film one long "wink" to their fans they would prevail in the end and have a fun time doing it.

The music of the 1960's paralleled the changes. The summer of 1965 was less than a year and a half from the Sunday evening when Ed Sullivan first introduced the Beatles and America's collective jaws hit the ground. Previously the pop charts had been topped by a habit-wearing Singing Nun with *Dominique*, sweater-wearing Bobby Vinton with *There! I've Said It Again*, and The Kingsmen, wearing crew cuts and college frat boy smirks with *Louie Louie*. Then there was The Beatles.

The screams of Beatlemania continued into 1965, but the four lovable lads in *A Hard Day's Night* were maturing. They were writing and singing about more than just holding hands. The Beatles had traveled across continents and lived experiences no one else would ever know in a lifetime. But they were still peers to the college aged young adults, and role models to teens and pre-teens who were forming opinions about what was happening in their world. The Beatles shared many of the same opinions, the youthful exuberance to express it, and a world stage to do it from. They had also matured into adults who didn't always want to be the agreeable Fab Four twenty four hours a day, eight days a week.

> **"He invited me to be one of the MC's for The Beatles concert at Shea Stadium. I said, 'Of course,' and proceeded to flip out at the thought of it." - Scott Ross**

Their simple pop hits from early 1964 were already on the shelf waiting to be rediscovered through Classic Rock Radio, still more than a decade away. Men in their early to mid-twenties wanted more than just whisper in a girl's ear and the Beatles were no different. *Beatles '65*, their U.S. follow up album to *A Hard Day's Night*, included the Lennon and McCartney compositions *Baby's In Black*, *I'll Follow The Sun*, *No Reply* and *I'm A Loser* that were more confessional and introspective than *Please Please Me* and *She Loves You*. Paul McCartney's *Yesterday* was a longing for days "when all my troubles seemed so far away." John Lennon later claimed his rollicking *Help!* was actually a personal cry from within the hurricane of Beatlemania.

The music and imagery derived from these lyrics were a sharp turn from the carefree and exuberant songs that earned *A Hard Day's Night* an Oscar nomination for Best Soundtrack for a Feature Film. Within the year they would record and release the albums *Rubber Soul* and *Revolver*. In less than two years The Summer of Love would embrace *Sgt. Pepper's Lonely Hearts Club Band*.

But this was still 1965. They had proved to be more than a fad or a flash in the pan and were basking in the glory of being the world's most famous quartet. What they said and what they did was headline news and every new record was greeted by their legions of dedicated fans as if it was *the word* coming down from four heavenly teen angels. By August 1966 comments from John Lennon comparing them to Jesus would create a backlash of nightmarish proportions and ultimately help end Beatlemania as a world touring phenomenon, but they were still in the early phase of their love-in relationship with the press and fans, and could seemingly do no wrong.

In 1965 the Beatles hadn't yet grown tired of touring or performing together as a rock'n roll band. But the clock was ticking. The live shows would last only another year and the band would be broken up by the end of the decade.

Cousin Bruce Morrow

Rock'n roll, thanks to the Beatles, became the first true international and multi-generational genre of music ever in history. Everybody all over the world started understanding it. Even if you didn't speak the language, you understood the emotion and the Beatles are greatly, greatly involved in that particular transition.

In about six months after they arrived, thanks to the Beatles helping it, parents decided they invented rock'n roll and it was their genre. They started liking it. Up until then they would just put it down and call it... "Hey, listen to Cousin Brucie and you'll grow hair on your hands." You know? It was that kind of thing. And all of a sudden, thanks to groups like the Beatles, it was now becoming acceptable to humanity and growing up into the adult world. Up to that point it was non-human music.

Clay Cole

There's a dividing line: everything before The Beatles and everything after The Beatles. I refer to it as *The Age of Innocence*. They were so influential and important. They changed everything; our whole culture, fashion... They inspired the Women's Movement, the Gay Liberation Movement and all that stuff.

•

America seemed to be growing in many directions at once. Parents used to the security of being middle class in the 1950's were set on maintaining the status quo for their children and generations to come. However the hidden undertones bubbling under what was considered normal a decade earlier was beginning to explode by 1965.

U.S. forces were being sent to Vietnam. A military draft that had continued since The Second World War and through The Korean War made healthy males over eighteen and without student deferments the armed defenders of freedom ordered to enforce government policies. And with voting age still over twenty-one; these potential soldiers didn't have any say in the matter. It planted the seeds for war protests that would explode on college campuses and in the streets within months and bitterly divide the nation.

"We don't like it if there's any segregation or anything, because we're not used to it, you know. It just seems a bit daft."
- Paul McCartney (5)

Streets and neighborhoods were already exploding in August 1965 when black protests in the Los Angeles district of Watts turned into riots over racial discrimination. The fight for equality would spread into violence through major cities such as New York, Newark, Cleveland, Detroit and Chicago, despite the peaceful protests urged by Rev. Martin Luther King and The Civil Rights Act signed by President Lyndon Johnson.

The Beatles were well aware of the potential for violence and discrimination in America, but were still shocked by it during the southern portion of their tour in 1964. According to journalist Larry Kane's book *Ticket To Ride*, detailing his experiences traveling with the group, concert promoters in Jacksonville, Florida had planned to segregate the audience into white and black sections.

Joan Murray

Yes, there were some performers who would do that and not play in front of segregated audiences. Then there were some who were afraid not to. But the Beatles learned a lot of their music from black artists. It was rock'n roll and that's where they learned it. It was the same with The Rolling Stones. It was everybody from Buddy Guy to Howlin' Wolf.

CBS New York hired me to work in News and Public Affairs. I was the first African American, black... ah, they called it Negro at the time but I'm saying black, to work on that staff. I met everybody who was anybody and it was fabulous.

I moved to NBC and worked on a show called *Women On The Move*, which was exactly like *The View*. Kitty Carlisle was like the Barbara

Walters and I was the requisite black girl. From there I went back to CBS, became a news reporter and then a newscaster. I met the Beatles in 1964, '65 and '66.

I was the only black girl with a microphone. I was very, very different, but the thing is I was always very nice. So when someone met me in an interview, they were very solicitous of me. But I'm sure there was underlining racism in the newsroom. That I know. I had a writer, one of the staff news writers who threw a script at me and said, "I won't do any nigger scripts." And that was in New York City at CBS in the mid '60s.

When I was in the newsroom they gave me a lot of different assignments. And because I had worked in the press department, I knew Ed Sullivan from writing press releases. So they said, "Joan, why don't you go and cover Ed Sullivan?"

Ed Sullivan was a very dear person. He helped people who needed to be helped. And yet, nobody knew it. He didn't want people to know how good he was to, for instance, black entertainers. He gave black entertainers a thumbs-up very, very quietly. He stopped some racism in the entertainment field very, very quietly. I think there was someone in Las Vegas who had a problem and Ed Sullivan picked up the phone and said, "This is Ed Sullivan. I just won't have this. I don't know if they call it racism, but you give this Negro artist everything you can. You give him a room."

At that time you couldn't stay in some of the rooms. I can't believe I went through all of that. But he was very gracious as far as giving me interview time. He and Bob Precht, his executive producer, both knew me. They gave me carte blanch and that day at *The Ed Sullivan Show* with the Beatles was a wild, wild scene.

When I went out to do interviews, I could see why people would be fascinated by me, as was the Beatles. They knew I was a news reporter and my microphone said CBS. But they were English, so they didn't know how everything worked in America.

Shaun Weiss

My father was friends with the Sullivan family and asked if he could get us tickets to Shea Stadium. So Ed Sullivan got the tickets for us and wrote a thank you letter to United Artists that said, "Thank you very much for The Beatles tickets." I have the letter framed and hanging on my wall. We came into possession of it because Nat's office became a

Beatles office. United Artists sent the letter to the Beatles and when Nat became a part of them, that letter was in a file system. I retrieved it when Nat closed his office. So we actually got the tickets to Shea from Ed Sullivan who got them through United Artists.

Nat became involved with the Beatles in late '64, but it really wasn't official until '65. He was a divorce lawyer and was at JFK when they flew in on February 7, 1964. He knew of the Beatles, but he never knew he was going to be involved with them. He went to England, met Brian and it just so happens they hit it off. He didn't go there to seek a position with Brian Epstein. He went there as an attorney doing a divorce and it just happened. I guess it's part of the mystique of The Beatles. They just mystically appeared.

When Brian came to New York he called Nat and they had lunch. That's when Brian proposed him working as the Beatles' attorney. So with me it was all coincidental. Who knew that when I met Mal Evans and went to *The Ed Sullivan Show* in '64 that a little over a year later Nat would be totally involved with them and was Brian's partner in NEMS? It was a… It was really a shock.

•

"America was where they really began to see for the first time this type of hysteria." - Nedra Talley- Ross

On Friday, August 13th the Beatles arrived in New York and were immediately escorted to their rooms in The Warwick Hotel on Manhattan's West 54th Street. NEMS press manager Tony Barrow had arranged a press conference in his suite, giving the boys another opportunity to trade wisecracks and quotable lines with reporters.

From transcripts and recordings of the event, it's obvious the Beatles were more self-assured than during their first press conference at Kennedy Airport in 1964. But in the eyes of the media and their fans, they still carried an image of being the lovable mop tops from England. Paul was pretty, George was quiet, Ringo was funny, and John was… John.

The questions asked by the harder edged New York press were not much different than potential cover stories for teen magazines:

"John, do you always do press conferences chewing gum?"
"Ringo, what are you gonna name the baby if it's a boy or a girl?"
"Is matrimony in the immediate future for the two unmarried members of your group?"

Only one question in particular reflected the mood of the changing times. Answered by John Lennon, he offered a glimpse into not only his future as a leader in the peace movement, but also the attitude of many young American males who would have to make a decision when the government was not offering one:

"Any plans for going to Vietnam and entertaining the troops?"
John: "I wouldn't go there, no." (6)

As the day continued WABC deejays Cousin Brucie and Bill Ingram kept listeners updated on all that was fab during live broadcasts from the Beatles' hotel suite. Later that first evening the group was visited by Bob Dylan and the next day they would tape their final in-studio appearance on *The Ed Sullivan Show* to be broadcast on September 12th.

Cousin Bruce Morrow

When they came back in 1965 I interviewed them in their hotel room. There's a photograph of me interviewing the four boys and it's a very interesting picture because according to their biographer and photographer, that's the only time they ever saw the boys paying attention to one person at one time. Yeah, they were always all over the place. They were characters. They carried on like crazy.

Steve Marinucci

I was living in that area at the time and the radio craziness with the Beatles and the New York stations was just totally insane. They'd break in during the day and play Beatles songs and do live reports from the street with the crowd. It was really exciting to be in that area at that time.

Peter Altschuler

When it came time for the Beatles to give this massive concert, Murray the K had already been their primary host in America. When they went down to Washington, he introduced them. When they were at

Carnegie Hall he introduced them, along with a number of other deejays. He was there and kind of expected that he was going to be the big honcho for Shea Stadium and they gave it to Ed Sullivan. Well, nobody was going to get in the way of Ed Sullivan. His clout was unmistakable and his power was absolute. If you got on the wrong side of Ed Sullivan, you might as well have kissed your career goodbye.

Cousin Bruce Morrow

Sid Bernstein, a very good friend and a colleague personally and in the business said to me, "How would you like to host that show at Shea Stadium with Ed Sullivan?" And I said *let me think about it…*, and it took me three seconds and I said "Yes!"

WA-Beatle-C as it became, was very instrumental in exposing the Beatles' records here in the United States because of the huge reach of that radio station. It was on in over forty states. So I was very involved with the Beatles and I was very friendly with them.

Peter Altschuler

To be honest, Murray wasn't as big a part as he expected to be. Because granted, Ed Sullivan gave the Beatles national exposure, which my father could not offer them under any circumstances at that point. I think everybody was pretty realistic about it. Ed Sullivan got the central part and they all played supporting roles. In the New York market television trumped radio, particularly national television. So everybody said okay, Ed's going to make the final introduction. We'll do the preshow stuff. Bruce Morrow was there and Murray was there.

Scott Ross

I'd been on stage and MC'd all the Rolling Stones concerts and that sort of thing. So when Sid called and said, "You've really got a following," he invited me to be one of the MC's for the Beatles concert at Shea Stadium. I said, "Of course," and proceeded to flip out at the thought of it; me at the Beatle concert and on stage yet? Man, what a goof. I wasn't supposed to be there, you gotta know that. I wasn't one of the elite like a Good Guy or an All American. I was from left field and a small station with no big things going for it. No promotion, important sounding jingles, or an echo chamber. It had to be done via the people who were listening and they did it. They had put me in Shea.

Sid Bernstein was a beautiful man; the Santa Claus of the music business. He was producing the concert and decided that I belonged there. That took guts because he had previously been pressured by various persons in the business to not have me there. I was not an All-American Good Guy. But Sid said, "Booo!" to those little Gestapo people and I was set for The Beatles at Shea Stadium.

•

Saturday was devoted to *The Ed Sullivan Show* beginning with a rehearsal at CBS Studios in front of a live audience. The Beatles performed five songs that would also be included in their set list at Shea Stadium: *I Feel Fine*, *Ticket To Ride*, *Act Naturally*, *I'm Down* and *Help!* The additional song was Paul's solo performance of the newly recorded *Yesterday*.

_____ Shea Rocks _____

"Saturday's rehearsals took almost ten hours because of horrendous sound problems that the boys insisted upon sorting to their satisfaction. A year earlier when The Beatles did their first appearance on Sullivan's show, I doubt his people would have let us go into so much expensive studio overtime in the pursuit of better quality sound. Sullivan himself was far more friendly to us than last year, which helped to ease the atmosphere." – **Tony Barrow** (7)

After working out the sound problems, a new audience was brought in to watch the 7 pm taping of *The Ed Sullivan Show*. The fresh audience provided fresh vocal chords for the screaming that would accompany the national broadcast.

Joan Murray

I went to the studio and interviewed Ed Sullivan. He came off the studio stage and in the background you could hear all of these thousands of teenagers screaming at the top of their lungs. After I interviewed him, I went over to where the Beatles were standing backstage and security was trying to protect them. I then decided to go outside to some of the

Joan Murray and autographs from *The Ed Sullivan Show*

fans who were screaming the Beatles' names, "George! John! Ringo! Paul!" It was just chaotic.

I went outside with my microphone and interviewed a lot of the fans that were standing behind those police wooden cross horses. They knew me from television and they shouted, "Joan, Joan! Can you get us autographs?" So I said, "Sure."

I went backstage to the Beatles' dressing room and said that their fans wanted autographs. I had my reporter's notebook and each one of them signed page after page. They stood there. They didn't sit they stood there and autographed all of these pages for me. George would sign four or five, then Paul, and then John and Ringo. I tore some of the pages out the book and was heading outside to give the autographs to some of the fans, but I was stopped by security. They told me not to go over there with the autographs because it was too dangerous. The kids were just out of control and they could be hurt trying to get these autographs. The police were all around and that was my experience. So I ended up with a lot of their autographs in a reporter's notebook. I saved them.

The Beatles were very, very nice. They were not star struck; not at all. Now today you find these young, I call them *artistes*, and they are so taken with themselves. No talent, no *IT* factor, no nothing. And yet the Beatles were very, very... *Accommodating* is the word that I want.

Judith Kristen

The cops, the Beatles' organization, the politicians and everybody that had any kind of control over the masses had become real savvy by this time. They weren't gonna let anyone get within fifty feet of them at their hotel or wherever they happened to be. And at Shea Stadium they weren't putting the Beatles in a little boxing ring sort of thing like I saw them on at the Washington, D.C. Coliseum concert in '64. At Shea they were gonna have barbed wire fences going up and cops on the field. They were really, really smart about that.

•

Among the many reasons that might have influenced The Beatles' decision to stop touring a year later was their lifestyle away from home. In London an appearance by all four together would attract a mob of fans, but separately they could live semi-normal lives. John, George and Ringo had homes in a quiet upscale neighborhood outside of the city, while Paul was part of London's trendy theater and art scene attending premieres and gallery openings with his girlfriend, actress Jane Asher. The Beatles could go to nightclubs and restaurants and walk to their favorite hotspots after recording sessions at EMI Studios.

Tours were a different story. Their hotels were staked out and surrounded by thousands of screaming fans. Police would shut down city blocks to protect the group or quickly transport them by limos or armored cars to and from airports and concert venues. The Beatles were essentially prisoners of their own fame except for occasional and well planned secretive outings. One would occur later in August when they met with their idol Elvis Presley in Los Angeles. But in reality, the Beatles rarely saw much of any city where they performed.

Nedra Talley-Ross

Oh yeah. We talked with them about that. The Beatles honestly were, like, *we don't know what this is all about. This is crazy.* They didn't get it. Because they had been in England when they were struggling and playing clubs trying to make it. And then America did a whole 'nuther thing for them. America was where they really began to see for the first time this type of hysteria.

For performers in America, we were artists. It wasn't until we went to England that the fans were very different. We had never had our cars rocked. It was like, *oh my, they're gonna kill us!* They got hysterical over us in Europe, Britain and all those places because we were from America. Then back in America, it was *you're OUR artist.*

When The Beatles came to America the hysteria was on a different and much higher level. They sat there going, "What the heck?" It was shocking to them.

They were young. We all were young. Everything began to be available in a way that was not good. Girls were literally going crazy. Girls would do anything to be with them. So when you get all that thrown at you at such a young age, it's hard for a young person to keep their bearing. And then we did have the '60s in there too…

Judith Kristen

I followed through with the same plan to meet them that I used the year before because it worked. I had met George Harrison at their hotel in 1964. Here's how it went. I could find out where they were performing because as soon as the tour schedule was up, good'ol Cousin Brucie, Murray the K and all the disc jockeys would be telling you. So you knew where they were gonna be on any given date in the summer. You just didn't know where they were staying.

So I got this idea, which was not bad for being blonde, that I know they're staying in New York City. Brian's not gonna put them in a Sleazy Sal's Motel in Hoboken. He's gonna put them in a snazzy hotel like The Algonquin or even The Plaza again, because that's the way Brian was. So I got the addresses to all of those hotels and requested reservations. All you had to do was send a letter. Not like these days when everybody uses credit cards.

My girlfriend and I wrote letters to all of these high end hotels like The Americana, The Warwick, The Delmonico, The Plaza, The Knickerbocker, The Hudson… You name it. We said, "We would like reservations for August 15th and 16th at your hotel for a wonderful family reunion we're having in the city. My name and address are as follows…" We got all the reservations back and kept them in alphabetical order. We had one for The Warwick that day.

Well, let me tell you. When I saw three or four thousand girls on February 7, 1964 outside The Plaza Hotel it was nerve-wracking. But at The Warwick there were fifteen or twenty thousand girls in a two or three block radius. There were girls everywhere.

My girlfriends and I had our pocketbooks and one suitcase. It was one of those round Sandra Dee white hat box suitcases. They were snazzy. But as we got closer to The Warwick there were cops on foot and cops on horses and nobody was letting us in. I said we had reservations. I was adamant, but forget about it. They weren't gonna let us in without an adult. Are you kidding me?

I kept saying, "But we're at a family reunion!" They said we had to bring an adult from the family reunion before they would let us in. So we're trying to accost people at Nathan's Hot Dogs. You know what I mean? At local hot dog joints! We're going, "Can you please say you're my aunt Marian?" And the people were looking at us like, "No honey, I don't think so." But we wanna get into the hotel! We have reservations and they won't let us come in! "I'm sorry sweetheart…"

They were all really, really nice to us, but they didn't want anything to do with it. They didn't want to walk through fifteen thousand girls and I don't blame them. So we didn't get into the hotel.

•

Following *The Ed Sullivan Show* taping a police escort drove the Beatles back to The Warwick Hotel. But rather than spending the night imprisoned in their suites, a different plan was in the works. Without the slapstick fanfare that accompanied the famous scene in *A Hard Day's Night* when they escaped from the television studio and ran wild in a deserted field, ("Sorry we hurt your field, mister," was George Harrison's famous quip after the *Can't Buy Me Love* romp), the Beatles quietly slipped out of The Warwick and were taken to New York's Rockefeller Center.

Mimi Schwensen

I was still with The Rockettes. Fortunately I didn't get fired the year before when I missed a show because we couldn't get out of our dance studio when the Beatles arrived for *The Ed Sullivan Show*. Across the street from Radio City Music Hall is the GE, General Electric Building. It's also called the NBC Building and 30 Rockefeller Center. The Rainbow Room was the famous nightclub and restaurant on the top floor. If any of the Rockettes felt like going out after the last show, we'd just walk across the street.

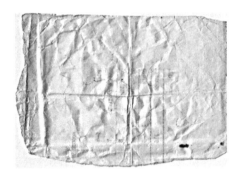

Ringo Starr's (very) faded autograph
on back of Rockette rehearsal
schedule

The Rainbow Room- August 14, 1965

This was a Saturday night and I was going out to dinner with a friend who worked for Capitol Records. I didn't know where we were going; just out for dinner after our last show at the Music Hall.

We went across the street and took the elevator up to The Rainbow Room. When the elevator door opened I saw that the Beatles were there. I guess their manager was there also and there were other people who worked for Capitol Records. It turns out we were having dinner with the Beatles.

I didn't see it as a big deal. Honestly. The Rockettes would meet a lot of famous people and I really thought the Beatles were more for teenagers. I remember thinking that they needed to wash their hair.

The nicest one was Ringo, so I sat next to him at dinner. I told him my twelve year old cousin in Ohio was a big fan and would love his autograph. Ringo took my Rockette rehearsal schedule, folded it and tore off a square. He signed his name and gave it to me for my cousin.

About a month later, in September, I was visiting my parents in Ohio. When my cousin came over I remembered having Ringo's autograph for him in my purse. When I gave it to him he asked why I didn't get the other three to sign it and I said I didn't like them that much. To this day he tells me if I had gotten all four autographs he could retire. I don't think anyone knew then that they would still be as popular as they are now. That was over forty years ago. If I had known that, I would've asked for all their autographs. And a few copies from each.

Oh, one last thing. That night in September was the Sunday they showed *The Ed Sullivan Show*. My cousin said it was taped the same evening I met them at The Rainbow Room. It looked like they'd washed their hair for that.

**"When the elevator door opened I saw that the Beatles were there... It turns out we were having dinner with The Beatles."
- Mimi Schwensen**

Nedra Talley-Ross

At that time we were working and enjoying it. We weren't sitting around thinking, *oh down the road this will be worth this and get this for these reasons.* You know, you hang with people and you don't sit around thinking about getting autographs and things like that.

Oh sometimes we did with the rock'n roll shows. They would make up the booklets and we would say, "Sign this, do that..." You know, for each other. And that was fun, but we didn't… Well, I didn't. I shouldn't say *we.* I did not think of it as *down the road this would be valuable.*

For instance, Jimi Hendrix was The Ronettes' guitarist. He was Jimmy James at that time and was traveling with us in probably '64 and '65. It was someplace in there. We weren't sitting around going *oh; this is going to be the future Jimi Hendrix.* We would be doing a week with Lionel Hampton and you just thought you were doing a week with Lionel Hampton. You didn't think of who was doing your guitar backup, just if they could work it out and make the sound right.

So you didn't look at all of the things that I think we would look back at today and say, "Take time and smell the roses." They were teaching no pop culture classes about this when we were in school. It was not something we even thought about down the road or thinking that you will be a part of history. It was just work.

On the Way to Shea

There was one thing both sides of the generation gap could agree on. The summer of 1965 in New York City was one of the hottest they had ever lived through. Rain had been almost non-existent, the water supply in area reservoirs was shrinking and all five boroughs that made up the city were under a drought emergency. In Manhattan, heat vapors sizzled off concrete sidewalks, blacktopped streets softened and tall buildings stifled any slight breeze, making temperatures feel hotter than they actually were under the baking sun.

On Sunday August 15th, the afternoon temperature in Central Park hit eighty four degrees. In only a few hours The Beatles were scheduled to perform in front of 55,600 sweltering ticketholders at Shea Stadium.

East of Manhattan in the borough of Queens, visitors to The New York World's Fair celebrated technology and communication between nations. The official theme was *Peace Through Understanding* and a twelve story high, stainless steel replica of the earth dubbed *Unisphere* stood as a symbol of hope for a united future.

Sharing Flushing Meadows Corona Park with The World's Fair was Shea Stadium. Officially known as William A. Shea Municipal Stadium, it was a state of the art sports complex built in a circular design with five levels of seating. Opened in April 1964, it was worthy of being paired with the futuristic World's Fair.

Michael Sergio

My mother used to work for Harry M. Stevens, the people with the concession stands. It was during the World's Fair when they first opened Shea Stadium back in '64. I was in there when they were building it out. I used to go there all the time and run around in the rafters under the stadium.

Shea Stadium was originally built not only for the New York Mets baseball team, but also football; The New York Jets. The infield bleachers actually would pivot so that the stadium could become a square stadium for football. So under the infield box seats, that's like a shell and under that is all empty. There's like this boardwalk... It was kind of like a little suspension bridge to get from the locker room to the dugout. From the bottom of the stadium you went across this boardwalk for about fifty feet until you got to the dugout. As a kid I used to go under there and run around so I saw all that stuff. It was very, very cool.

That was during the World's Fair and it was just really a wonderful and incredible time. And it was the same with the Beatles. It was unbelievable. When the Beatles first came I must have been about thirteen and living in Astoria. Our black and white TV wasn't working so we had to run down to the pizza place on the corner to watch on the little screen they had when they were doing *The Ed Sullivan Show*. That was just amazing. It was just amazing to see that.

Judith Kristen

We weren't gonna get into The Warwick, so we decided to go out to Queens. One of the girls actually said they might have gone to Shea already because they'd never been to The World's Fair. And for some reason, somehow she thought she knew they wanted to go to the Fair. And I thought *what if they're at the Fair? Oh my God, what if they're at the fair! Maybe they're in disguise!*

So these poor guys, anybody who was five feet, eleven inches tall who had a hat on or sunglasses, I'm like staring at them because it might be Paul McCartney, John Lennon... Or is it George?! And then I'm looking at all these guys that are like my height, because I'm about five-eight. You know, looking for shorter guys with large noses and stuff like that, praying it was Ringo. Ah, that didn't happen, so... We met a few interesting guys, but it wasn't any of the four that I wanted to meet.

I'm thinking this is what it must be like when you die and go to heaven. You stuff your face with Belgian Waffles and then you see The Beatles at night. What else do you need?

•

It had been less than four years since Brian Epstein first saw the Beatles perform a lunch time show at Liverpool's Cavern Club in November 1961. He had predicted, mostly out of frustration at being turned down in his early efforts to secure the band a recording contract, that they would someday be bigger than Elvis. But it's unknown if he could have ever dreamed his boast would come true on a level they were about to achieve.

Epstein had proved his worth as a manager and a businessman many times over. He knew the value of good publicity and shaped the image each of his artists presented to fans and media. Even the rebellious John Lennon had been coaxed into wearing suits and his biting, sarcastic humor and penchant for making fun of "cripples" on stage had been toned down and softened in the press for teenaged consumption as being witty and cheeky in a typical Liverpudlian style.

As a businessman with an eye to the future, Epstein also understood the historic proportions of Shea Stadium. So did Ed Sullivan. No other pop music act, including Elvis himself, had even dared to attempt an event this massive in the media capital of the world. It was too good to only happen once, so Epstein and Sullivan made sure it would have a second life. NEMS Enterprises and Subafilms, which was owned by both Epstein and the Beatles, joined with Sullivan Productions to have the concert filmed for a television special.

> **"Anyway, the big day came and probably, I guess one of the most memorable days in my career."**
> **- Cousin Bruce Morrow**

Arthur Aaron

Sid asked Ed Sullivan to introduce the Beatles at Shea Stadium and Sullivan agreed. About six or eight weeks before the concert, Sullivan calls Sid and he says, "Sid, would you mind if I filmed this concert?" And Sid said, "No, go ahead."

That was Sid. There were no contracts.

Michael Adams

My dad, M. Clay Adams, formed his own company in the early 1960's called Clayco Films. He hired sound guys and camera guys, and they would do exterior shots for different shows. If somebody had a television show that was filmed on a soundstage but they needed some outside pictures of buildings or sound of the traffic, my dad's people would go out in sound trucks and film that stuff.

My father at that point had already been working for some years with Ed Sullivan. His show was filmed on a soundstage in CBS Studios, but when he needed a *man on the street* kind of thing or when they were doing a skit and needed to show traffic or whatever, my dad's company did that. Any exterior shots were handled by them, so he already had a connection with Sullivan.

> **"I got my great seat and behind me was every screaming teenager on the planet as far as I could tell." - Peter Altschuler**

As a matter of fact, I was at *The Ed Sullivan Show* the first time the Beatles were on. I also went to the dress rehearsal, which was filmed for the third week. When everybody says they know where they were that night, I know exactly where I was.

Clayco Films was hired by Sullivan Productions and NEMS to film the concert. This was a joint production and would be shown on ABC over here and the BBC in England. My dad already had a film crew and sound people and that's how he got roped into doing the thing. Of course technology still being what it was back then, they weren't prepared for Shea Stadium with all the screaming.

Judith Kristen

I can tell you what I was wearing that day because I always thought, "How can you go out like that? What if George Harrison would see you?" Such a chick thing, you know?

The day before I drenched my hair in Clairol Hair Conditioner because it was really long and I wanted it to be beautiful and shiny. You're only supposed to leave it on for forty five minutes and I left it on for three hours. My hair was stiff, but it came out really nice. And I was wearing this mini skirt, but they weren't so *mini* like in the late 60's. Mini skirts then weren't up to your butt. They were just maybe a little above your knees. That was risqué enough. So I had this green outfit on, these real funky sandals, and big, hoop earrings and everything and I just thought I was the bee's knees. And I thought if George sees me he'd go, "Pattie Boyd who?" and we'd live happily ever after. It was a lovely thought.

Cousin Bruce Morrow

Anyway, the big day came and probably, I guess one of the most memorable days in my career. The place would be packed with over 55,000 kids. Most of them were female of course, because at that time the boys were kind of jealous. Boyfriends were very jealous of the Beatles because their girlfriends were all in love with their new heartthrobs. So they became sort of enemies to the boys. Maybe not enemies, but they became adversaries so most of the place was packed with girls.

Judith Kristen

Before we got to Shea we went over to The World's Fair. They had these futuristic phone booths and I had, thanks to seeing *A Hard Day's Night* fifty seven times and *Help!* about two dozen times, perfected quite the Liverpool accent. The New York cops had kept us from getting into the hotel, so I said to my friend, "Okay, here's the plan…"

When you're kids you always have candy wrappers or something going on. My friend liked Chuckles and they came in plastic. I was like a Hershey's kind of girl and that came wrapped in foil. They make a crunchy noise when you roll them between your fingers. I wanted a sound like we're far away because I remember calling England just wanting to talk with someone who had a Liverpool accent. For what, I don't know. But I would find out a telephone number and call. Of course we'd get a thirty five dollar phone bill and my mother would have a fit, but anyway, that's the way it went.

I always heard like a disturbance in the background. It's not like now. I can call Germany and it sounds like they're next door to me. But back then it always sounded like this "shhhhh" kind of thing going on in the background and little crackles every once in awhile. So I had my friend Shelly stand right next to this phone speaker and make "shhhh" and crackle noises with the candy wrappers so it gave that long distance sound to it.

You could always reach a hotel operator. To get a Beatle on the phone or even anybody in their entourage would be a different story. I thought we would have a better chance if it was from Cynthia Lennon or Louise Harrison in London than to say, "Hi this is Mary MacAfee from Yonkers, can I talk to Ringo?"

So I pretended to be an operator. I knew from my times calling Liverpool that unlisted numbers back then were called x-inquiries. I thought I had all my ducks in a row, but of course I did not. But it was worth a try. If you don't try nothing's gonna happen. If you do, at least you tried.

So my girlfriend is crackling the Chuckles and Hershey wrappers. I got on the phone and hear, "The Warwick Hotel. May I help you?" And I said in a British accent, "Hello, I'm calling from Great Britain. We have a person to person phone call for Mr. George Harrison."

She said, "Excuse me, can you just hold for a minute." And I was like, *oh no, could I be this lucky just the first time out? Did I sound that good? Please, please... Come on, come on...* But then she gets back on and says, "Do you have a number or a code?"

I said, "All I can tell you is we have an x-inquiry." And she asked me what an x-inquiry was. I said, "Well, I can't give you the number because it's what you call in America unlisted, which is what we refer to as an x-inquiry. Is there any way at all you could mention that?" And the candy wrappers are crackling in the background.

She goes away again and then comes back on and tells us it's not possible at the moment. I said, "Thank you very much. I will tell my party to try a little bit later."

It was only a dime for a phone call, so we called back. I wasn't gonna ask for George again, so I asked for Ringo. I was doing the same accent and the wrappers are going "shhhh" and all that stuff. We tried for Ringo because Maureen was calling him. We tried for Paul because his Aunt Gin wanted him on the phone. We tried Aunt Mimi and Cynthia, but nothing was flying. We even tried Mrs. Louise Harrison and Mrs. Louise French Harrison, which was George's mom's maiden name. And we also tried his sister Louise Harrison Caldwell. But do you think we get through? No.

My plan had worked the year before, but in 1965 there was a whole new awareness of fans trying to get to the Beatles. I guess it could bring a smile to American fans back then because we were pretty slick. In 1964 a lot of us were getting into hotels and were meeting Beatles and getting through barriers where we shouldn't. A lot of us were getting through with phone calls that were answered by a Beatle. But in '65 they kind'a pulled the reins in on us. I still look at a Hershey wrapper and a wrapper of Chuckles with a smile on my face.

Shea Stadium in Flushing, Queens, NY

George Orsino

I got there through a friend of mine, Mike Goffredo. We used to call him the unofficial mayor of South Philadelphia. He was a promotions man and did a lot in rock and roll and with disk jockeys. I would do a lot of work with him and take pictures of the celebrities like Elvis Presley, Tom Jones and whoever was coming into town. I wasn't a journalist. I had a photography studio. I did Fabian's wedding and others from the area, but I did mostly everyday people. That was my livelihood.

He asked me, "George, do you wanna go to Shea Stadium to see The Beatles?" And I said not really. I wasn't a fan. But then he said he could get me on the bus and if I bring my cameras I could take some pictures. So I said alright, I'll go.

So I met him at the bus in South Philly; Center City. It was sponsored by the radio station WIBG, number 99 on the dial. It was the number one station at the time and they were taking ninety-nine contest winners to Shea. I got on with my camera and case and the teenagers on the bus were asking me what I was doing. I was a little old for them. I was thirty-five. And I said I'm going to be taking pictures of the Beatles and they got all excited. They wanted to hand me all kinds of notes and things to hand to John Lennon, to hand to Ringo Starr and so on. I said I didn't know if I could do that or not.

Peter Altschuler

It was like what happened in 1969 when the Mets got into The World Series. The crowds going to the stadium were larger than usual. On top of that there was the traffic going from Manhattan to Queens. That was already annoying because I never went to Queens. I was either in Manhattan or I went to Brooklyn for Murray's Brooklyn Fox shows. For me, there was pretty much nothing in-between.

So I went out there and got into the stadium with my little free ticket in my hand. I was seventeen years old. I got my great seat and behind me was every screaming teenager on the planet as far as I could tell.

Fans arriving at Shea Stadium - August 15, 1965

The Fans Arrive

Shirley Kellar

I was fourteen years old from Massachusetts and went to the concert with two girlfriends. My friend Suzanne and I liked John and dressed alike with John Lennon hats and polka-dot dresses so they wouldn't miss us.

I remember it was so hot. But the thing I really noticed was how big the stadium was when we got in and saw where our seats were. We were at the top of the stadium and didn't even bring binoculars. I had never been to a baseball stadium or New York for that matter. It was a real experience. We had no idea how big it was going to be.

Judith Goodspeed

I was about ten and my dad got tickets to the concert. It took us about an hour to drive there from the middle of Long Island. When we got there, what I noticed right away was the crowd. There were girls… There were some boys too, but I saw mostly girls in their young teen years. The crowd was people my age. It was awesome to see this and feeling like I belonged. It was overwhelming to see this type of crowd.

I remember having to walk up the steps to get to our seats because we couldn't have had worse seats. We were in the top tier and the very back row. It was as far back as you could get.

Doug Fernandez

I was fourteen and living in Ardsley, a near north suburb of New York City. I took a local bus and then two subway trains to make my way to Flushing, Queens. I had purchased the ticket for my older brother as a birthday gift, his birthday being August 16th. But he didn't want it. So very quietly this fourteen year old set out to meet the Beatles.

Shea Stadium was a mad house and there was a lack of order as fans piled in. The audience was mostly girls and at fourteen, I only noticed the girls. It was very unlike attending a Mets game.

Eve Hoffman

It was very hot and humid and we were dropped off at Shea Stadium sometime in the afternoon and there was already a line of girls waiting outside to get in that evening. We took our place on line in the heat and after a while we started seeing limousines drive by us. We naturally thought that the Beatles would be in one, so all the girls swarmed each limo that came by. We stood outside for hours until the stadium gates opened about 6 pm that evening.

Bob Eaton

My cousin lived in New Haven, Connecticut and I lived in Rhode Island. He got the tickets and invited me to go. We left his house and took the train to New York. At every stop kids would get on with homemade signs and banners. One of my biggest memories of the trip was almost everyone had a transistor radio. When a Beatles song came on, everyone would tune to that station and we would be treated to an early version of surround sound.

I don't remember how we got from the train station to Shea, but I remember how hot it was. They were hauling people out before anyone ever was on stage.

Diane Gunther

From Valley Stream you would get on a bus and go into Jamaica and get on the subway at 69th Street. Then you would change to the elevated subway at Roosevelt Boulevard and go to Shea Stadium. I was a big baseball fan, so I had been to Shea a number of times and that route was very familiar to me. It was a quarter for the bus ride and fifteen cents for the subway ride.

We went early because we knew it was going to be really crowded. I guess they let us in early because I remember sitting in the stands with very few people around me. I had a good seat behind home plate in the very first tier. And since I knew I'd be sitting for awhile, I brought my summer reading. It was August 15th, getting close to the beginning of school and like most kids I put it off until the end of the summer. So I had all that reading to do. It was a Shakespeare play and I can't remember which one. So I was sitting there basically by myself doing my summer reading. I was fifteen years old.

Janice Bartel

I never saw so many Beatles fans in all my life. I kept wondering what the Beatles must of thought of seeing all these fans waiting for them.

There were thousands of handmade signs. The two I recall were "Give Us A Kiss" and "Happy Anniversary John."

Debbie Stern

We were too young to drive, so my parents dropped us off and went to The World's Fair. We made our way through a sea of fellow Beatlemaniacs to our seats in the mezzanine section and proudly hung our lovingly handmade sign, which proceeded to fall off the railing we taped it to in about thirty seconds flat.

Shirley Kellar

We were very excited and we came into the stadium, we asked someone where our seats were and they pointed to a middle area of the stadium at the very top. Since we had sent away for our tickets, I guess we couldn't expect the seats to be very close. So we decided that we would sit in the section where we came in near the third base dugout until the people came that really owned the seats. Our one friend, Gayle, got scared and went to her seat at the top of the Stadium. But Suzanne and I stayed. When the people came for their seats, we just kept moving to empty seats until there were no more seats left. We ended up standing in the aisle right behind the dugout.

Mary Troumouhis

It was an experience that, to this day when I think about it, makes me feel fifteen all over again. We had nosebleed seats at Shea Stadium, but being there was all that mattered.

Marc Catone

Our tickets were sort of like a package deal because it included a bus to get us there and back. One of the pluses and minuses was that they needed chaperones on this bus because we were all kids, teenagers for the most part and they wanted chaperones. And low and behold my parents volunteered to be chaperones. So I'm on this bus with my parents, which I didn't think was very cool at the time, going to Shea Stadium.

We bought tickets through a particular agency and they were a block of seats. I'm not sure if that was something done in a lot of little cities, but they would have a block of tickets and everyone would be sitting together. So we knew most of the people who were from Danbury and were in the rows all around us. I even knew the girls sitting in front of us from my high school classes. So it was kind of a *Danbury Goes To Shea Stadium* type of thing. They were all from our hometown, so that was kind of cool.

My parents didn't have tickets to go into the stadium. They went to The World's Fair while we were watching the Beatles. And my mother to this day, and she's eighty-three now, always remembers that she got a glimpse of Ed Sullivan outside Shea Stadium. I don't know if he was entering to announce the Beatles or leaving shortly after, but she got to see him and that made her day. She was all excited because she got to see Ed Sullivan in the flesh.

Marc Catone's ticket

Back Stage

The Beatles had eluded fans and media during their Saturday night visit to Rockefeller Center following *The Ed Sullivan Show* taping. But if everyone knew in advance where they would be and when, as they did with Shea Stadium, the only way the Beatles could travel was with a police escort.

Before they even arrived in New York, the city police department had decided it wouldn't be safe for the group to travel by car from Manhattan to Queens. Traffic through the Midtown Tunnel or across the 59th Street Bridge would be stop and go at best, while the streets and highways would be worse than the midweek evening rush hour. With the amount of cars and buses converging on Shea, not only from New York and Long Island but also the surrounding states, there was a chance the Beatles wouldn't even make it to their own concert. And any sightings by fans of John, Paul, George and Ringo stuck in traffic could be a potentially dangerous situation that had to be avoided.

The plan called for the group to be escorted from The Warwick Hotel to the East River Heliport in Lower Manhattan and then flown by helicopter to Queens. An earlier thought of making a grand entrance by landing on the field at Shea Stadium was cancelled for safety reasons. Instead the helicopter would land on the roof of a building at The World's Fair and the Beatles driven to the stadium inside a Wells Fargo armored van.

The subsequent television special, *The Beatles At Shea Stadium*, showed the group, Brian Epstein and their entourage flying over the Manhattan skyline toward Queens. Reportedly the pilot thought they would enjoy a scenic tour past some of the taller buildings and over Central Park. George Harrison, who was not a fan of flying, was quoted later as saying the next time he would drive.

Finally they were over Shea Stadium and even the reluctant flyer Harrison had to gaze down in amazement at what was below them. It wasn't yet dusk, but the banks of lights illuminated the playing field and more than 55,000 people who were waiting impatiently for their arrival. For four young men who had already known world fame and achieved more than anyone would have ever dared to predict it was a sight and experience none of them had ever witnessed before. The only way to describe it would be breathtaking.

_____ Shea Rocks _____

When we reached the airspace around Shea Stadium even George forgot to be nervous and smiled broadly. Below us some 56,000 fans realized that The Beatles were circling the stadium and thousands of flashbulbs popped off almost simultaneously to create a momentary display of dazzling light that lit up the evening sky. For the first time as we looked down at this unforgettable sight, it dawned upon four awe-struck Beatles that this might just turn into the greatest gig the group had ever done. Utterly overwhelmed, we descended in stunned silence to the landing site of The World's Fair, a mile or so from the concert venue, and transferred into a waiting Wells Fargo armoured truck. - **Tony Barrow** (8)

Russ Lease

When they were getting out at the stadium there was sort of a little mock ceremony. They were deputized for the night and presented with gold Wells Fargo Agent badges. The Wells Fargo guys who were driving the truck were Jack Lee and Mike Boyle. When the Beatles got out of the truck, that's when they gave them the badges. Then at some point in the locker room when they were getting dressed, McCartney suggested they wear them on their coats.

The badges are even kind of interesting. They've sort of disappeared, the four original badges. There's a picture of Lennon at home in the fall of '65 where he's sitting on his couch with his son Julian. And Julian's got this little sweater on and Lennon's Shea badge is hanging off the front of the sweater. I can only guess he gave it to Julian to play cowboys and Indians with.

Those badges have never turned up or been put up for auction. Of course if they did, unless it was being consigned by one of the members of the group, it would be hard to authenticate something like that. But that's always sort of puzzled me. Whatever happened to the badges?

George Orsino

For me, one thing led to another. I got off the bus and don't know how I left the crowd, but I made my own way and got through. A security guard put his hands up and I just stopped, kind of raised my camera and said, "I'm taking pictures." He might have felt embarrassed and he put his hands down and stepped aside. Before I knew it I was walking down the hallway to the locker room and a couple minutes later I see the Beatles coming in. Other people had tried to stop me, but I just raised my camera.

I didn't have a press pass. I had a 4x5 press camera with a big flash strobe on it and a battery pack. That was intimidating to these people. If I'd had a small 35mm hanging around my neck, forget about it. I wouldn't have made it. So security moved aside. I mean, how many times did they have something like that going on at Shea Stadium? That was it. It was the first time. They didn't know how to act and I just moved in. Before I knew it I was in the dressing room with them, which was in the clubhouse that the ballplayers used. I just tried to be nonchalant. I didn't want to go in there and just snap pictures of them and acting like a fan.

Scott Ross

I arrived at the stadium in the proper style. In the front seat of a right-hand drive Bentley. In the back seat we had two of the Ronettes. It was a nice entrance. We walked under the stadium. It was all kinds of concrete and steel; a monster cave. It was massive and scary. When I came out from under the grandstand, my breath literally left me. I had never seen such a mass of humanity in one place in my life. There were thousands of them and they looked like white specks. Individual lives crammed together, fifty-five thousand of them. I was ready to split for home. It was cozy and safe there.

Ed Sullivan would introduce The Beatles. King Curtis was on the bill, so I was there to introduce King Curtis and that's what I did.

Shaun Weiss

When Ed Sullivan showed up one the girls working for him, I think it was Geri, was looking around at the crowd. I saw her and she brought my sister and me down and stuck us in the dugout. A male in the dugout wasn't bad, but a female in the dugout screaming...

Scott Ross with The Ronettes - Veronica, Nedra and Estelle

We were going to be there when the Beatles ran out. But while I was sitting in the dugout, what really amazed me was that The Rolling Stones were there.

Peter Bennett

For the 1965 concert, I was with The Stones. We were on a yacht touring the East River. I told Mick Jagger and Keith Richards that the Beatles were at Shea Stadium. I said maybe we should go. And they said, "Oh yeah, let's go. How are we going to get there?"

I called the police department in Queens and said we'd like to see The Beatles. So what happened was we docked the boat at the marina in Flushing and had a police escort to Shea Stadium. We got right in. In fact, I saw Sid Bernstein and I also saw Bobby Vinton. We went into the dugout.

Shaun Weiss

Yeah, the band was on a boat cruise. You know, people didn't believe Peter. It took many years and I don't think anybody believed that he brought The Stones there until *TV Guide* did their exposé and Peter was in it. There was a picture of Peter with Mick. He was with the Stones on that boat cruise and then came to the stadium. He was there.

Peter was so important in the history of The Beatles. Much more than even Nat was because Peter promoted them. He had an insight. It wasn't until I went to England that I realized how important Peter Bennett was to the history of The Beatles. And he's taken a backseat because he didn't promote himself. His main concern was getting people number one hits.

Ron Schneider

My uncle Allen Klein was managing The Rolling Stones at the time. I was the business manger. I did all the deals and all that. I was a promoter in effect, and I hired tour managers.

It's a memory that's stayed with me to this day. Actually, I have a picture of us on that yacht. It was one of the first times I met Mick and Keith. But anyhow, I didn't know you could go to Shea Stadium via the water. We took the yacht up and docked in the basin. I believe Peter arranged the whole thing. Mick, Keith, Allen and all of us walked to the stadium. The thing that shocked me most was the fact that we could pull the yacht into the harbor and walk to Shea Stadium. That's what surprised me most.

I don't remember the other Stones being with us. What I do remember is Mick and Keith. We went down to the dressing room and it was just mobbed. It looked like a big sale at Macy's or something. It was shoulder to shoulder people and we had to push through. I'm a little guy and I could always squeeze through. Mick and Keith were just ahead of me and I was walking close to Keith. We were pushing through and my uncle, Allen Klein, was trailing and people were getting between us.

We all pushed through into the main dressing room where the Beatles were with all the people crowded around them as well. And Mick went right over to John first. It was just that kind of a small intimacy in the sense that they all knew each other and went over and hung out together. Whereas I pushed through and got by the security guys, but they grabbed my uncle and held him back. And he's like, "Ron!" and screaming out to me.

I turned around and looked at the guard and I said, "He's with me." And they let him come through. And afterwards we were laughing because the only connection I had was that I was standing close to Keith and walking with him. That's why I guess the guard allowed me in. And then when I said it was okay for Allen, the guard said, "Oh yeah, come on in."

We met and all hung around for a little while. Then they had to get ready to go on.

Scott Ross

I knew Pete and I remember them in the locker room. I knew The Stones quite well. I was very close to Brian and Bill and then Keith, in that order. Mick and I had a lot of altercations.

> **"We went down to the dressing room and it was just mobbed. It looked like a big sale at Macy's or something."
> - Ron Schneider**

Peter Bennett

The Beatles knew me because I had met them before they did their concert at Forest Hills Stadium the year before. I was involved with the concert, promoting it, and met them with Murray the K who introduced The Beatles on stage. Murray and I were close. I was managing him at the time.

So at Forest Hills Stadium, Murray was telling the Beatles and Brian Epstein that I started The Stones' career in America. I was their promotions manager and promoted their records. Now, John Lennon was close to Mick Jagger and said the guys knew that. The Beatles knew me because of The Rolling Stones.

At Shea Stadium Mick and Keith were saying, "You know Peter." And they said, "Yeah, the big promotions guy. We know that. We know him and Murray the K." I was managing Murray and the big Stones' record that I was promoting around the time of Shea Stadium in '65 was *Satisfaction*. When Brian Epstein died I wound up being the promotions manager for The Beatles and also promoting Apple Records.

Nedra Talley-Ross

Backstage could be very boring. You're just sitting there and really not thinking about it because it was work and you're doing a gig. You didn't think, *well, this is where I'm performing*. You had the dates and you had a time. You're out for two weeks, one week, one show or whatever. Then you had another place to go and you were sort of guided. Someone is taking you there, you're flying, getting off the plane, doing whatever, you perform, they take you from there and you go home. So you did not sit around going; *oh I'm going to this city and I'm going to take a tour and see what's in that city.* You missed all of those things, because it was just work.

If you didn't have people to sit with and laugh with backstage, it could be very boring. People must think *my goodness that's crazy* or *are you crazy?* Well, I guess if you don't know that, you have your imagination of what it must be.

Cousin Bruce Morrow

That dressing room was crowded. It was what I call a gang Beatle thing. Everybody and their brothers and sisters were trying to get into this. This was the hottest room in town. Everybody wanted to share space with them and it's continued for many years. Everywhere the Beatles went.

You know, it's like human nature. People love to hang onto the coattails of a winner. That's why everybody became The Fifth Beatle. They didn't like that, by the way. They didn't like that Murray-thing and a couple of the other people calling themselves Fifth Beatles. Every market had a Fifth Beatle. They didn't like that.

Nedra Talley-Ross

I was never one to sit there and go *I've got to be in there...* I didn't have that in me. I didn't like the feel of it because there were people you looked at and thought *who are they?* Are these people really there because they love this person, or are they there because of who this person is now? Would they be there for you later? Is it that they want something from you? It's almost like the star-gazing side of things, that *oh my gosh, I gotta be at that party* or *I've gotta be in that room* or *I need to be there.* The Beatles were aware of all of that.

When we would sit around and really talk about life and some of the decisions of life, who is there because of *you?* Who really knows you and wants to be your friend because of you? Or do you want to be my friend because I'm what the world sees as a celebrity? Whenever I see that somebody's clinging or whatever, it's because they want to get in more. You know why those people are there and want to meet them. There was so much of that and it was so much of a turnoff for me because it was just climbing. Everybody was just social climbing.

What was different with the Beatles was that they were very guarded in who they were in a lot of ways. So people really couldn't say, "Gee, let's just be friends." That was different too because then people just wanted the limelight of saying, "I touched them. I've been near them. If you go to the party I want to be there." You know?

With us, we had met them before they came over here. We were performers. You hung with people because those were our peers. So I don't think they were guarded around us at all.

Scott met The Beatles and The Stones through me. Because he was from Scotland and they were from England, all he needed to do was speak with his accent and they were, "Oh, you really are one of us!" He had his rapport going and then went on and did things with them that I didn't even do. I mean, The Stones came to dinner at my house uptown on Riverside Drive. The building high rise was in an uproar because The Stones were there.

Scott Ross

I was with the Beatles backstage because I had been with them previously and they knew who I was. There were all kinds of disc jockeys and Ed Sullivan and the Fifth Beatle, Murray the K. There were about three hundred Fifth Beatles throughout the U.S. There were even deejays from California to get exclusive bits of information about the Beatles. Maybe even an interview with one of them. "Pardon me, George, but could you say hello to all the listeners on WLSD who love you?" Or, "Paul, are you and Jane Asher really father and mother to seven children secretly?" "Ringo, why did you get married?" "John, could you tell us what time you went to the bathroom this morning?"

A couple of the Rolling Stones were standing off to the side. If they couldn't get the Beatles they could always talk to the Stones. "Hey Keith, what do you think of The Beatles?" "Hey Mick, what time did you take a bath this morning?" *Hey*, I said in my head, *go stick it up your nose colonist.*

Nedra Talley-Ross

I was backstage, but I was in the midst of… That night when I left there, I had to go meet with my mom to call off my engagement to Scott. It was that night, so the whole evening for me was sitting there knowing that I had to deal with my mom. Scott and I were planning to get married and she was very much against it.

I was just twenty I think, or maybe nineteen. He was not what she saw for me. He also had long hair. Okay, for the Beatles, but not with my mom. She could say, "I grew you to get you to where you are and you're going to marry him?"

Friends were appearing and we were hanging with them and all those things, but my life was dealing with… My mother's very strong and it was like somebody getting ready to go to the principal's office. You can't enjoy the day at school when they say, "At three o'clock meet with the principal." I was going to meet her afterwards. So that evening for me was major. I did delay our marriage for a year.

George Orsino

A security guard at one of the doors asked me if I could get an autograph for his daughters. I said I didn't know if I could do that or not. I'd kind of feel funny because now I'm not a photographer. I'm a fan. And then they'll kind of look different toward you. I always tried not to make these guys overpower me. I'm thinking that I'm the important guy there. The photographer's the important guy there, not them. I try to make them get that feeling. But I said, "Let me see what I can do."

So I went over and Ringo Starr was sitting on a bench drinking a soda. I said, "Ringo, could you do a security guard here a favor and sign these?" Two pamphlets, papers, whatever they were. And he goes, "What should I say?" Meaning what should he write as far as their names. I think we got Marie and Dolores from the security guard. Ringo was fine and he wrote down their names and signed his name. I gave them to the security guard and he kind of flipped-out. It was great and that was it.

I was trying to be cool. I took a couple pictures in there. John Lennon and Paul McCartney were talking to PR men around a table. And a girl that was a friend of theirs, I guess, was sitting at this table. They were just talking.

Joan Murray

I was backstage and they were absolutely adorable. They were so nice to me. Now I don't know if it's because… Well at that time, I was the

Quiet area backstage after Ringo signed autograph for security guard
Ringo seated left, George standing center, Paul seated at table
Man in front and men talking with George are unidentified

cutest little thing. I must say that because I was very unusual. I was an
interesting butterscotch color and I wore a lot of eye makeup that I
learned from Twiggy. I was the first reporter to interview Twiggy when
she came to the United States. I had a lot of heavy eye lashes and a lot of
hair. I don't know what I was thinking! But the Beatles were adorable.

I think they were nervous because they did not expect this kind of
reception. They did not know what to expect. Today they have concerts
with what, a 100,000 people? I mean if you look at the Tina Turner
concert down in South America, I think there were 100,000 people.
56,000 people at Shea Stadium in the mid-60's was a huge, huge event.

So I would image that they were nervous and it seemed like they clung
together. There was security, but today there would be much more
security. In fact there would be an enormous amount. But I think
because there was not that much security I just felt that they felt, and I

don't want to overdramatize it, that they felt in fear of their lives. I really did, because there were so many people around them.

I'd been around that also with other celebrities. They would go into a car and fans would rock the car or they'd pull at their hair or pull at their clothes and whatnot. And it's very frightening. And I think that they were startled; frightened. I don't know if I want to say *feared for their lives*, but it was just something that had never happened before. Plus they were in a foreign country.

Ron Schneider

I recall everybody being very nervous because it was a big event. So I do remember them being nervous. Everybody just seemed to be on edge. And there was a lot of electricity in the air as it was, because it was such a big thing at that stadium at that time.

Peter Bennett

The experience of Shea Stadium was the size. So many thousands of people… I was used to shows with about 16,000. And at Shea Stadium they were going crazy before the Beatles even came out with screaming and yelling and all that. I remember when we got there and seeing all the buses and the field full of police and everything. I was nervous myself. I said to myself, w*hat the hell did I get involved in here?* I shouldn't have said anything, you know? I was scared myself.

The guys were so nervous. They were smoking cigarettes like mad. They had cigarettes sitting all around. And they were shivering, you know?

Ron Schneider

They were smoking cigarettes. I would've smelled weed. You'd smell it in that dressing room. There wouldn't be any place… There was no room to move; it was definitely that packed. So it's not like they'd even be able to light up. I didn't smell anything. I think the excitement of the crowd was enough energy for everybody.

Scott Ross

They were nervous. But you know I think they always handled that stuff with their cynicism and their humor, especially John. There was an anxiety about it. The whole thing was so insane. Nobody had ever seen anything like that. So yeah, they had anxiety about it.

•

For the 55,600 fans outside that couldn't get past security and into the Beatles dressing room, the show had already started. A small stage about thirty feet square and five feet high had been constructed on the baseball playing field over second base. Compared to the massive stage used by The Rolling Stones at Shea Stadium almost a quarter of a century later, it would hardly be large enough to hold all the amplifiers used by Keith Richards. But in 1965 there was more than enough space for four Beatles and their equipment.

Another stipulation placed on Bernstein would not allow him to have any seating on the field. For crowd control and safety purposes, ticketholders were restricted to the stadium seats and almost two thousand security personnel were on duty to keep them there. If field seating had been approved, the sea of people from the upper deck to the stage might have doubled the size of the crowd. Instead the closest seats were more than one hundred feet away from where The Beatles would be playing.

At approximately 7:35 p.m. everyone was asked to stand for the singing of *The National Anthem* accompanied by The King Curtis Band. Cousin Brucie welcomed the audience and introduced Murray the K, who announced The Discotheque Dancers, five girls and one boy, to demonstrate various dances such as the *Frug* and *Watusi* to a medley of hit songs including *Can't Buy Me Love* and *A Hard Day's Night*. Next up was Scott Ross to introduce The King Curtis Band.

Scott Ross

The show had started, but no one had really noticed. Then somebody said, "Hey Scott, you're on." It was about a hundred yards or a mile from where I was in the dressing room to where I was supposed to be on stage. I decided to run.

I took off and was slammed in the back of the neck by a cop who said, "Where do you think you're going, buddy?" I told him up on stage and that I'm a talent. I'm booked. Somebody pulled him off and I ran for the platform on second base. Cousin Brucie introduced me.

I jumped up on stage and faced the crowd for the first time. It was unbelievable. I didn't have an act or a bit and no idea what I was going to do. I looked up in the stands and a lot more people than I had anticipated were yelling, "We love Scott!" We love Scott!" Man, they were beautiful and nuts.

Some kids had made signs out of bed sheets and they were hanging down over the tiers of bleachers with things like, *Beatles Forever!* and *Long Live The Beatles.* I also saw one that said, *Scott We're With You.* What was that doing in there? I introduced King Curtis and split. I don't even remember what I said and of course, no one paid any attention to me or King Curtis.

•

WMCA's Frank Stickle and the WMCA Good Guys sang a jingle about the Beatles and their radio station before bringing up Cannibal & the Headhunters. Following their hit song *Land of 1000 Dances,* Cousin Brucie introduced WABC deejay Hal Jackson to welcome singer Marvin Gaye, who did not perform. Following a set by Brenda Holloway and backed by The King Curtis Band, Cousin Brucie introduced WABC deejay Charlie Greer.

Over crowd chants of "We want The Beatles," Cousin Brucie read off some of the signs hung by fans throughout the stadium while the instrumental group Sounds Inc., also managed by Brian Epstein, took their places on stage. Their opening song was *The William Tell Overture.*

_____ **Shea Rocks** _____

"The Beatles everybody, they are the greatest. Ladies and gentlemen, they will be here soon. They're ready for'ya! Are you ready for them?! I bet you are. Ladies and gentlemen, they'll be up in a few moments. They're getting themselves ready and let me tell you they told Cousin Brucie they can't wait to make this their greatest appearance. What do you think of these fabulous Beatles? Let's hear it for them! Let'em hear it in their dressing room!" – **Cousin Brucie on stage at Shea Stadium** (9)

Judith Kristen

What always makes me feel really bad, even when I go to concerts now, are the opening acts. At Shea Stadium it just never ended. Did you ever see a tape of what we had to sit through? Those disco dancers with white go-go boots? Oh please…

Now I always cheer for the opening acts. But I remember at Shea my girlfriend said we didn't have to cheer for these people because they got to meet the Beatles. They were spending all this time back in the locker room with them. You don't have to cheer for these people. And I remember the go-go girls because my girlfriend was saying, "I wonder how many of them might have…" No! Sorry, don't talk to me about that.

"George Harrison peeked out to see what was going on out there." - Shaun Weiss

Peter Altschuler

I couldn't hear anything that anybody was saying on stage. Every time anybody showed up on that stage at any point while I was there, the crowd went wild. I don't know who they expected it to be, but it was like, *well, if it's The Beatles let's scream for them!* Well, it was never The Beatles. It was somebody setting up a microphone or somebody prepping the stage for the first act, or whatever it was. I couldn't hear anything.

Shaun Weiss

I got caught up in the things that were happening in the dugout that people couldn't see. Like The Stones and Ed Sullivan being there. I was also trying to take a peek inside to see where the Beatles were. I would get to a certain point and then stop because there were guards. There were things happening that the fans didn't see and that's what I got caught up in.

George Harrison peeked out to see what was going on out there. He came and looked out of the dugout and ran back in. I don't know if anyone else was behind him because I got asked to go to the other side. But I could see George coming down the walkway. Remember, backstage on those walkways was filled with people. It was The Rolling

Stones, Pete Bennett, guards, Beatles people like Tony Barrow, and Brian's clan of people.

I could hear the crowd in the stands, shuffling around and yelling things out. But knowing George Harrison came in and peeked and that they were no more than fifty feet from me, that's what I was caught up in. All that stuff.

Michael Adams

I had a ground pass with Clayco Films, so I was on the field. They had a little setup, like a dugout for the cameramen that was closer to the stage, so I could sit in there. It was a makeshift dugout or whatever. I don't even know what it was, but it was between the pitcher's mound and the stage.

> **"This was The Big Apple. It was the major experience that they would have so far in the United States, so they were very, very nervous."**
> **- Cousin Bruce Morrow**

It was for the cameramen and they were hunkered down in it. If you see the film, you'll see it at one point because one of the camera guys sweeps past and there you go. He's got the other camera guys in the shot.

I was there with my dad. I caught the concert, but I didn't catch it sitting down. It was a long haul before The Beatles came on. Once The Beatles came out I was pretty much standing the entire time.

•

In the locker room John, Paul, George and Ringo were very aware of being filmed for the upcoming television special they were co-producing with Brian Epstein and Ed Sullivan. When the cameras were aimed in their direction they smiled, opened gifts from fans, played guitars, watched television and generally fell in line with the images they had portrayed in *Help!* When the cameras turned away, they talked with friends, gave interviews and smoked cigarettes. Backstage quotes from all four were recorded and later added to the edited television footage:

_____ Shea Rocks _____

"We always get dead nervous before we go onstage and nine times out of ten we suddenly feel tired about half an hour before when we go to get changed. All of a sudden everybody's tired and changing into the suits and putting the shirt on you feel, ah, no... And then just as soon as you get on it's alright." – **John Lennon** (10)

"I think it makes us less nervous playing to a big crowd than a little crowd. Because if you're playing to a little crowd they're gonna hear what you're playing." – **Paul McCartney** (11)

_____

At one point John, Paul and George sat down with their guitars to rehearse the songs they would play. According to a voiceover in the television special from McCartney, they had meant to do it the day before but had forgotten.

Eventually it was time to change into their stage clothes. Instead of the business style suits Epstein and the Beatles had favored since abandoning the collarless jackets that had caused a fashion stir during their 1964 breakthrough in America, they had another look that would forever be related to their concert at Shea Stadium.

"The whole thing was so insane. Nobody had ever seen anything like that." - Scott Ross

Russ Lease

The information I've found from researching over the years was that the Shea Jackets were McCartney's idea. He had the overall design. The inspiration was the Bahamian police jackets they saw in February 1965 while filming _Help!_ The police in the Bahamas wore an almost identical jacket except it was done in a very stark white and had belts over it. McCartney thought the jacket was very cool looking, so that was the impetus for the idea he took back to Dougie Millings in London.

Millings made all of their stage clothing starting in '63 with the collarless suits. When they all moved down to London from Liverpool,

Paul McCartney's Shea Jacket

Millings was well known for doing stage clothing, clothing for the stars, all the West End plays and all that kind of thing. Brian Epstein hooked up with him and all the way through their touring years he made all their outfits. So McCartney sat down with him when they got back to London and kind of described and showed images of the Bahamian police jacket. That's what the Shea jacket was born out of. The first time they wore them publicly was in April of '65 at the New Musical Express Poll Winners Concert in London.

I'm not sure where the name Shea Jacket came from. In England it was referred to as the Beatles Military Coat or the Beatles Military Tunic. That's what the Beatles referred to it as and that's what some of the auction houses referred to it as. To me, ever since I acquired McCartney's I've always just naturally referred to it as the Shea Jacket because for the most part, that's where everybody saw it for the first time.

Now universally it's known as the Shea Jacket, but I really don't know where that came from, really. Certainly the description in the Sotheby catalogue whenever the McCartney one was being sold or Lennon's that's been sold a couple of times as well as Ringo's, it's always referred to as the Tan Military Tunic or the Khaki Military Tunic. I don't know. I might have had something to do with that being called the Shea Jacket because it just seemed like the natural name to me.

It's funny because they really didn't wear the jackets that much. They're wearing them in the promo videos for *Day Tripper* and *We Can Work It Out*, but only wore them six or seven times on stage. It's not nearly as much as everyone thinks. With the Shea Stadium show being the most famous and filmed for the television special, that's why it's so well known.

Nedra Talley-Ross

When The Ronettes went to England, we met The Rolling Stones first. We were headlining and they opened for us. I remember The Stones coming to our dressing room and hanging out and talking to us. I said, "We're going to need to get ready. Don't you guys need to get ready for the show?" And they were like, "No. We're dressed." And I was thinking *what are they wearing?*

Whatever they wore it was rumpled looking or just average. And coming from America you had groups like The Temptations and different ones that knew how to dress to go on stage. Even the girl groups... You know, The Ronettes were known for our look. Nobody just went on stage in dirty clothes.

Russ Lease

Initially the Beatles were going to wear black suits. This story comes from Larry Kane, the journalist that traveled with them and wrote a couple books. Larry told me that there frequently was discussion backstage about what they were going to wear on stage each night and Lennon felt he didn't like the Shea

jackets very much. He used to say that he didn't like the way the collar rode up when he had the guitar strap on. But mainly he didn't like the sort of quasi-military suggestion of the Shea jacket or the look of it. He was just very anti-military and he argued with McCartney backstage about that.

They were going to wear black suits, but McCartney wanted them to wear the tan Shea jackets. There was a little bit of discussion and McCartney won out. It was also McCartney's idea to wear the Wells Fargo badges on their jackets that they had received when they arrived at Shea.

George Orsino

We left the locker room and were going down the hallway and now we're kind of picking up all kinds of people. I don't know where everybody came from and I'm trying to stay in front of them. I was walking along the side of the wall. In fact, I'm in the video. You can see me sneaking up, trying to creep up in front of the Beatles as they're walking. I'm going alongside the wall, trying to work my way through.

I finally get in front of the crowd and I'm walking backwards taking pictures. I had a camera that would hold eight pictures. I'm taking a picture and trying to wind the film up. You got a crank on it and you crank the film. I'm walking backwards and I holler to John Lennon to slow down. "You're gonna run me over!"

He said, "That's not my problem." And he kind of said it with a laugh and a smile. *That's not my problem.* And I'm walking and I took a couple more pictures.

The crowd had us stopped at one area. That's where the door was that led us to the dugout and then the field where the stage was on second base. They got jammed up by this door and the security guard is trying to get all the Beatles in the front. I took a picture and you can see George Harrison, Peter Bennett, Allen Klein, Mick Jagger and Bobby Vinton. And Bobby's looking like he's saying, "Wow, what's going on?!"

They were trying to get Ringo Starr up in front. He was in the back somewhere. In one of my pictures you can see John Lennon near the door and see the handle of a guitar with four strings on it, so you know that's Paul McCartney's bass guitar. You see George Harrison is there. All but Ringo Starr and they're waiting for him to come up from the back so they can leave together.

Waiting for Ringo before running onto the field. From left - Peter Bennett (behind policeman's cap), Allen Klein, Bobby Vinton, George Harrison and Mick Jagger. Top of Paul McCartney's bass guitar is seen at right edge of photo. Standing behind Paul's bass is John Lennon.

So meanwhile I'm jammed up with this 4x5 camera, which is pretty big. And I can't take any more pictures because I was running out of film. Then I see these swinging doors alongside of me. I pushed them open and there were commodes for the ballplayers. *Wow, a private room here!* So I went in there and stood on the commode. I'm hanging on and shooting over a cinder block wall. I've got my elbow on the top of the wall and was taking a couple pictures.

I unloaded a black and white roll of film there. Maybe two or three shots were left, that's all I had. I used that to take the shots of Mick Jagger and Bobby Vinton. I knew Bobby Vinton because I had done some work with him. I didn't know who Mick Jagger was until one day I had the pictures in my studio window and a bunch of teenagers were outside screaming and jumping up and down. I said, "What's wrong?" And they said, "Mick Jagger! He's in one of the pictures!" I didn't know.

Anyway, I finished the roll of film at that point. I got down and walked out toward the guard and said I had to get to the stage. So he opened the door for me and I ran out to the field. That's when I changed my film to color. I only had one more roll and it was color film. I wish I'd had a ton of it. I got in position and waited for The Beatles to come out.

Shaun Weiss

Ed Sullivan came into the dugout and The Rolling Stones were in the walkway. I could look in and see them. I saw them walking down with Peter Bennett. I think Peter was in front and Mick was behind him. It was an interesting sight.

Peter Bennett

We walked from the locker room and the Stones were in the dugout with me. And of course some of the fans could see the Stones in the dugout. You couldn't see that clear into the dugout, but what happened was they probably saw Mick's head or Keith from the opposite side of the field. And they started yelling, "The Stones! The Stones! The Stones!" We were getting nervous.

"They didn't even want to go the stage because they were so nervous. We were in the dugout and they were shaking" - Peter Bennett

---

Shaun Weiss

All the girls started to notice them when they came into the dugout. They started chanting, "The Stones! We want The Stones!" And Peter turned around and said they should probably leave because it was a show for the Beatles and not the Stones. So I know they ended up leaving early. They stayed for maybe one or two songs.

Peter Bennett

The Beatles made it to the dugout and got more nervous. They didn't even want to go on the stage because they were so nervous. We were in the dugout and they were shaking. They were so nervous and scared.

It really got bad when we were in the dugout, because they saw bottles flying down. At that time they were using glass bottles for beer and soda and they were flying down on the field. Some of the kids were throwing things. The Beatles were not used to doing a stadium like that.

Cousin Bruce Morrow

We were in the dugout. Ed Sullivan was right by my side. Lennon and McCartney came over and John Lennon said to me, "Coo'zin'…" That's what he used to call me, *Coo'zin*, instead of Cousin. He asked, "Is this gonna be dangerous?" Because you know, they felt the pressure of the audience, the power.

Now with all of the things they had done in the past, all the amazing things in Europe and all over, this was probably the most exciting and, they felt, the scariest. It was because of the pressure of the audience. The audience was so large and so loud.

I explained to them, "Guys, there's no problem here. This audience is here out of love and they're here to share this space with you," which John Lennon, by the way, never really *got*. He never really understood that. And he still didn't years later when I was with him in Central Park during one of his last appearances.

We were in the dugout and they asked, "Are you sure?" And I said yes.

They were very nervous at that particular thing. And with all the experience they had, they were still sort of wet behind the ears and not very secure about what they were doing because this was a major thing. This was The Big Apple. It was the major experience that they would have so far in this country, so they were very, very nervous.

Ken Mansfield

For the Beatles to have experienced that, I think they would probably reflect on it as being a big moment in their lives. You know, just to have experienced it. And I don't think they expected it. I don't think they expected a lot of things.

I got in a limo with Paul in 1968 when we had to go through a crush of people leaving a hotel. We slammed the door and he looked at me like he didn't get it - even then. So I don't think they really expected any of that at Shea Stadium.

Peter Bennett

In the dugout, John Lennon did most of the talking. He said there were all sorts of bottles coming down. "I could get hit in the head." And they were nervous. They saw that crowd. They peeked out and could see the whole crowd.

I got nervous too because I had been hearing "The Stones! The Stones!" They had been yelling. And what happens is word gets around. You know what I mean? More and more kids were yelling, "The Stones! The Stones!" And they were throwing bottles and more stuff on the field before the Beatles even came out.

•

Shea Stadium was electric with emotion and anticipation. Everyone within screaming distance knew what was coming next and the stands shook with excitement.

On stage Mal Evans arranged amplifiers and set up the rented Vox Continental Portable Organ John had used the day before at *The Ed Sullivan Show* taping. The guitar and bass amplifiers had been custom made by Vox to push out one hundred watts of power each, compared to thirty watt models used during their first concerts in America. The sound would also be pumped out through the stadium's public address system. Since no pop group had ever played a venue this big in front of an audience this size, they hoped at least some of the sound generated by the group on stage would be heard.

Cousin Bruce Morrow

So we got ready. I was standing with Ed Sullivan and Bernstein came over to us and said, "Okay, guys. Let's get it going."

We went out and were walking up to that little stage to announce The Beatles. Ed Sullivan mounted the stairs before I did. I was right behind him about two steps and suddenly about half way up he turns around and he said to me, "Cousin Brucie, is this dangerous?" John Lennon had asked me the same question.

I'm looking at Sullivan and I'm thinking this guy is such a stiff... So I felt like I just wanted to get him. Did you ever feel like you wanted to, you know, give someone a little shot? And I said to him, "Ed, very."

He looked at me and his eyes, he had these big bulging eyes anyway and his eyes bulged more and he says, "Really?" And he continues up the stairs and he turns around again and he goes, "Brucie. What do we do?"

I said to myself, *I got him*. And this is exactly what I said to him. "Pray Ed. Pray." He looked at me and continued up the stairs.

The Fans In The Stands

Rosemary McKinley

There was great excitement and anticipation. What I remember most is the roar of the crowd coming into the stadium. It was deafening in a good way. Everyone was excited to see The Beatles live. No one knew how and when they were going to enter the stadium. Everyone was looking at the dugout or the entrances to the field. When the helicopter came from overhead the crowd was wild with excitement and girls were yelling and fainting.

Dotty Poirier

There were other bands and singers at this concert, but I don't remember any of their names. It seemed to take forever for The Beatles to come out.

Diane Gunther

I could not tell you who the opening acts were. I remember every time they introduced somebody, everybody groaned. It was that kind of thing.

Arlene Levine

I know there were acts before them, but everybody was like, "Just get off!" Those poor opening acts... We just wanted to see The Beatles. I guess the really popular acts at that time weren't going to put themselves through it. They wouldn't want to perform before the Beatles.

Janice Bartel

The acts prior to the Beatles taking the stage were somewhat of a blur because all I was doing was screaming, "We want The Beatles!" One of the opening acts, Brenda Holloway, kept yelling into the microphone, "We love the Beatles too and they will be coming out soon." Of course then everyone would scream.

Marc Catone

I also recall being very impatient with the opening acts. We just couldn't wait for these people to get done. I remember The King Curtis

Band playing and Sounds Incorporated in particular… I don't remember Brenda Holloway whatsoever, but I know she sang there. But the thing that stood out in my mind and the only song I remember was *Land of A 1000 Dances* by Cannibal and the Headhunters. But we just couldn't wait for these people to get done so we could see The Beatles.

Pattie Noah

I remember being bored to tears by the opening bands and dancers. I had my sight set on one prize only. I remember the helicopter coming in, but at the time had no idea that they were inside it. People were screaming so loud you couldn't hear the rotors of the 'copter.

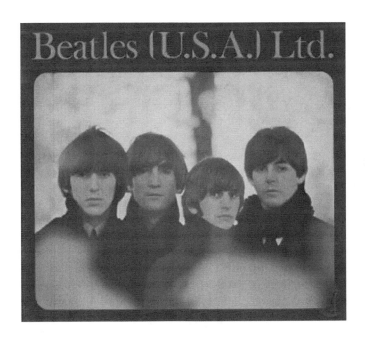

1965 Tour Program

Here They Are The Beatles!

At approximately 8:45 pm everyone in Shea Stadium knew what was coming next. Waves of screams and the energy of anticipation from over 55,000 people were aimed at the stage as Cousin Brucie walked up to the microphone. Facing the crowd for his final time that evening he introduced Sid Bernstein, who only two years earlier had taken a chance when he promoted an unknown beat group from England for two shows in New York City.

_____ Shea Rocks _____

"One of our finest newspapermen, the number one showman of the world, and most important of all, a truly great American, Mr. Ed Sullivan." – **Sid Bernstein**

"Thank you very much Sid. Now ladies and gentlemen, honored by their country, decorated by their Queen and loved here in America, here are The Beatles!" – **Ed Sullivan**

Peter Bennett

Ed Sullivan was up there and Bruce Morrow. And the stadium shook. Even in the dugout it was shaking a little bit. Just talking with the Beatles in the dugout we were scared. The dugout is open, but we had a top over us. We weren't outside on the field, but we were right near it. If we walked out, we'd be right on the field.

So we were right there. I told them, "Good luck." I told the guys, "Fellas, good luck." And they were, "Oh, yeah, oh yeah…" And they were shivering.

Ed Sullivan announced The Beatles and all of a sudden when they went out the whole place is going crazy. As far as the stadium shaking and the whole thing, it actually started shaking more when they went on.

Shaun Weiss

I was standing there and the guards told me to get away because they were coming through. The Beatles were in that walkway right where the door was and then they came running out of the dugout.

Arthur Aaron

There was a constant roar, "Aaahhh!" It never stopped. When you go to a baseball game and somebody hits a home run there's a roar that subsides after ten seconds or whatever. This roar never subsided. It never subsided for the entire three hours that I was there. Can you imagine that? A roar that never subsides...

If you go to Niagara Falls and stand right where the water starts to drop over the falls, all you hear is, "Aaahhh..." Because it's constant; it never stops. It's doing that right now. That's what it was like.

Nedra Talley-Ross

It was a roar of people. It was a roar of sound. It was the hysteria of America at that time.

Joan Murray

It was already loud. I wondered how they would hear themselves with all that noise.

•

The police, reporters and photographers waiting outside the dugout opened a path for Paul, Ringo, John and George as they ran up the steps and onto the field. The screams were deafening, soaring into a high pitched roar of solid noise filling the air and seeping into every crevice of the stadium. The sound was electrifying and emotional and it seemed as if all 55,600 in attendance rose at once to watch one of the most famous jogs ever onto the playing field at Shea. Hundreds of Brownie Cameras aimed to capture the moment sent bright flashes of light pulsating through the stands.

Dressed in their tan jackets and black pants, Paul, George and Ringo presented the unified group image Epstein had in mind when he first insisted they wear matching tailored suits instead of the more dangerous looking black leather they preferred. John admitted in later interviews he had agreed to Paul's wishes to wear the military style jacket, but as an individual protest he refused to button it. His Wells Fargo Badge was pinned over the left pocket while his open jacket revealed a black t-shirt. In what might have been another personal statement or only a result of dressing in a hurry backstage, George was the only Beatle to wear the badge over his right pocket.

Russ Lease

Yeah. That's right. But Lennon didn't often do the top button of his shirts and things like that. The images I have from the Portland show where they also wore the jackets, it's fairly buttoned up. At The Hollywood Bowl show, he's got it open just like at Shea.

Everybody also thinks they just wore black t-shirts underneath it, but that was strictly at the Shea show. Out on the west coast when they did The Hollywood Bowl show, they actually wore white button down shirts and ties just like they would with any other suit. And in England for the NME show and the videos, they wore black turtle necks underneath. I guess the t-shirt thing was because it was a hot night in New York and they didn't want to put too much on underneath. But that's the only time they wore black t-shirts underneath it. It was just that night. Otherwise they wore their regular button down shirts.

•

Once they reached the infield dirt of the baseball diamond, security stopped the press from following and the Beatles emerged from the pack giving fans their first unobstructed view of the famous foursome. The noise raining down on them never let up. Excited girls stood in the aisles, screamed and waved their arms trying to gain the attention of their favorite Beatle. Some cried and held onto each other for support while others slumped in their seats overcome with emotion. Boys stood and watched with smiling envy, shocked disbelief, or a teenaged combination of both. Parents and adults dealt with the high powered onslaught of Beatlemania by handing out tissues, calming fans, or just watching the chaos unfold around them.

Surrounded by adulation and shadowed by a group of police standing between third base and the stage, The Beatles continued moving. Smiling and waving, John with his open jacket and Rickenbacker guitar and Paul steadying the Hofner bass strapped over his right shoulder, set the quick pace toward the stage. Following closely behind, George held onto his Gretsch guitar while Ringo offered a slight wave to the crowd. After glancing around with amazed expressions, each set his sights on the stage and kept walking.

Then looking like he was impatient to start the show, Paul took off in a run for the stage. He was immediately followed by John.

Joan Murray

They ran out and I was running behind them. We ran out through the tunnel, but it was so fast. I mean they were not walking, they were running.

I was behind them with my microphone and my cameraman, dragging him along. In those days the cameras were different. The cameras were very heavy. They were these huge cameras and they were on tripods and if you had a microphone you were hooked up to camera, lights and the electrician. You had three with you and then four, with me as the reporter.

As The Beatles were running I was dragging my cameraman with me, trying to keep up with everybody. But then the security told us that was it. That's enough. They put their hands up and said that's it. And they knew me. They said, "That's it Joan." So they stopped me before I could get anywhere near the stage.

> "It changed everything as far as concert venues and the fact that it could be done - that there could be stadium rock."
> - Ken Mansfield

George Orsino

They were running across the field and I was already at the stage. I was loading the color film into my camera and trying not to look conspicuous. There weren't that many people with cameras near the stage taking pictures, so I took whatever I could.

Michael Sergio

I went with my brother Brian and we sat all the way up in the bleachers. All the way on top and literally, you couldn't hear anything.

When The Beatles ran out on the field you couldn't hear anything except the crowd screaming.

The only thing similar to that was when I went to Woodstock later on and it just had this event feel to it. So sitting up there in the nosebleed seats high over home plate, looking down at this whole thing and watching the Beatles come out and the screaming... It was really an event.

Judith Kristen

When they ran out of the dugout I almost strangled my girlfriend because she had binoculars. When I saw them come out, oh my God...! I didn't even think about it. I just wanted to see George real fast so I grabbed the binoculars and almost strangled her. I was like, "I'm so sorry!" And she was like, "Judy! My God!"

It was like an atom bomb going off in my heart. When I saw the four of them walk onto the field, I'm telling you it was as if my entire body had gone on reset. I just felt like I'd flown to Heaven and back in enough time it took me to count four shaggy heads. That's all I can say. It was amazing. Oh my God!

•

Before they reached the stage, Paul slowed and waved again to the crowd allowing John to overtake him and assume his roll as the group leader. He was first up the stairs and onto the stage and walked straight to a tan and smiling Ed Sullivan.

Only the Beatles could ever know what thoughts were racing through their minds at this moment, but John's expression as he moved toward Sullivan had the sly appearance of someone who might be enjoying an inside joke. *How could four friends from Liverpool cause such a scene?* Their lives had changed many times over during the past few years. Almost daily there had been new adventures, experiences, achievements and accolades, but never before on this level for a live performance.

Ken Mansfield

That first concert at Shea Stadium is a defining moment. And what I mean is that it was something we had never seen before. Like with

Woodstock. It just changed everything about the potential of live concerts.

Think about it in terms of equipment. You look at their equipment for that concert and it looks like it's for a garage band or something. So there was the evolution out of this small equipment and into major productions. It was just something that I think changed everything as far as concert venues and the fact that it could be done - that there could be stadium rock.

_____ **Shea Rocks** _____

"It was like being in the eye of a hurricane. It was calmer right in the middle. You'd think, 'What's going on?' That was about as deep as it got. 'What is happening?' You'd suddenly wake up in the middle of a concert or a happening. 'Wow, how did I get here? The last thing I remember is playing music in a club and the next minute this.'"– **John Lennon** (12)

The eye of Hurricane Beatle had never been as intense. It was roaring at them in the media capital of the world and playing out before 55,600 people under the bright lights of Shea Stadium. Whatever feelings of excitement, elation, accomplishment, nervous energy or fear they were experiencing was powered by the anticipation of the crowd. And it was all centered on four young men who still remembered playing music in a club.

The Fans In The Stands

Shirley Kellar

We kept hearing stories about how they were going to arrive. Everybody thought they were going to land a helicopter in the stadium and drop them off on the stage. So we didn't expect them to be right underneath us. We just stayed in the aisle until the concert started and were both right behind the dugout on the third base side when they came out. Right from under us! My friend Suzanne fell on top of the dugout and the cop standing on the top of the dugout pushed her back.

Rick Andrews

The anticipation and excitement of the Beatles arrival was overwhelming. Stories were flying around everywhere about how the Beatles would actually arrive. We were convinced it would be by helicopter landing in the middle of the outfield. Every airplane noise above us would cause huge screams and roars. The tension was amazing and my friend Gary and I couldn't sit down. Everyone was standing, so we found a place atop the fence behind the field level seats.

As if the noise wasn't at fever pitch already it became even louder and completely hysterical. It's incredible though, at that moment when Gary and I saw the Beatles in person for the first time running through the infield towards the stage, neither of us made a sound. We both just stared in disbelief. It was surreal.

After awhile our almost catatonic trance was broken by two crying girls pulling at the back of our shirts pleading to let them up so they could see. The look on their faces was frantic so Gary and I got down and let the girls up. But we found another place further down the fence and that's where we stayed for the rest of the concert.

Pattie Noah

Our seats were on the second tier, to the right of the stage which was John's side. When Ed Sullivan came out to introduce them, I knew that was it. The moment had arrived.

I'll never forget seeing them coming across that field. It was just surreal. I could have died right there on the spot and that would have been okay because I got to lay eyes on John Lennon at least once. He was, and still is, the only Beatle for me. That's when the screaming started to escalate and the pounding on the stands started in. Despite the fact that I was beside myself with excitement, I got this wave of sheer terror because I thought the stands were going to collapse beneath us. My brother was doing his best to calm me down and in the end he had to hold me up not only for me to be able to see properly, but to make me feel safe.

Joyce Kaufman

I went with my cousin and had no idea where we were going to sit. My father had arranged the whole thing for us. When we got to our seats, we were at the end of the dugout that they came out of. I was standing there, of course, screaming. Everybody else is screaming and my ears were ringing and I didn't know why I was so excited, but I was extremely excited.

John Lennon came out, crumpled up an empty pack of Gauloises Cigarettes and threw it into the stands. And I got it! That was the highlight, but all I did was cry over this cigarette pack and have people, you know, that were around me offering me money for it. One girl wanted to beat me up for it, but there was no way I was giving it up. I came there loving George, but got the cigarette pack and became an instant John Lennon fan.

Janice Bartel

I still get chills when I watch clips of the Beatles running onto the field at Shea. Ed Sullivan introduced them and John, Paul, George and Ringo came running onto the field wearing tan jackets with badges and black pants. Flash bulbs were going off in every direction. It was like an electric charge.

Bob Eaton

I had never seen that many people in one place in my life. There was an electric feeling in the air, like something big was gonna happen. It was like the anticipation of an explosion, but you didn't know when it was gonna happen. Then Ed Sullivan stepped up and the tension rose another hundred points. When he announced their name and they ran out, the whole place went crazy! There was a girl sitting next to me and when The Beatles ran out she let out a blood curdling scream and promptly passed out for the entire show.

Arlene Levine

They ran out onto the field. There were people standing on the seats in front of us and on the sides of us. I remember my friend Maxine's sister and me just looking at each other and going "AHHHH!" I think she was starting to cry. A lot of people were crying around us. I didn't cry, but I was excited. I mean the excitement was just not to be believed.

Frank Branchini

When the Beatles came out there was a total pandemonium. What I remember most was the noise and the excitement.

Marc Catone

The noise… I'm sure everyone has talked about the noise. To this day I don't think I've ever heard such an explosive noise at anything I've been to since. It was unbelievable. You couldn't hear anything else.

I remember hearing Ed Sullivan's introduction. But I have to wonder at this point now if I actually remember hearing it in real time, or from watching it on *The Beatles Anthology*. But I do remember when he came out.

Then the Beatles came out of the dugout. We were sitting on the first base side and saw them emerge from the dugout. And just the amount of light bulbs popping made it look like a strobe light show. What a sight. It was unbelievable.

Dan Reznicak

It was like it was yesterday. I was only five years old, but I can remember every little detail. I looked to my right and there they were running out of the dugout. The screaming went up ten notches. I went nuts! What a feeling, what a rush and I still get goose bumps every time I see them or hear their music.

They walked and ran to the second base. They walked on stage shook hands with Mr. Ed Sullivan and I screamed and screamed. I will never forget the experience.

Judith Goodspeed

It was just noise because nobody stopped screaming the whole time. So I did not hear Ed Sullivan's introduction. I did not hear very much of the music. Maybe when they first started, I may have heard a little bit.

Diane Gunther

When they finally came out it was just magical. It was just something that you had anticipated for such a long amount of time and it was great. I was fortunate because of where my seat was. If you go back and talk about the sound system that was available at the time it's a wonder anybody heard anything. But I was close enough.

With all the screaming, and of course there was a lot of that, one thing I remember telling myself was *you're going to go and you want to listen and you're not going to scream*. But I do remember that when they came out I kind of screamed. After that I didn't do any screaming because I really wanted to hear them.

Doug Fernandez

The Beatles came out and the crowd went loud, then louder. Then they began to play and the crowd went even louder. During the entire concert I believe I heard broken pieces of instruments and voices, but nothing coherent. When it became obvious that I would not hear the music I took to watching the Beatles and the crowd.

Ray Robinson II

I was sitting up on the first tier, upper deck looking out over the field. They came on stage and the place went crazy. I was just overwhelmed.

THE
CONCERT

Twist and Shout

On stage the Beatles moved into their positions. John (black-finished Rickenbacker 325), George (Gretsch Tennessean) and Paul (Hofner violin bass) plugged their guitars into the Vox Amplifiers and checked the settings as Ringo stepped onto the drum riser and sat behind his Oyster Black Pearl Ludwig drum kit. George and Ringo waited as John and Paul shouted into the microphones:

_____ **Shea Rocks** _____

"Hello, hello! Oh, oh, hello! Hey, hey hey! Hello, hello!"
"Hello Paul."
"Hello John."

Whether they could hear him over the screams or would just have to read his lips, Paul turned toward the others and shouted: "One, two, three!" On cue they launched into a shortened version of *Twist and Shout* and the stadium rocked even harder.

The opening notes crackled with electricity and punch. The sound was harder and looser than fans would remember from *The Ed Sullivan Show* a year and a half earlier and delivered a clear message this would not be a laidback performance. The audience reacted with thunderous screams and the energy level generated by The Beatles on stage was cranked-up as high as the volume on their Vox Amplifiers.

"Well shake it up baby now, shake it up baby.
Twist and shout. Twist and shout." (13)

Twist and Shout still stands as was one of the highlights of early Beatlemania. It was the final song on their debut album in England, *Please Please Me*, where it succeeded in following the honored showbiz advice to always leaving the audience wanting more. They chose the song to end their two most important performances in 1963, *Sunday Night at the London Palladium* (Britain's equivalent of *The Ed Sullivan Show*)

and *The Royal Variety Show* attended by the Queen and Royal Family members. Both shows are often referred to as the true beginnings of the Beatlemania phenomena and John's introduction of *Twist and Shout* at *The Royal Variety Show* has given the song legendary status in Beatles history:

> "For our last number, I'd like to ask your help. Would the people in the cheaper seats clap your hands. And the rest of you, if you'll just rattle your jewelry." – John Lennon (14)

The Beatles also knew *Twist and Shout* was not just a great closer, but a guaranteed shot of adrenaline to start any show. They had used it to open their third appearance on *The Ed Sullivan Show* and throughout their 1964 North American Tour.

Twist and Shout was not written by John and Paul, but it had all the necessary ingredients to make it a Beatles classic. It included an infectious musical hook, a beat that was impossible to sit through, John's throat-shredding vocal, and answering backup vocals by Paul and George. When left-handed Paul and right-handed George brought their shaggy heads together at one microphone for a high pitched, Little

Richard inspired "*Woooooooo!*" female fans would answer with waves of equally high pitched screams, weak knees and tears of passionate joy.

Michael Adams

I was on the field, but didn't work with my dad and the film crew because I was only thirteen. My dad was all over making sure stuff was running properly. They had cameras all over the place and sound equipment. I can't say for sure, but I think they used about twelve cameras and it was technology at its finest for 1965.

Back then you got a bunch of alarm clocks and synchronized all the alarm clocks because the film would only go so far. You had to keep switching out film as you were filming. So everybody would have to pay attention to when they were switching. They had to know what time it was and when the clock said they had to put another canister of film in the camera. That's how they would do it. That's how they could sync everything up at some point and onto time code and whatever. Filming live like that, that's what they had to do.

"It was noise like you can't imagine. But it was joyful noise."
- Judith Kristen

I have the microphones; the film microphones they used to get the sound for the television special. If you look at the film, there are the public address microphones they're singing into. Those are the big ones. Then underneath are little microphones taped on the stands.

These are lavaliere microphones that the sound guys got their sound from. These are the ones that went directly to them and not into the public address system. If you look at the film you'll see on each microphone stand there are two microphones. The smaller ones, just below the big vocal microphones are the ones I have. Yeah, it's extremely cool that I still have those.

Michael Sergio

The sound system they had then is not like the sound systems we think of nowadays. They really just had like a speaker system on the stage. That's what it looked like. And you really couldn't hear anything. I don't think I heard them play a single note the whole time we were there. All I heard was the people screaming.

———————————— **Shea Rocks** ————————————

The Sound System

For fans to have a chance to hear The Beatles, microphones were placed in front of their 100-watt Vox guitar amplifiers and Ringo's drums. Together with audio from the vocal microphones, the sound was wired to the stadium's public address system and played through small speakers hung from steel support girders in the various seating levels that were basically designed for announcements during sporting events. The performance was also carried through tall, thin yellow speakers lined up along the first and third base lines of the baseball field.

The technology for stage monitors, which are on stage speakers placed in front of musicians allowing them to hear what they were singing and playing, was primitive at best in 1965 and not used by The Beatles at Shea Stadium. In smaller clubs vocal microphone speakers could be placed on the side of a stage and the volume adjusted at a lower level to prevent feedback caused by sounds going into a microphone, coming out of an amplifier behind it, and running back through the microphone. This continuing cycle would result in a loud, high pitched ringing "feedback" noise.

For any music to be heard at all over the screams filling Shea Stadium, the guitar amplifiers needed to be set at maximum volume. Any microphone speakers near the sides of the stage would have to be turned lower to prevent feedback. This meant the Beatles would hear their guitars when standing in front of the amplifiers, but could hear very little if any of their own vocals.

Michael Adams

There was so much going on where I was standing. I was there right in the middle of it and just the feel of the whole thing is what I really remember. I was just blown away by the whole deal.

This was before they had stage monitors and that's why there were problems later with the audio for the television special. They couldn't really hear each other once they started playing. The noise in the stadium was deafening, but I could hear them. I could hear them better because I was getting the music off the stage instead of through the public address hook up that went into the stands. So I got that, at least.

But if I didn't know I was there, I wouldn't believe it myself because I don't remember particularly the music so much. It was just the excitement of the whole thing. Quite frankly, I don't even remember what they played because of all the racket. By the time they hit the stage it was just pandemonium and it was the excitement of being there.

Beatlemania wasn't about listening to the music. Not live, anyway. That's why they got tired of doing it. People came and yelled and fainted and… you know, people went crazy and that's what it was all about I guess.

I could probably hear them better than the people in the stands. But then again, I didn't have the public address, PA system that they did. But what did they have for a PA? They had the regular baseball PA. Nothing more, so what I could hear was coming off the stage and not out of the PA.

Shaun Weiss

The music was over the Shea sound system, so it was really poor. You heard certain songs, but it was really more about being mesmerized by just being at the event.

Judith Kristen

They had to put it through the stadium sound system and I'm sure they used the same speakers that they would have used during a ballgame. This is another thing that I always point out. When somebody hits a home run in Shea Stadium, everybody is screaming their heads off but you can still hear the announcer go, "It's a home run!" You know what I mean? Whenever I mention that I went to nine Beatles concerts, someone always asks, "Could you hear anything?" So that's why I say of course you could hear them. But if you were surrounded by people who were screaming and just never let up, the relentless ones, I'm sure you didn't hear much.

I'm not saying it wasn't noisy. All you have to do is watch the film and listen. It was noise like you can't imagine. But it was joyful noise. You know? And did I scream and holler and sing at the top of my lungs? Yeah, of course I did. And I almost strangled my girlfriend grabbing her binoculars when they first came out. I was freaking out and "George!" was the first thing I yelled. But you could hear them.

•

The high wattage amplifiers were definitely louder and more powerful than any they had used before, but without stage monitors and a rehearsal to check the sound equipment the Beatles were playing on adrenaline and instinct. They bounced through *Twist and Shout* while close up shots for the television special caught their eyes taking in the full scope of the madness playing out in front of them. The stadium shook and the screams were deafening. From where they stood on stage, an entire baseball infield away from the nearest seat, the audience looked like a sea of people in constant motion from ground level to the upper seating decks. Bed sheets with messages painted in large letters hung over steel railings proclaiming *I Love John, P.S. We Love You,* and *Help!*

It could also be seen from their expressions the noise level would force them to rely on visual cues with each other. At the moment *Twist and Shout* could have followed their recording and taken off into the lead guitar break, Paul and George glanced at John for his assurance they would only perform an abbreviated version. Timing their steps with the final notes, John, Paul and George moved back from their microphones and with Ringo seated on his drum platform, ended the song. With the final note echoing amid the screams through the overheated stadium, they bowed in unison to the largest audience ever to attend a Beatles performance.

The Fans In The Stands

Steve Zisk

You could barely hear them. My father kept saying, "I don't hear anything!" Not that he cared. He only took us because we wanted to go and he wasn't really interested. But he kept saying, "I can't hear anything! I can't hear anything!" And you really couldn't hear. It was just constant, continuous screaming. I think they opened with *Twist and Shout*, but I wasn't sure...

Ray Robinson II

Of course I heard them! As good as you could hear with all those people screaming. The fans were just happy to be there. We were all thrilled to be there. They sounded wonderful.

Maxine Ascher

I don't remember what they sang. I just remember the bows they did at the end of the songs. *Beatle Bows*, that's what we called them. They were so deep and from the waist. You know, when you look back and you see Frank Sinatra and Dean Martin when they were on television, they had on tuxedos with handkerchiefs and flowers in their lapels and patent leather shoes. You just knew that their underwear was clean because that's how good they looked. Not like some of these performers today with tattoos and spitting and drooling. When the Beatles made that bow, it was just a sign of respect for their fans. And they probably had clean underwear on.

Dotty Poirier

As the Beatles came on it was hard to hear them, but I was able to focus and hear a few of the songs. Everyone screamed and ran closer to the stage. I sat overlooking first base in the second tier of the stadium. It's years ago but it seems like yesterday because I can still see myself there. Everyone around me was screaming. I was screaming too for awhile, but realized in order to hear them I needed to be quiet. I thought they sounded great. I had never been to a concert so this experience was and will always be the best.

Diane Gunther

I could hear them really very well. Then again, my friends who got tickets later on were way down in the left field upper deck and they really couldn't hear much of anything. I thought they sounded remarkably like the recordings. I guess I was pleased that they sounded so much like I was used to listening to on the radio.

I have pretty good recollection during that whole performance and I guess I went into the whole thing pretty determined that I wanted to be able to hear them. And it worked. My good seat had something to do with it too. I think that I was just amazed that I was able to be there.

She's A Woman

Without an introduction The Beatles went immediately into their second song, *She's A Woman*. John's opening chords sounded distorted and full as a result of the one hundred watts of full volume being pumped out from his amplifier. He set the song's tempo by practically pounding on the strings of his Rickenbacker guitar until Paul's bass and Ringo's drums joined him to fill in the bottom sound.

"My love don't buy me presents..." (15)

Except for the slight lyric miscue in the opening line by Paul, *She's A Woman* followed the same arrangement that appeared as B-side to the single *I Feel Fine* and on the Capitol Records album *Beatles '65*. After Paul's first verse, George's guitar under laid John's crunching chords with a melodic background originally played on piano for the studio recording.

"She's A Woman wasn't included in the television special because they had to change film during the song." - Michael Adams

The personalities displayed by The Beatles for the media and in their films also held true during live performances. John was the unpredictable rock'n roller and no one could be certain what he would say or do at any given moment. George was quiet and appeared more serious than the others about his musicianship. His playing held the songs together and he wasn't as inclined as Paul to excite fans when the others depended on him to deliver steady guitar backing and lead breaks. Ringo, except for a featured solo during each show, stayed in the background and supported the others by keeping the beat.

Paul was a showman who enjoyed the spotlight. Regardless of the situation or event, whether it was a concert, press conference or movie premier, he always seemed to be in control of the situation and himself. He smiled for the press, waved to the fans, and played *yin* to John's *yang* whenever any sharp edges in their public image needed to be smoothed out. Paul was a press agent's dream and the pin-up heartthrob for female fans.

As the group's natural showman, Paul's task was physically more difficult than the others at Shea Stadium. While George and Ringo concentrated more on trying to hear what they were playing and John bashed away on his rhythm guitar, Paul continually moved about his side of the stage singing and playing his bass to every fan in every section of the stadium. In between vocals and bass notes he waved, laughed, shook his hair, bounced in time to the music, winked and smiled. He had the ability to play to the last row of seats in the upper deck as effectively as he could to people in the front row. And in the process he made sure every fan in every section also had a good look at him.

Joan Murray

Shea Stadium was even more chaotic than *The Ed Sullivan Show*. I mean, there were more than 55,000 kids. Mostly girls and you could not hear anything. You couldn't hear the Beatles on the stage singing. I didn't know kids could make that much noise.

Scott Ross

It was insanity. It was almost 56,000 people and it was like a wall of sound. You could barely hear them.

•

During *She's A Woman*, John never let up on the rhythm and pushed the song with pure energy. On the Clayco recording of this performance, which never appeared on the television special, his playing dominated the song as much as Paul's vocal. Then quite suddenly following George's guitar solo, *She's A Woman* shifted away from the familiar arrangement and into a hard and fast, three chord rock'n roll riff.

The ending of this song is both surprising to hear and notable in showing their roots as musicians. The Beatles song catalogue would always include early rock'n roll influences, but their chart-topping hits were becoming more complex and musically sophisticated. When *She's A Woman* was released in late 1964 it's doubtful the average fan heard anything other than the hottest pop record from the world's hottest pop group. But to end the song at Shea Stadium, the rhythm easily slipped into the basic guitar chords and beat they had been playing since they were teenagers. The result easily compared to any Rolling Stones version of a Chuck Berry classic song. Whether it was a sweaty basement club in Liverpool, a dank, smoky bar in Hamburg, or a sold-out stadium in New York, The Beatles proved with *She's A Woman* they were first and foremost a rock'n roll band.

Michael Sergio

The stadium was so energized with the girls screaming and stuff. The Beatles were a group where every girl wanted to be with them and every guy wanted to be like them. Like James Bond. They had that kind of thing going where everybody liked them. It didn't matter if you were a guy or a girl. You liked them for different reasons, but you liked them. So when they came out and you had that much energy floating around it was absolutely electric. It was like going to a World Series game, the bottom of the ninth inning and the game is really on the line. That's how it felt. It's just amazing stuff, you know? The Beatles really were amazing.

Michael Adams

What I remember hearing from my father is that *She's A Woman* wasn't included in the television special because they had to change the film during the song. It was a film changing issue. They had shot so much of the other stuff before The Beatles went on that they had to put in new film. And the cameras that were still going when the others changed film didn't catch what they wanted. Whatever camera work they had wasn't usable, so it was decided they couldn't use it for the TV show.

The Fans In The Stands

—————————— Shea Rocks ——————————

"Thank you. Thank you very much everybody. Ta. Thank you."
– Paul McCartney

Marc Catone

When the Beatles first were on stage, we didn't know that they had already sung one song. They sang *Twist and Shout*. We could see them go through the motions of singing and playing their instruments, but we had absolutely no idea what song they were playing because it was so loud. We couldn't hear them at all. It wasn't until about the second verse of *She's A Woman*, which they went right into without an introduction after *Twist and Shout* that we realized *oh, that's what they're singing*. It was kind of funny.

Arlene Levine

The screaming was not to be believed. It was just screaming. People were screaming all around us. We were standing on the seats and holding each other up because the seats would fold us into them. So we were just standing on the seats and screaming. I couldn't even tell you what songs they were singing because it was just one big scream. The excitement was unbelievable.

Eve Hoffman

We couldn't hear anything above the screaming and crying, including ours. From where we sat, the Beatles were the size of ants. My friend Neli had borrowed a pair of opera glasses from a neighbor and I continued to grab them from around her neck to get a better look at Paul. He's still my heartthrob today.

I Feel Fine

Shea Rocks

"We'd like to carry on now... now... with a song which was one of our records a few months ago. And this song is called *I Feel Fine*." – Paul McCartney

The Beatles had gelled years earlier as musicians during all night sets in nightclubs and bars. Their talent and practiced ability to play rock'n roll had become second nature and could transcend the numbing assault of more than 55,000 screaming fans. The high energy ending of *She's A Woman* carried over into *I Feel Fine*. John again set a manic pace with the guitar intro that's as recognizable as the openings of some of rock's most famous songs including *Jailhouse Rock*, *Louie, Louie* and that summer's big hit for The Rolling Stones, *Satisfaction*.

> "What was happening was making this a historical event."
> - Shaun Weiss

Musically they're in sync. They played, bounced and moved with the song and appeared to be growing more comfortable facing the massive crowd than during their earlier moments on stage. John handled the lead vocals with George and Paul sharing a microphone to shout out their harmonies. Ringo shook his hair and knocked out the steady, rhythmic beat.

Cousin Bruce Morrow

It was a day I will not forget because first of all there was so much noise. The level... The volume of noise... I've always said it could've run the electricity of New York City for that entire day. That's how much the energy was. Of course to this day I can still, when I think about it, feel in my body and in my chest the amount of pressure and energy and electricity coming from that audience. It was pretty wild.

Peter Altschuler

I couldn't hear what was played on stage. I couldn't hear what anybody was saying. It was dumb. I mean I didn't have any particular need to see The Beatles perform. I just wanted to hear them live because all I'd heard was recordings. I figured maybe live was better. But to this day I couldn't tell you if it was, because I just couldn't stand it. So I left. I didn't stay for the concert. Maybe I thought there would be another time and I'll get to see them again. But I didn't.

Judith Kristen

Well the only thing I could say about not hearing them is that it may have been your section; where you were sitting. If you were surrounded on all sides by girls who were just totally freaking out, then you probably couldn't hear anything. I could hear the noise coming from everywhere else, but our section was pretty good.

•

I Feel Fine had been their first number one single after the success of *A Hard Day's Night*. It was a clear signal the Beatles would not remain stagnant as songwriters and musicians. The driving guitar riff, created and played by John, gave the song a rougher electronic edge than other pop records when it was released with *She's A Woman* just before the Christmas holidays in late 1964. The guitar feedback opening the song was the first time feedback had been used in a recording. The Beatles didn't attempt to reproduce the sound in concerts, but John, Paul and George could still blend their familiar harmonies over the fans' high-pitched screams.

The terms *heavy metal* and *hard rock*, like technology for stage monitors were still a few years from being invented. But the harder sound generated by The Beatles on *I Feel Fine* can be viewed as a preview for what future stadium performers would build on. Pop stars were becoming rock stars, even though most of audience at Shea Stadium couldn't hear it happening over the hysteria of Beatlemania.

Shaun Weiss

I looked over the top of the dugout and at those girls that were in that first couple rows and could see the emotion they were letting out. That emotion isn't something you could forget. It was looking in their faces and seeing the tears and hearing them scream. They yelled for me to give them some dirt from the playing field or rip up the grass for them. But the reality was the emotion that they were putting out. They were sincere. They idolized these guys, as well as I did. And that's emotion that you can't bottle. It's emotion that's hard to express.

"The volume of noise... I've always said it could've run the electricity of New York City for that entire day. That's how much the energy was." - Cousin Bruce Morrow

When you look back at '65 when the Beatles just were so big and breathing the air in these girls' presence and you looked in their faces and saw their tears, you knew it was true tears. They weren't pretending. That's what touched me at Shea Stadium. What was happening was making this a historical event.

We didn't know that it was historical. And I didn't know that I was being caught up in a whirlwind that would affect my life many, many years down the road. We were just at a point in time where four men came together and touched over 50,000 peoples' hearts. And they touched our hearts all in the same way. You know? That's not a coincidence. That's a spiritual power that comes from within.

The Fans In The Stands

Shirley Kellar

I just remember all the screaming. That's really all you could hear. We could barely hear the music, but that didn't matter. I lost my voice and probably some hearing that day, but it was worth it. We were diehard Beatle fans.

Debbie Stern

We were breathing the same air, occupying the same space; albeit several thousand feet away, and screaming our little teenage heads off. People always ask me, "Did you even hear them?" And my standard answer is, "You had to scream to hear them." There was something magical in the way their voices transcended those high pitched screams.

Marc Catone

Shea stadium was so close to LaGuardia Airport and the planes would fly right over it. It was either the final approach or taking off, but they would fly right over the stadium. And the noise level was so huge that you could not hear the jets. I mean you could see the jets flying over, but the noise of all these girls screaming and yelling drowned out the noise of the jets. You could still feel the reverberation of the jets flying over, but you couldn't hear them.

Janice Bartel

I bought a program, a Beatles record charm that I think said *Beatles at Shea, August 15, 1965*, and I must not forget a pair of binoculars that cost one dollar. I could not believe I was seeing The Beatles. Well actually, I was not seeing them very clearly because my one dollar pair of binoculars were worthless. Anyway, it didn't matter because I was screaming and crying and then just felt numb.

Dizzy Miss Lizzy

"Thank you very much everybody." (To the other Beatles: "Can they hear me?") "We'd like to do a song..." (To the others again: "What LP is it on?") "...off our LP, album, *Beatles VI*, I think. Can you hear me?! Hello! And it's called *Dizzy Miss Lizzy*!" – John Lennon

There was no drop in energy anywhere on stage or off during *Dizzy Miss Lizzy*. George played the opening lead notes and the band took off on another breakneck revisit to their rock'n roll past. The song had been included on the British version of the *Help!* album, though it was not part of the film soundtrack. Fans at Shea Stadium were already familiar with *Dizzy Miss Lizzy* since it had been released earlier that summer on the U.S. album *Beatles VI*.

"You make me dizzy Dizzy Lizzy, the way you rock'n roll..." (16)

Featuring a solo vocal by John, *Dizzy Miss Lizzy* had fit the unspoken pattern of including one song on each Beatles album that would stretch his vocal cords to the limits. John's strong performances on earlier recordings of *Twist and Shout, Money, You Can't Do That, Slow Down, Mr. Moonlight* and *Rock'n Roll Music* would stand as an impressive legacy for any rock singer. *Dizzy Miss Lizzy* was the latest addition to that list.

The song needed a powerful delivery and at Shea Stadium John didn't hold back. He screamed and shouted the lyrics while George, Paul and Ringo provided an instrumental backing that rocked along with him.

"We were performers in Liverpool, Hamburg and other dance halls. What we generated was fantastic when we played straight rock and there was nobody to touch us in Britain."
– John Lennon (17)

Ron Schneider

We stood there for about ten or fifteen minutes. It wasn't a long time. We gave it time, but after awhile it was just... You couldn't hear anything except for screaming. It was just screaming and it wasn't going to get any better. The Stones wanted to listen to the music, but all there was were girls screaming.

We went out to the side and were along the fence area. Since it was in Shea, it might have been a batting fence behind home plate. I remember looking through a chain link fence into the thing and holding our hands up and watching. We weren't in the dugout.

You'd start hearing the band play and the crowd was just so loud. You know, they could've just been standing there doing nothing and it wouldn't have made a difference because you couldn't hear anything. This went on for awhile and we realized that it just wasn't going to be enjoyable. There was nothing to hear, so we left and went back on the boat and went back to the city.

Peter Bennett

We stayed for probably twenty minutes and you couldn't even hear them. You couldn't hear the Beatles sing at all. And some of the kids were still yelling, "The Stones! The Stones!" It was getting bad, so I told Mick and Keith let's get out of here before we get bombarded. So we left. I got the police and they escorted us back to the yacht in Queens.

Michael Sergio

Yeah? Well if The Stones couldn't hear anything down there imagine what it was like at the top of the stadium.

Peter Bennett

The experience was you couldn't hear them at all or what they were singing. The audience... There were so many people screaming and yelling and girls fainting. I saw stretchers coming out all over the place. When we left there were people fainting all over the place. We had people fainting every minute.

Judith Kristen

This girl, and God love her, she was two rows behind me and to my left. And she passed out. I remember hearing a shrill kind of shriek, different than the, "George! John!" Because, you know, they would yell and scream, but they were usually screaming a name. It just sounded painful. And I don't remember seeing a lot of cops near us because we were kind of in the middle of the row, but this girl passed out and they were there to help her right away.

**"The Stones wanted to listen to the music, but all there was were girls screaming."
- Ron Schneider**

I guess they gave her smelling salts or she came to because she yelled, "I wanna go back to my seat!" She was back in her seat for the end of the concert. So that was the only one I saw. It was very close to me. And I know her girlfriend was freaked out. She was a nervous wreck. But then she was fine. I guess she was hyperventilating and it was warm. It was an August night and crowded and there's The Beatles right down there singing their hearts out to you. It's just one of those things that happened.

The Fans In The Stands

Judith Goodspeed

I screamed. I went with my girlfriends to their movies and we screamed. But what amazed me at watching other people screaming was seeing them cry. Now, I didn't get emotional. I was too excited. I was too young to feel that kind of emotion. But I saw girls crying and leaning back and falling into people. It was hysteria. It was just unbelievable to see it all. People fainted all the way up in my tier.

I could never believe that people would faint over that until I got older. I can see what people felt then because I can feel emotion now towards The Beatles where I didn't when I was ten years old. I can see how awesome it is to have that kind of dream come true.

What was really neat was that through the binoculars we were able to see the fans closer to the front. It was almost like they were trying to rush the ball field and were being held back. I imagine there were a lot of police there.

Ray Robinson II

They were doing all the crazy things that kids do, especially young women at a show like this. I can imagine what it was like when Sinatra was playing at The Paramount, because people were passing out and it was unbelievable. I was like, *okay, if that's what you're gonna do so be it!* Passing out wouldn't have been my idea of the thing to do.

But it was wonderful. I was high on just being near my idols. They were my idols. I had them as heroes in my life. I was thrilled to be there.

Maxine Ascher

It was loud and it was crowded and it was very exciting. Everybody was jumping. The stadium was just bouncing. I remember everybody was running around and everybody was jumping because they were so excited to be there. It was a contagious thing. And I didn't see that many boys, just millions and millions of girls. I must have been eighteen or nineteen years old and there were a lot of younger girls.

View from Marc Catone's seat in the upper deck

Marc Catone

The worst part of the whole thing was we were stuck way up in the upper deck at Shea Stadium, the typical cliché nosebleed area. That's where we were. If it wasn't for the fact that we had a pair of binoculars that my sister and I shared throughout the concert, I don't know if I would've really been able to see them too well.

Frank Branchini

Our seats were on one end of the top tier of the stadium. From the nosebleed section, the Beatles looked like ants on the stage. I have a few photos taken with a Brownie camera of these very tiny figures. They're quite amusing actually. But it was glorious.

The Fans on Parental Control

Judith Goodspeed

Some of the kids in my neighborhood said I was too young to go because I was only ten years old. That was when my dad decided I wasn't too young to go and he took me. From then on it was just all about me and my dad and The Beatles.

Once we got there, we were thrust among thousands of screaming teenagers. It was very intimidating for a ten year old. We couldn't possibly have had worse seats. We were in the last row of the top tier. My father braved the summer heat, the crowds, the screaming, just to look through binoculars and see The Beatles for his pre-teen daughter.

We didn't hear a single sound of music from all the screaming. Even with the binoculars, the Beatles were still tiny.

Steve Zisk

I fall into the group where my dad took me to the concert. But don't assume from that that he was at all interested in them or thought they were any good, because he didn't. He made fun of The Beatles a lot and pretended to not remember their names. He called them George McClannahan and Ringo McClanahan and Paul McClanahan. He liked the music from his era, like Tommy Dorsey and whatever.

But there were points in his life where he would begrudgingly show some interest in them. I think later on there were songs that he thought were good, but I can't say they ever won him over. He was there just to take us and maybe because there was some slight interest on his own part.

Cindy Salvo

I remember that the fans were screaming so loudly that you couldn't hear the Beatles perform. It was just screaming. You could barely hear anything as far as the performance. I remember my father getting really angry about this because he thought it was like the silliest thing that he had ever seen. I remember him saying, "If I was the Beatles, as soon as there was one scream I would stop performing that song and go onto the next one. Then the whole concert would be over like in two minutes because they would just do a little of each song and then it would be over." I remember laughing about that.

My dad liked The Beatles too. I think he liked them. And he was supportive in that he knew how much we really wanted to go and we couldn't go without him. But the screaming made him furious. He was so mad at the screaming. He never said he had a headache, but he said it was ridiculous because *you can't hear anything!* He was mad about that.

Frank Branchini

Every one was jumping up and down and my mother remembers that she was terrified because the whole upper deck of the Stadium was bouncing and she thought the deck would collapse. My mother is afraid of heights and we were at the very front of the top deck so it must have been totally miserable for her.

Ticket To Ride

<hr>

Shea Rocks

<hr>

"The next... The next song that we'd like to sing now ... This... Yeah, this one which was our, uh, last one record, the one before this... And the record... This is called *Ticket To Ride*." – Paul McCartney

<hr>

The first four songs had been fueled by the outpouring of excitement and emotion from the audience. It was contagious and evident in the Beatles' performance. They played with an energy that fed off the crowd and each other and made it look easy and fun.

The intense screaming had become a numbing noise and continued unabated, regardless of what song was played or which Beatle shouted into a microphone hoping to be heard. But on stage, *Ticket To Ride* was a change of pace. The Beatles appeared to be growing more relaxed and confident. During the song's introduction, John mimicked Paul's hand gestures. With exaggerated waves of their index fingers through the air they looked more like a comedy team keeping count of their bits, "... last one record, the one before this..."

It was a hot night and when the film cameras moved in close on John and Paul it was obvious they had worked up a sweat. During the introduction John was seen catching his breath after a wild *Dizzy Miss Lizzy* and Ringo adjusted the collar of his jacket, which would have been constricting and overheated for any drummer playing outdoors on a summer night.

Russ Lease

It was hot and the Shea Jacket is not a light jacket. It's not extremely heavy, but it's a heavy one hundred percent wool jacket with a full lining and everything. When I think about the Beatles wearing them on a hot, humid August night in New York City, I can't imagine... With the excitement and the adrenalin pumping, I mean, yeah, they were soaking wet a song and half into the set. This is definitely a hotter jacket than you would prefer to be wearing on a night like that.

McCartney's jacket still has the sweat stains on it. If you open it up it has an acetate lining on the inside and it's stained to a degree. You can certainly see where it was heavily sweated in. Even with subsequent dry cleaning, and I've never dry cleaned it since I've had it, but whatever dry cleaning was done, it wasn't able to get all of that out. So you can obviously see the lining is stained a little bit.

•

Ticket To Ride was the third Lennon and McCartney song performed that evening and is another important milestone in their development as writers. Recorded barely a year after their 1964 debut on *The Ed Sullivan Show*, it demonstrated how far they had grown from the innocent pop songs that launched the first wave of North American Beatlemania. The biggest chart-topping hits from only a year earlier, *I Want To Hold Your Hand*, *She Loves You* and *Please Please Me* were no longer part of their live repertoire. *Ticket To Ride*, along

"With the excitement and the adrenalin pumping... they were soaking wet a song and a half into the set." - Russ Lease

with other Lennon influenced songs from the *Help!* soundtrack such as *You've Got To Hide Your Love Away* and *You're Gonna Lose That Girl* had more honest and darker lyrics about love not always working out the way he had hoped:

"I think I'm gonna be sad. I think it's today.
The girl that's driving me mad is going away." (18)

The song also incorporated a heavier beat from Ringo that emphasized the darker tone and lyrics. George filled the background with a steady lead guitar riff under harmonies from John and Paul who thrilled fans even more by singing into the same microphone.

"...one of the earliest heavy metal records." – John Lennon (19)

Only five months earlier *Ticket To Ride* had hit number one on the music charts. The song was on their current album and used over the skiing sequence filmed in the Austrian Alps for the movie *Help!* To the screaming fans, the four young men on stage were not just The Beatles, they were also movie stars.

Shaun Weiss

I got caught up in the hoopla. The fact that it was a Beatles concert; the fact that I was sitting in the dugout; the fact that The Rolling Stones and other people were there and the fact that I was able to feel the emotion from all the kids because I wasn't caught up with them. I was away from them. But I could feel and hear the tears and the girls crying at the fence and that's what I got caught up in. All of that...

Standing out of that dugout and looking at these girls... It was mostly girls and their moms. There were guys, but it was more girls. And just hearing them screaming, "John, I love you!" and "Paul I love you!" and the Beatles trying to sing and all you heard was screaming. Their mouths would open and you'd hear screams. I still get emotional about it.

The Fans In The Stands

Marc Catone

It was so hot… To give you a little background, it was hot as hell that summer and the whole New York Metropolitan area was going through a drought. In fact, there was a blimp that was flying around the stadium. I don't know what company it was, that might have been pre-Goodyear at that point, but they had a little, like electronic message board on the bottom of it that spelled out, "Save Water." That was the big thing. Everybody was trying to save water because the reservoirs were getting low all around the whole area. I remember that.

I was sweating and everybody was sweating. It was really hot. And I had hair in those days, which I don't have now. But I had hair and I would comb it down. I remember my bangs, or my Beatle-like cut, just full of sweat. Yeah, thanks for reminding me of that...

Judith Goodspeed

We were there a long time and it was hot. It was summer and my dad's concern was keeping me hydrated. He spent a lot of time while I was looking through the binoculars making sure that vendors were coming up the stairs so people in the top tier could order stuff. But I don't remember the heat bothering me. I was just too excited.

Maxine Ascher

It was very, very hot. It was the middle of the summer and Shea was a very hot stadium in the summer.

Pattie Noah

That day was just beastly hot. I was dressed for warm weather to be sure, but I had never been in a crowd that size in my life and that massive crush of humanity raised the temperature in the stands by at least 20 degrees.

Arlene Levine

It was very hot. And if it was any other thing I wouldn't sit through it. When I get that hot, I just get annoyed with it. They wouldn't sit there for me, so why would I sit there and go through this for them? But for

The Beatles it just didn't matter. I remember it being hot, but I don't remember complaining. It was like, o*h yes! We'd do anything to see The Beatles!* It didn't matter.

Everybody's Trying To Be My Baby

_____ Shea Rocks _____

"Thank you. We'd like to carry on with a song that was, um...
(In the back ground John has turned on the organ he'll use later
and is running his fingers over the keyboard). ...on an album...
On the album before last, (now John strums a chord on his
guitar), and it's called _Everybody's Trying To Be My Baby_." – George
Harrison

For his featured vocal at Shea Stadium and during the entire tour,
George sang Carl Perkins' reliable country flavored rocker, _Everybody's
Trying To Be My Baby_. Similar to _Dizzy Miss Lizzy_, this was the basic style
of rock'n roll The Beatles could play by instinct over the deafening sound of screaming fans. The song had been part of their grueling all-night sets at The Star Club in Hamburg, played live on the BBC Radio program _Pop Goes The Beatles_, and finally recorded in late 1964. It was released by Capitol Records in the U.S. as the final song on _Beatles '65_.

> **"I don't believe there
> is any footage... That's
> the kind of stuff that
> was left on the cutting
> room floor."
> - Michael Adams**

Everybody's Trying To Be My Baby
included two lead guitar breaks by George and no harmony input from
John and Paul. The simple arrangement followed the recorded version
and the live performance had no surprises except one:

It was filmed, but has never been seen.

Unlike _She's A Woman_, which didn't have usable film footage,
Everybody's Trying To Be My Baby was edited out of the television special.
For many fans not there, this absence made it unclear whether George
even sang a lead vocal at Shea Stadium. The definitive answer came

more than thirty years later when the live audio was included on *The Beatles Anthology 2* released in March 1996.

Michael Adams

My dad prepared the first version of the film and presented it to them. It was a judgment call on time constraint. An hour TV show, because of commercials, means about fifty minutes of actual show.

The Beatles, Brian Epstein and their producer George Martin had the final say. There wasn't anything they could use from *She's A Woman* and with *Everybody's Trying To Be My Baby* and seeing that it wasn't a song they had written, it was a Carl Perkins song; they decided that would be the one taken out for time constraints.

There was also the feeling that everyone should get something. *Act Naturally*, Ringo's song, was included because it was just coming out on a new album and he was more in the background during the film. There just wasn't time for both.

The audio on *Everybody's Trying To Be My Baby* is fine and that's what you hear on *The Beatles Anthology*. But they mixed it down to mono. There's a true stereo version but for some reason it's locked up in the Apple Records vault.

I don't believe there is any footage of *Everybody's Trying To Be My Baby*. That's the kind of stuff that was left on the cutting room floor. I remember my dad telling me they just had yards and yards and yards of film. And a lot of that film was just left on the floor. They cut stuff down and just tried to make it as cohesive as possible. The film that wasn't used was just thrown out, so whatever footage there was of that song was edited out and gone almost right away.

The Fans In The Stands

Maxine Ascher

Oh, they were just so cute and every one was different. My sister and I made George our favorite. This is why, and it sounds so crazy to say it, but we didn't think he had as many fans as the others. So we stood a better chance of marrying him. Everybody loved Paul.

Joyce Shelfo

Our seats were in the second section up from the field, but it really didn't matter. I was there, in their presence, spilling coke all over the guy in front of me because I was jumping and screaming with abandon like everyone else. And yes, it's true what they say. We couldn't hear one word of any song because of the screeching, but who cared?

Steve Zisk

I was thrilled. I couldn't believe that I was actually seeing them in the flesh. That The Beatles really did exist. That was my feeling all along. They were like superheroes. Intellectually you understood that they were human beings, but at fourteen or fifteen you really didn't believe it somehow. You felt like they were somehow beyond that and to see them there in real life, breathing the same air that you were breathing at the same time was amazing.

Karen Bernstein

My boyfriend, who later became my husband, and I were so excited to be going. What I remember most were the energy and excitement of the crowd all screaming in anticipation and wishing I could hear them sing because the crowd noise was so overwhelming. After a while I didn't even care that we couldn't hear them sing. We were just so glad we were at a *happening*. It was an amazing night.

Can't Buy Me Love

_____ Shea Rocks _____

"Thank you very much." – Paul McCartney
"Thankyouverymuch!" – John Lennon

"Thank you. We'd like to sing'a a'little song for ya'now. And'a this'a song… We'd like everybody to ah… Everybody, all along there and all along there and all along there… Everybody! Everybody join in and clap your hands! (Paul claps his hands and then runs his fingers along the strings of his bass guitar while doing a quick dance). Smashing. And'a this'a little song'a is'a one'a which'a I hope you like and it's'a called'a, _Can't Buy Me Love_!" – Paul McCartney

It's doubtful Paul's impression of Lawrence Welk, the German accented band leader and star of his own weekly television variety series, reminded anyone at Shea Stadium of Champagne Music, bubble machines and The Lennon Sisters, who were a trio of sisters featured on his show. Instead fans were more focused on the musical trio of Lennon, Harrison and Starr providing backup to Paul's lead vocal on another former number one song.

In addition to their talents as songwriters and musicians, the Beatles as performers and recording artists stood out from other groups because they had two legitimate rock'n roll lead singers. Most other bands in 1965 only fronted one: Mick Jagger with The Rolling Stones, Peter Noone from Herman's Hermits, Eric Burdon with The Animals, and Mike Smith from The Dave Clark Five to name a few. The lead singer's distinctive vocals made each group recognizable on Top 40 Radio, but every new Beatles release had to be heard before listeners knew whether it was sung by John or Paul.

Their music was also more diverse since John and Paul were also adept at delivering ballads, pure pop, and blending their voices together in tight harmony. And when it came to full throttle rock'n roll, both were equal to the legendary singers who first inspired them such as Little Richard, Fats Domino and Elvis Presley.

Can't Buy Me Love was rousing and thrilling with Paul belting out the song that is often pointed to as forerunner to the modern music video. In a memorable scene from *A Hard Day's Night*, The Beatles break out from the prison of their own fame by racing down a fire escape and are shown running, jumping and fooling about in a vacant field. *Can't Buy Me Love* is the musical soundtrack played over the sequence, but unlike previous pop stars that had songs featured in movies the Beatles never pretended to play their instruments or lip-sync the lyrics during their great escape.

The same joy and playfulness was in the song's performance at Shea Stadium. The Beatles seemed to have as much fun as the fans, though it's unlikely many of them stopped screaming long enough to take Paul's advice to, "Join in and clap your hands!"

Shaun Weiss

The Beatles really had a magical thing about them. And their power was contained because it was controlled by Brian Epstein and the regimen that had made them untouchable. It made them bigger than life and when you were in their presence, you got caught up in that. It's not something you can even really explain.

Nedra Talley-Ross

There's nothing wrong with that. I have people I'm a fan of. There are people I love. I'm thinking *you don't know how much I love you! How many times I played your record!* Yeah, we all have people that we look at and go, *boy, there's something that resonates there that makes you want to go, "Gee, you're special."* Your sound is special or you look special or there was a time in my life where your song was special to me.

The Fans In The Stands

Joyce Kaufman

The stadium vibrated - the whole place. You didn't hear any music, so I don't remember them playing. All you heard was screaming. I don't understand how we screamed for so long. It never stopped. You go to a concert today and they scream and then they stop and you hear something and then they might scream again.

It was just perpetual screaming where I was. Shrieking and then falling down and just calling out names. Everybody had their favorite Beatle. My cousin, who I was with, was screaming out, "Paul! Paul!"

They were so far away. They were out in the middle of the field. They looked like little ants and I didn't have any binoculars. And there was just so much screaming.

Steve Zisk

All you would hear were the intros. Like John would say, "Here's our latest record." And then they'd start the song and there'd be screaming. You couldn't hear what the song was. My remembrance of it is that they screamed and yelled the name of whatever Beatle they loved. They screamed especially for Paul when he winked or gestured to them, almost like he was saying, "How you doing?" They would scream and shriek louder and louder.

Arlene Levine

It was just the main event in our life. Everybody was just in love. We stopped everything. It was just love. That's really all I remember. I couldn't even tell you what they sang. I heard there was a good reason for that because they couldn't even hear what they sang. And they didn't even have to do anything. If they just stood there it would've been the same thing.

Frank Branchini

Words are really inadequate to describe the sense of exhilaration and joy at being part of the event. And the audience and the mania were an essential ingredient. There was a delightful feeling of community among tens of thousands of teenagers sharing the experience of seeing the Beatles live.

Howie Altholz

The overarching memory is not about anything specific. It was just a feeling. It was very surreal with an all encompassing sense that something very big was happening and that I was in the center of something very powerful, and that major changes were taking place all around me and in me. There was kind of a sense of limitless possibilities.

Baby's In Black

"Can you hear me?! Hello? We'd like to do a slow song now (breaks into gibberish while looking at the stands to his left)... And it's also off *Beatles VI* or something. I don't really know what it's off. I haven't got it. Haha. Hoho! It's a waltz this one! Remember that. Anyway the song's called, hopefully enough... Ah, look'it there, (watching fans running onto the field and being chased by police). Ah... Ahaaaahhh! It's called *Baby's In Black*!" – John Lennon

During the Shea Stadium concert, John was the Beatle who cut loose the most. It was evident during his introduction for *Baby's In Black* that he wasn't sure anyone could even hear him over the constant screaming.

He was also quite aware of being surrounded by sheer pandemonium. From where he stood the tiers of stadium seating would have looked to be in complete chaos with fans waving and jumping up and down to get their attention. Both girls and boys made daring runs onto the field in a vain effort to reach the stage, only to be chased down and carried back by police.

Everyone was over-excited, hot and sweaty, and completely involved with what was happening. It was madness and mania and the chief Beatle was standing on a small stage in the middle trying to make sense of it all. In some ways he probably couldn't and decided to go along with the craziness by acting a little crazy himself. He mixed in gibberish nonsense during the song's introduction, probably thinking no one would know the difference anyway.

"John was having a good time at Shea. He was into his comedy, which was great. That was one of the great things about John. If there was ever one of those tense shows, which this undoubtedly was – you can't play in front of that many people for the first time and not be tense – his comedy routines would always come out. He'd start the faces, and the shoulders would start going, and it was very encouraging: 'OK, that's good – at least we're not taking it seriously.' He kept us jolly." – Paul McCartney (20)

John also acknowledged fans running onto the field and trying to dodge police to get closer to the Beatles. "Ahh, look'it there. Ah... Ahhhh!" Like everyone else he was also watching a show that was developing around him and because of him. But his view was from a different perspective. This time he was an observer from inside the eye of Hurricane Shea.

Shea Rocks

As he watched the whole show from a vantage point on the grass to one side of the stage, Brian Epstein's face glowed with pride. Tears of joy ran down his cheeks long before the boys finished their set. The main reason for this very special performance was that John, Paul, George and Ringo were hugely excited by their surroundings, by the unprecedented size of that stadium audience and the sheer electricity that was sparking away across the field between the stage and the stands. Inspired by the grand setting and the fantastic reception from the fans, their performance was thrice as large as life. They exaggerated every facial expression and bodily gesture in order to reach out to the crowd on the far side of this vast field. Never before had I seen the Fab Four play and sing with greater energy and enthusiasm. - Tony Barrow (21)

Scott Ross

I have never in my life, ever, ever heard anything like that. It can't be described unless you were there. I have photographs, but even then you can't quite conceive. John, Paul, George and Ringo...

Brian Epstein was standing off by himself. Watching and absorbing. Even he was awed by what was happening. But he had seen it before. I hadn't.

The screams were solid. Like a wall. It hurt. It was frightening. Cops were all over the field. Kids made a run for the Beatles and were stopped repeatedly by the police. They wielded their power, sometimes harshly. Maybe they had to.

Then one little girl made it. She was in the open. She had outmaneuvered five massive cops and she was going for broke. Lennon was her goal and he saw her. He took in what was happening in an instant, raised his hand and encouraged her on. She was wide open and the whole stadium was concentrating on that one girl. Everyone wanted her to make it except the police. One came flying out of nowhere and literally tackled her. The Beatles smiled at her, saying they were sorry. John said, "*Ahhhh...*" I felt sad.

**"The screams were solid. Like a wall. It hurt. It was frightening."
- Scott Ross**

Ken Mansfield

Shea was when they started realizing that nobody was really listening. And that's, I think, when they started fooling around with lyrics and stuff. It's either that's when they started or when they decided they could because they got really discouraged with all the excitement. Nobody was really listening to the music.

You know, this was a rock band. This was a band that was used to playing in clubs and having feedback. They got off on getting the people off. So I'm not really sure of the sequence and things like that, but Shea might have been one of the starting points to where they were just so drowned out that it was like, you know, why bother after awhile.

•

John's description of *Baby's In Black* as a waltz would have offered a calmer crowd another change of pace. Like *Ticket To Ride*, it's a story of unrequited love and would be the nearest song to a ballad they would perform that night. But with the chaos in the stands and on the field, and the thrilling sight of John and Paul once again harmonizing into the same microphone, the fans screamed with joy. During George's instrumental breaks Paul waltzed on stage with his bass and John did little to hold back his smile.

George Orsino

I was going around the stage taking pictures and kept watching, making sure everything was cool as far as I was concerned. There were lots of kids trying to get on the field and a lot of policemen around the stage, but no one looked at me cross-eyed at all.

Michael Adams

It was almost sort of surreal. I mean it was all business for my dad, of course. That was a working day for him. But I'll tell'ya one thing, he had a camera and he took a whole mess of stills. He was right there, so he was able to walk up and take pictures. While the whole thing is going on he's snapping pictures. Then the next day he took them to some film place and just dropped them off. Of course they never came back to him...

The Fans In The Stands

Pattie Noah

From that first opening chord of *Twist And Shout* the noise never stopped. But I have to say that I actually do remember hearing a little music and oddly enough, I could hear them speak between songs. I have the distinct memory of John saying, "Aw....look'it 'er!" when the girl was running from the cop across the field. My brother said that I was screaming too - right in his ear! He held me up for the entire show. I don't think I blinked for over twenty minutes.

Marc Catone

If you've seen the film of Shea Stadium, there's a moment when John is introducing *Baby's In Black*. My memory is that all of a sudden there were people climbing over the center field wall and he makes note of it. In fact, I can remember hearing that. I actually remember him saying and pointing over there going, "Look at that." And the kids were climbing over. But the minute they got twenty feet into centerfield there were cops on them and just dragging them off. Their goal obviously was to reach the stage. They were thwarted in their efforts to do that.

Eve Hoffman

Our seats were only about a dozen rows from the very top of the stadium and I remember looking down at the ball field and seeing more policemen than I'd ever seen in one place. They were standing with their shoulders touching in a single row starting at the front two corners of the stage and ending at the gates of the front row seats.

I can still see the girls who were brave enough to run out onto the field being scooped up by the policemen in the lines and carried off the field. There was not a single lull of quiet in the crowd for the entire concert.

Howie Altholz

I was eleven years old and remember every minute. We sat over the first base dugout and there was a constant buzz of intense screaming the whole time. The energy was amazing and nothing like I ever experienced. It still gives me chills. It no doubt led me to a life of loving and being very involved with music, as a musician and later a music business lawyer.

I could hear the music fine, but with a backdrop of steady massive screams. It was almost like white noise, if you know what I mean. Girls were running all over the field and being chased by New York's finest. Some girls made it quite close, but were scooped up almost like some sporting event by New York City cops.

Act Naturally

"Thank you. And now…" – Paul McCartney
"Hello." – Ringo Starr
"And now…" - Paul McCartney
"Hello!" – Ringo Starr
"…before your very eyes, we'd like to introduce to you at great expense brought 'specially from the other side of the earth for you tonight. Singing a song off our new album called _Act Naturally_, Ringo!!" – Paul McCartney

Ringo was always considered the newest Beatle in England, taking over the drummer slot from Pete Best on August 16, 1962 just as the group started their recording career and catapulted to world fame. The day following the Shea Stadium concert would mark only his third anniversary as a Beatle, but he had already been considered a local celebrity in Liverpool as a member of the popular group Rory Storm & the Hurricanes. During each show Rory Storm would give up the spotlight for Ringo to sing one song in a fan favorite segment called _Starr-Time_.

In America, Ringo was as new as the other Beatles and always one of the more popular. "Ringo For President" signs popped up after their first visit and a young singer named Cher, using the name Bonnie Jo Mason, recorded the song _Ringo, I Love You_, co-written and produced by Phil Spector. Even the actor Lorne Greene, star of the hit television show _Bonanza_, released a single titled _Ringo_. The song was actually about a cowboy outlaw named Johnny Ringo, but in 1964 he was also riding on the wave of Beatlemania and Starr power. Anything with the name Ringo on it was sure to sell.

In _A Hard Day's Night_, Ringo had earned the best notices as an actor for his dry sense of humor delivered with sad eyes under a fluffy mound of hair. In _Help!_ he was the featured Beatle with the plot centered on a sacrificial ring he couldn't get off his finger.

Act Naturally was Ringo's *Starr-Time* at Shea Stadium. Paul's grand introduction, "...'specially from the other side of the earth for you tonight," gave up the spotlight from the other three singers and aimed everyone's attention to the solitary Beatle sitting on his drum platform at the rear of the stage.

"No one knew what the song was because it hadn't yet been released in the United States." - Marc Catone

Ringo was a country music fan and *Act Naturally* had reached number one on the Country Charts for Buck Owens and the Buckaroos in 1963. With the Beatles' version two years later, the song has since gone on to become as much associated with Ringo as it is with Owens. Thanks to his featured role in the film, the lyrics gave an impression the song was specifically written for Ringo to sing in *Help!*

"They're gonna put me in the movies.
They're gonna make a big star out of me." (22)

Despite the lyrical reference, *Act Naturally* was never heard in the movie. At this time it was only on the British version of the *Help!* album and not available on the U.S. release, which only included songs that actually appeared in the film and the instrumental soundtrack. The Beatles had performed it the day before during *The Ed Sullivan Show* taping, to air in September when it would be released as the B-side to the single, *Yesterday*. In the U.S. *Act Naturally* did not appear on an album until Capitol Records released *Yesterday...and Today* in June 1966.

Marc Catone

I thought this was unusual about their performance. When Ringo did *Act Naturally*, no one knew what the song was because it hadn't yet been released in the United States. It was on the *Help!* album in the U.K. but it hadn't been played yet here in the United States, unless some deejays in some cities had advance copies. It didn't show up until it was the flip side of *Yesterday*, which didn't come out until September. So throughout the whole song, we were listening and watching and we know Ringo is singing, and we're going, "Is he singing *Boys*? *I Wanna Be Your Man*?

What is he singing?"

We just had no idea until afterwards that he had sung *Act Naturally*. Let's put it this way, I don't know if anyone else in the stadium knew, but the people that were around me had no idea what he was singing.

•

For the fans it didn't really matter what song Ringo was singing since they reacted to *Act Naturally* the same way they had for every song the Beatles played that night. The screaming never stopped.

Ringo sang and kept up a steady beat while John, Paul and George played electric country with a Beatles' flair. Paul's vocal harmony for whatever technical reason is never heard on the live recording, but it didn't turn out to be a problem. When the television show aired, *Act Naturally* was included. But it wasn't the version played at Shea Stadium.

Shaun Weiss

The concert just took me off my feet because even in the dugout I couldn't really hear them singing. The noise was coming from over our heads, but it was almost 60,000 kids just screaming. You could only hear certain parts of songs.

Steve Marinucci

They always said they couldn't hear themselves, so I think they just got tired of it all. And they cared, but a lot of their live performances were lost in the screaming. An example of how they were playing live at the time would be the recordings from The Hollywood Bowl. Capitol Records recorded those shows and as a band they sound really good. I'm sure after awhile it all got on their nerves and they decided playing live wasn't necessary anymore.

The Fans In The Stands

Frank Branchini

As Ringo has pointed out in interviews, people came to *see* The Beatles. You couldn't hear anything but the screaming. It was like being in a jet engine. Occasionally the noise level would drop just enough so that I could figure out what song they were playing, but you really couldn't hear the music at all.

Judith Goodspeed

We had binoculars and were able to see. But even with binoculars they were very small. So I was just overwhelmed with the crowd and the noise. It made me feel, I guess kind of like how the older teenagers and the twenty-something's felt at Woodstock. I just felt that I couldn't believe I was in this place with all these people trying to see this concert. It was just awesome.

For me it was more the emotions of being there, rather than experiencing the Beatles' music because I just couldn't hear it. It was just like in the Beatles movies. People really, really did scream and faint and mash up to the front of the line. I mean everything you saw in the movies actually happened and that just amazed me.

Bob Eaton

We were sitting behind the first base dugout, so we could see pretty well. But hearing them was just about impossible. It was like the whole stadium was alive. We could pick out a few words, but not a whole song. Occasionally someone would run out on the field but was quickly intercepted.

Cindy Salvo

One thing that made a huge impression upon me was all the girls that were running out onto the field. There were so many. They had cops all over the place but they were teenage girls that were running out on the field. Constantly, they were trying to run to the Beatles and then they would get stopped by the cops and taken back wherever they were taken to. But I remember thinking why would anyone do that? Because they know they're going to get caught. They know they're not going to be able to get to the Beatles. But many, many, many girls kept running onto the field. There were a lot. I remember thinking they kept doing it and doing it throughout the whole concert.

I also remember thinking that I wished I was older. Because in one way I thought the girls were being so silly to run out to the field, but then I saw one who got pretty close to Ringo. I do remember that. One got pretty close to Ringo. Maybe he was my favorite at the time and I was thinking, *Oh, I wish I was older and then I could run out there!*

A Hard Day's Night

Shea Rocks

"Thank you." – Ringo Starr
"What a show!" – Paul McCartney
"Thank you, Ringo." – John Lennon
"The next song we'd like to sing… (John speaks nonsensical gibberish and throws his hands in the air). When George is ready. We'd like to do the title song from our first film we made. Remember that. The black and white one. Hahahaha. And it's called *A Hard Day's Night*." – John Lennon

John Lennon had a sense of humor that could be sarcastic and biting. Authors of his many biographies claimed it was developed as a defense against unsettling events in his life. Usually he's described as the young rebel with a sharp tongue who wasn't afraid to speak his mind. His stinging humor could be used as a way to quickly end a situation or cut short a conversation he had grown bored with.

John was an artist and his creativity and interests flowed continually from one phase to another. He proved this throughout his life by throwing himself completely into what he was doing until his spirit as an artist would send him into another direction. His humor, whether using sarcasm, putdowns, or generally making faces and acting a bit crazy while making fun of someone or certain situations could signal he was ready to move on to something else.

It's apparent from watching film of their performance at Shea Stadium that John and the other Beatles were enjoying the experience. They were idols being worshipped by thousands upon thousands of people and could seemingly do nothing wrong. But for John it might have been the true beginning point signaling the end of The Beatles as a touring act.

The equipment and technology in 1965 could carry their music over the screams in smaller venues like the CBS Studio during *The Ed Sullivan Show*, but stadiums filled with hysteria presented other problems. The

Beatles often said they couldn't hear themselves play since most of their audiences were young fans more intent on seeing them and screaming rather than sitting back and listening to their music. For an artist, composer and musician who wanted his work to be heard, it could be a frustrating and overwhelming situation.

John was the one most anxious to throw off the restraints of being one of the lovable mop tops. He had played that role already, singing *I Want To Hold Your Hand* and *She Loves You* on *The Ed Sullivan Show* and during their triumphant tour of North America in 1964. He had already moved on as an artist creating songs such as *I'm A Loser*, *I Don't Want To Spoil The Party* and *You've Got To Hide Your Love Away*. These new expressions of his life could be difficult to perform live under the smothering squeals of Beatlemania, so instead he had reverted back to the smiling pop music character he portrayed in *A Hard Day's Night* and *Help!*

His work was becoming more personal with confessional lyrics and his opinions and concerns were maturing. John had already shown signs at Friday's press conference of his future outspokenness against war and for human rights. Even before leaving the dressing room he had expressed his distaste for the military style Shea Jackets. He had worn it since The Beatles' image still required them to look like a group, but had refused to button it like the others.

The popularity of The Beatles was also becoming more and more absurd for him. In his 1971 *Rolling Stone* interview, John claimed they had been, "Just a band that made it very, very big, that's all." (23) But mentally, physically and emotionally the experience had to entail much more than his simple explanation. Sometimes mocking the situation would be the only way he could deal with it and perhaps express his feelings about the intense fame that surrounded his life. This was undoubtedly the case during their June 1964 tour of Australia when John stood on his hotel balcony in front of over 350,000 people, the largest crowd ever gathered to see The Beatles. According to a description in *The Beatles* by Bob Spitz:

> Another roar went up, this one even more deafening than the first, as John put a finger across his upper lip, threw the Nazi salute, and goose-stepped jauntily across the platform, screaming, "Sieg heil! Sieg heil!" (24)

Within the next year John would talk in an interview about the absurdity of The Beatles' popularity and how fans made it seem they more popular than Jesus. He would later use his fame in more positive ways to end war and promote peace. But on August 15, 1965 he looked out at more than 55,000 fans at Shea Stadium who would scream and cry over anything – and it didn't matter what – he would say or do next. It had to be more than a bit surreal.

> **"I understand that John Lennon was saying a few dirty words because nobody could hear what he was saying."**
> **- George Orsino**

The Beatles had played with intensity worthy of the all-night amphetamine fueled nightclub sets that had been their norm only a few years earlier. Sweat plastered John's hair onto his forehead as he appeared to finally give in to the craziness swirling around him. The fans wanted him to talk and sing, but wouldn't stop screaming long enough to hear him. Similar to the mad dictator standing on a balcony overlooking thousands in Australia, he threw both his hands into the air and ruled over the adoring masses by shouting out nonsense gibberish.

George Orsino

Standing by the stage with all the noise… That was ridiculous. Why were they even playing? I mean you couldn't hear a sound. All you heard was screaming. I was saying to myself, *I don't believe this. You can't hear them sing!*

And I understand that John Lennon was saying a few dirty words because nobody could hear what he was saying. No one could hear him. He was just clowning around on the microphone. Maybe earlier when they first started it might have been different. He might have been serious. But by this time it was like, *what are we doing up here? They can't hear us.*

Judith Kristen

There's a picture of John with his hands up in the air. And I can say with all of my heart and soul that at the exact moment that picture was taken my hands were up in the air along with, I don't know, five hundred other girls in our section. Because it all started by crossing our hands over ourselves making like an *X*, you know? When crossing your arms over each other it's an *X*. Because how else were we going to get any attention? What, we were going to holler for them? Yeah, they'd notice us because we were hollering for them. That wasn't going to happen.

I started waving my hands and I told a couple others, "Wave! We gotta wave! We gotta wave!" I turned around and our whole section, I mean it was just a mass of crossing arms and everything. We didn't stand up. We were just sitting in our seats and all waving in unison. It was like this big massive bunch of crossing hands and we'd bump into the next person, but we didn't care. We just kept going and going until...

We didn't care who it was, but it just happened to be John. He turned to us and waved back to us exactly the same way we were waving. So we knew that he saw us. And it was just a genuine thrill for all of us. *He saw us! Oh my God!* And we were just ranting and crying and it was wonderful.

John had turned to our section and just when that picture was taken he put his hands up. We freaked. I laughed, I cried, because I thought, you know what? There are 55,000 plus people at this stadium and what are the chances that John Lennon is gonna spot anyone in particular? But he saw our section. He made that gesture like, *I see you!* He was waving back to us and it was just the coolest moment.

It seems like such a small, tiny thing, but you know what? Every time I think about it or see that photo, I know exactly where I was, I know exactly how I felt, and it never fails to put a smile on my face. It was just awesome. It was amazing.

•

John's adlibbed introduction gave George time to switch to his electric twelve-string Rickenbacker guitar. Then all four Beatles joined together to hit the distinctive opening chord of their first movie's title song and once again they were the four mop tops in *A Hard Day's Night*.

"It's been a hard day's night and I've been working like a dog. It's been a hard day's night; I should be sleeping like a log. But when I get home to you I find the things that you do will make me feel alright." (25)

Unlike *Act Naturally*, every fan at Shea Stadium knew *A Hard Day's Night*. Paul, also visibly sweating in the summer heat, traded lead vocals with John and harmonized. Whenever it was Paul's turn to sing, John gave an acknowledging hand wave in his partner's direction asking fans to at least try and pay attention to which Beatle was singing.

It was all still crazy and it was all still absurd. It was *A Hard Day's Night* in New York.

The Fans In The Stands

Eve Hoffman

No words can truly express the experience accurately because Beatlemania was truly the energy of Beatle lovers that one had to live through and experience to know the feeling and fully understand. I don't think there will ever be anything like it again.

Steve Zisk

I remember the stadium shaking, but I don't think people back in '65 were accustomed to stomping and jumping. First of all, people didn't stand all through concerts the way they do now. That wasn't the custom back then. But people were screaming continuously and the stands were shaking. And it was a really, really hot day.

I remember girls, three, four or five girls, trying to get to the Beatles who were on second base. The girls were running onto the field and the security guards were grabbing them.

Rick Andrews

What we heard all night wasn't the Beatles singing. What we heard was screaming in the middle of pandemonium that I haven't experienced since. The Beatles were gods to my friend Gary and me. We knew every word of every song they performed that night even though we couldn't hear a note. There was the incredible awe of being caught up in the fever of that night and that was way more than we were ready for. Even though the screaming hysteria was all around us we didn't or couldn't scream, yell or even cheer.

I do remember having a big lump in my throat and letting out many, "Oh man… I can't believe this!" Thinking back maybe it was because we were eighteen year old guys and a little older than most there. Maybe that was part of it. But it was mostly that the Beatles were too important and we didn't want to waste a second of it by not paying attention to everything they did. Even so that night was an emotional roller coaster that neither of us knew how to handle really. The comments made by the other fans are interesting in that we didn't expect to be so overcome with so much emotion either. But in our case, the experience numbed us into catatonic silence.

Marc Catone

As a guy, we had a little bit more of an advantage because we weren't screaming. I guess if you have ever tried to scream and try to hear somebody talk at the same time you can't do it because you're drowning them out. So unlike the girls who were screaming, crying and moaning, which added to their inability to hear, at least at some point I could hear because I wasn't drowning myself out by yelling. So I did hear a little bit towards the end of the performance.

I think with the girls, their voices were pretty raw and they were getting tired screaming. It got a little less noisy. The last few songs could be heard a little bit better because the girls' screaming had sort of dwindled out of sheer exhaustion. Again, I'm doing this from a guy's perspective.

Help!

———————————— Shea Rocks ————————————

"Thank you. Thank you! Yeah!" (Paul looks to his right) "Yeah!" (Paul looks to his left at George and Ringo). "Oh yeah. Haha. What a show! Yes, yes..." (Sees police chasing fans on the field behind the stage). "Booo! Booo! Booo!" (John talks to him). Now we'd like to carry on with a song which is the title song from our new film. This is our latest record here. And the song is called *Help!*" – Paul McCartney

Comedy may have helped John cope with the madness and mania, but he wasn't the only one on stage feeling the effects. It was the biggest show for all four Beatles in their career together and being the showman of the group, a lot of that pressure was also on Paul.

John could act crazy and get away with it. Even during the rehearsal for their second appearance on *The Ed Sullivan Show* in Miami Beach he had shouted at screaming fans to "Shut up! Pauley's talkin'!" And when he'd make grotesque faces and stomp about making fun of "cripples," no one in the New York or national press wrote a bad word about him.

In The Beatles, John was the unpredictable one to rule as a mad dictator speaking gibberish to his subjects. But Paul's role was as the charmer who'd ask fans to join in and be a part of the group as he did with *Can't Buy Me Love*. Then he would take that excitement up to another level with a high energy performance that could have persuaded fans to actually join in and clap their hands - if they hadn't been screaming so hard instead.

If there was a moment when the excitement and magnitude of Shea Stadium may have affected Paul, it was at the end of *A Hard Day's Night*. Instead of immediately addressing the fans to introduce the next song, he grabbed his microphone, looked to his right and sighted a few girls running through the outfield. He laughed, spun to his left and appeared excited about what was happening behind the stage.

"What a show! Yes, yes..."

Unlike modern stadium concerts, there was no backdrop behind the stage. Between Ringo and the baseball home run fence was a long stretch of outfield grass. George and Ringo turned to see police chasing girls who had scaled the fence and were making desperate runs for the stage. They dodged, jumped and waved trying to catch any Beatles' attention. Paul, still clutching his microphone turned toward the audience in front of the stage and began to boo the police.

"Booo! Booo! Booo!"

John, usually the instigator and protagonist for any Beatles rebellion, hurried across the stage and confronted Paul. It would only be speculation what he might have said since the microphones didn't record any dialogue, but John's expression appeared to be saying, "What are you doing!?"

John may have liked to tease fans to the edge of madness, but it wouldn't help anyone, especially The Beatles, to turn the crowd against the police by booing. Without security, the field, the stage and most importantly The Beatles, would have surely been overrun by fans.

Cousin Bruce Morrow

After we introduced them, the police asked me to escort them around the perimeter of the field in Shea Stadium, which I did. The Beatles were on second base and they had the wire behind home plate and barriers and all kinds of things to keep the kids away. They had to stop them from getting over these to run to where The Beatles were.

We walked around the perimeter with the police and the kids were going... Well, I remember prying their hands off the wire and the gates that were set up. They were just excited. Nobody was there to do any damage, you know. The kids were just great.

•

By the time they'd finished *A Hard Day's Night* John and Paul looked like marathoners coming to the end of a race. Both were sweating profusely and appeared flushed from the heat and excitement.

In the almost thirty minutes they had been on stage, The Beatles and Paul especially had been going at full speed. There was no chance to rest with a set of slow acoustic songs where they could sit on stools and slow the pace of the show. There were also no bottles of water or anything to drink since Epstein had decided against any drinking, eating, smoking, or swearing on stage during a Beatles performance.

Adrenaline was pumping through his showman's heart and Paul had given it his all since walking on stage. Out of breath and with sweat running down his face and neck, Paul continued with the song's introduction:

"And the song... (breath)... is called... (breath)... *Help!*"

Joan Murray

I had been backstage and ran with them from the dressing room. Then I went out into the crowd, which became dangerous because they would pull at you. If you had even touched one of the Beatles they wanted to touch you. And there weren't that many black people there, so me with a microphone stood out. They knew me from all the

"I went out into the crowd, which became dangerous because they would pull at you. If you had even touched the Beatles they wanted to touch you." - Joan Murray

interviews I did on the television news at six o'clock and eleven o'clock. So the fans knew who I was and that I had been with The Beatles.

Michael Adams

I was on the field for the whole show. It was quite exciting. It was a total privilege to be there and have this opportunity. It was almost sort of surreal. But it wasn't like going to a concert and standing on the floor and watching them. You weren't getting close no matter what. This was The Beatles and you weren't getting close because it was still Shea Stadium. You still weren't *close* close. It's not like going up to a band playing in a bar and getting drenched in their sweat. But it was quite the scene and pretty amazing to see the camera and sound guys doing their thing. And I was just standing there. I just thought to myself, *stay here. This is a good spot for you to watch from.*

I was as involved in the show as anybody else in the stadium. But even being in front of everybody in the stands it was still... The screaming was amazing. The amount of noise was amazing and it all happened so quickly. You waited through the whole buildup and the guys play twenty minutes and they're gone.

Judith Kristen

My seat was on the second level. The only way I could've even been on the field was if I had leaped into the first section a hundred feet down, then crawled over some fences and gone onto the field. There was no chance. We were just very far away.

That was the one bad thing about shows back then. Today you could be in the worse seat in a stadium anywhere and they have those big screens. You could be looking at this little twelve inch figure, but see the sweat pouring off his face on the big screen. We didn't have that back then. We were far away from the stage, but we were fans. There was no mistaking, you know, who was singing.

The Fans In The Stands

Frank Branchini

There was a huge line of police on the field facing the audience, catching girls as they jumped onto the field. One girl made it past the police line and a considerable distance onto the field before she was caught. The audience booed loudly and Paul joined in.

Dan Reznicak

I was only five years old and it was my first time coming into a strange country, from Canada. I went with my sister, brother-in-law, nephew and niece. My brother-in-law complained about the noise because girls were screaming and I was a little scared. Girls were holding on to this mesh wire fence and their hands were bleeding. I saw this one girl bleeding because she was holding on the fence so tight.

Marc Catone

My sister and I were sharing a pair of binoculars all throughout the whole show. *Help!* was their single that was out at the time and my sister really loved that song. She especially liked the third verse, the final verse where it kind of slows down and John sings the first verse over again. Obviously we could hear it because she knew it was coming up and she grabs the binoculars and says, "I wanna see John sing the third verse!"

She forgot that the strap of the binoculars was around my neck! So she was choking me! I just remembered that I wanted to yell for help because I was being choked by my sister with the binocular strap during that whole latter part of *Help!*

I'm Down

Shea Rocks

"Thank you very much. Ta. Thank you. Well, this next song now, is the one where we want everybody, everybody to clap their hands. Okay? Yes? Clap your hands. Okay? To this song." (John plays a few chords on the electric organ). "Alright. And this song will have to be our last song for tonight! Yes! Well, we have to go home, you see. So... Yeah, so... So we'd like to say to everybody thank you very much and good night. See'ya. With this song! So clap your hands to this one, okay? Alright, alright."
– Paul McCartney

Since this was the first date on the 1965 North American tour, none of the fans knew in advance what songs would be played, what order they would be performed, or even how long The Beatles would be on stage. After joining the theater circuit with their first hit records in England, their scream-filled performances were cut to about half an hour in length. The reasoning was that no one would hear the music anyway, so fans could at least see them in person. Then after a short period the Beatles would be rushed safely out of the venue before the mania became too overwhelming and dangerous for both the audience and police.

Without any prior warning Paul answered the question of how long they would play when he announced this would be their last song. And since he wasn't sure if anyone could hear him over the screaming, he mimed to his words to demonstrate the end was here:

Shea Rocks

"Yes, well..." (Paul looks at his watch). "We have to go home you see..." (He points at the watch and then lays his head on his hands like it's time for bed). "So..."

Judith Kristen

Nobody did encores then. When they were done, they were done. And The Beatles always announced it. You go to a concert now and if you don't get at least two encores at a Green Day or U2 or whoever else you happen to be watching, or even Paul McCartney, people would get mad and storm the stage and that kind of stuff. So now you get two or three encores out of everybody. The Beatles? Forget it. When Paul said that was it - that was it.

•

I'm Down was another new release, appearing as the B-side on their single, *Help!* It was written primarily by Paul to take the place of the Little Richard rave-up, *Long Tall Sally* that had been their concert closer during the first North American tour. It was the same style of 1950's three chord rock'n roll also played by Elvis and Chuck Berry that had inspired both John and Paul and brought them together in their first group as The Quarrymen and continued with The Beatles.

During Paul's introduction, John took off his guitar and pulled his microphone back to where Mal Evans had set up the rented Vox Continental Electric Organ. Since he and George shared backing vocals, they would be anchored toward the rear of the stage leaving Paul as the front man for the final song.

The continuing noise and chaos around them grew even more intense when fans realized this would be the end of the show. They screamed, cried and fainted as parents held on knowing it was almost over. Teenage girls and boys who had waited to make a mad dash onto the field leaped from the stands and raced past barriers that had been placed around the baseball infield trying to outrun the police.

On stage Paul hadn't bothered to announce the name of the song. At this point, it didn't seem to matter. None of the Beatles knew if anything they played had been heard and whatever fear or nerves they might have had earlier about performing looked to have melted away in the heat.

John's smile had broken into laughter. While waiting for Paul to start *I'm Down*, he stood behind the electric organ taking in the final moments of this experience. It's doubtful even he knew his upcoming performance would be as entertaining for himself and the other Beatles as it was for the audience.

_____ Shea Rocks _____

"If you look at the film footage you can see how we reacted to the place. It was very big and very strange. I feel that on that show John cracked up. He went mad; not mentally ill, but he just got crazy. He was playing the piano with his elbows and it was really strange." – Ringo Starr (26)

Paul's jacket was wet with sweat stains around his collar and shoulders, but he wasn't about to slow down. Invoking the spirit of Little Richard and demonstrating why he also possesses one of the greatest voices in rock, Paul gave a full out performance.

"You tell lies thinking I can't see.
You can't cry cuz you're laughing at me, I'm down." (27)

Though *I'm Down* is rarely included on any official greatest hits list by the Beatles, it's lived on as arguably the most memorable song performance from that night. Everyone in Shea Stadium knew there would be no encore and like the audience, the Beatles held nothing back - especially John.

_____ Shea Rocks _____

"Because I did the organ on *I'm Down*, I decided to play it on stage for the first time. I really didn't know what to do, because I felt naked without a guitar, so I was doing all Jerry Lee (Lewis). I was jumping about and I only played about two bars of it. I was putting my foot on it and George couldn't play for laughing. I was doing it for a laugh. The kids didn't know what I was doing." – John Lennon (28)

John's solo break saw him running his elbow over the electric organ's keyboard while he waved to the fans. The entire stadium seemed out of control and his reaction was to act out of control. Dissolving into laughter, he and George could barely shout out their backing vocals,

("I'm really down!"). And when Paul caught sight of them he also broke into laughter as they rock'n rolled together into the ending of *I'm Down*.

The laughter, sweat, exhaustion and joy radiating from their faces amid the screams of adoring fans will forever be an image of the height of Beatlemania. Their performance of *I'm Down* was so exhilarating and comical that it was later used as both the opening and closing sequences for the television special.

Steve Marinucci

They sounded like they're having fun that night, as opposed to later on. It looks like they enjoyed it. The part with John at the end with *I'm Down* is absolutely hilarious. It's one of those things you can watch over and over again and you get a smile every time. He just kind of took off and had some fun with that. They all kind of did. They all seemed to enjoy it that night.

You can hear it in the interviews they did for the TV show. They really enjoyed it. They were really glad about it and that's another good thing about this concert. That the Beatles had fun. And in spite of things that happened later on when things started turning sour, it wasn't Shea Stadium that did it. They were enjoying themselves then.

•

The song ended with John playing swirling notes on the organ while George rushed to the center of the stage for their final *Beatle Bows* of the night. Paul grasped the neck of his Hofner Bass and raised it high over his head in what has become a symbolic gesture of their triumph at Shea Stadium. To this day when he repeats the move at the end of his concerts audiences erupt into loud ovations and cheers. The direct lineage for this tradition can be traced back to August 15, 1965 and the ending of *I'm Down*.

Still waving to the audience, Ringo, Paul, John and George hurried down the same steps they had used earlier on stage right and into a waiting cream colored station wagon with the New York Mets baseball team logo on the driver's side door. Fans continued to scream while some attempted to chase the car as it was driven out of the exit near left field and away from Shea Stadium.

Judith Kristen

You know what? It was a very happy song. And you could tell they were really having a good time. You know, John was playing that organ thingy that he had with his elbow and everything. And Paul spun around and they just… I don't know if they were like, *thank God this is over* or *my God we had such a wonderful time*, but they really looked like they were having a ball.

When it was over I was still so high from seeing them and hearing that song. It was just so up. It was just super charged and the guys were all bouncing around and happy and laughing and all that kind of stuff. I couldn't feel down. No pun intended. I wasn't down at all.

Then I just watched them go and that was sad. But I remember leaving my seat and asking the girl behind me how she was feeling because she had passed out.

> **"In spite of things that happened later on when things started turning sour, it wasn't Shea Stadium that did it. They were enjoying themselves then." - Steve Marinucci**

Michael Adams

The fact is that the Shea Stadium concert is still revered. And it's great that there's an actual document. Of all the Beatles' big concerts, this is the one. It's still pretty cool. They did better concerts in places before and maybe even after when they were doing other stadiums. But this is the one that was filmed and this is the one that is the most famous.

And you know what? They sounded good. I've got the recordings, the raw tapes from the show. The raw tapes came out of my dad's stuff for the television special and they sound pretty good.

•

From Ed Sullivan's introduction to their final bows on stage, The Beatles performance at Shea Stadium lasted just over thirty seven minutes. It had been loud, exciting and fun. It had been hot and sweaty, amazing and absurd; emotional, chaotic and more than a bit crazy. And for the more than 55,600 who were there, it would be remembered.

The attendance and gross revenue at the time was a world record for a pop music concert. The Beatles' share of the $304,000 box office takings was also a record - $160,000. (29)

Most of all, it was an experience shared by four young musicians from England and the fans who were part of it. It was the height of Beatlemania. It was the birth of stadium rock.

The Fans In The Stands

Maxine Ascher

It was a very loud night. And it was fast. It was like they sang their songs and they were gone. I don't remember hearing too much of anything except everybody screaming. I think you had to scream out of self defense.

Janice Bartel

I could not believe I was watching The Beatles who meant more to me than life itself. The concert ended all too soon with Paul announcing, "This song will be the last song of the night," and they went on to sing *I'm Down* with Paul on lead vocals. To this day I don't know if my sister Bonnie and I took the subway home or walked.

Frank Branchini

Ringo said in a much later interview that he thought John cracked up during the show. But at the time and looking at the video years later, it simply looked like a good rock and roll stage move.

Bob Eaton

When Paul announced the last song, I wondered how they were gonna get out of there in one piece. People were starting to head towards the field like a small river that was about to turn into a raging torrent. They went into *I'm Down* and they all went crazy on stage. When they finished and started leaving the stage I thought, *how are they gonna get away?* Out of nowhere, a white Rambler station wagon appeared and they got in and were whisked away before our very eyes. I turned to my cousin and said, "This is the greatest day of my life!"

I don't remember how I got back to my cousin's house, but I woke up and saw the ticket stub next to my glasses and realized that it wasn't a dream.

Marc Catone

My favorite song, my favorite moment actually from the entire concert was *I'm Down*. I remember it happening exactly the way that I saw it later when Ringo was interviewed on *The Beatles Anthology*.

After my sister almost choked me grabbing the binoculars I said I had to watch the last song. So I'm watching *I'm Down* through the binoculars and looking at Lennon. And I'm going, w*hat the hell is he doing?* He's playing the organ with his elbow. He's waving to the crowd and acting really funny. And George was kind of laughing too. I just really remember that sequence. Of course I couldn't see them that close up to know that both George and John were cracking themselves up during that performance. It was pretty cool watching them do that. It was probably the most manic that they got on stage that night. I mean no where is that kind of mode in their performances. You know, they would get done and bow, which is kind of quaint now, but John sort of broke lose there.

Then thirty years later *Anthology* came on and Ringo was talking about how that was the night John went a bit manic. And that's exactly what I was thinking when I saw him do it live. So I just really enjoyed that. It was nice to see them cut up and to be loose and free at that moment.

Steve Zisk

I remember that the concert was about thirty minutes long. We didn't know, obviously, any better than that. I hadn't really been to a concert, so we didn't think it was short.

Doug Fernandez

It was electric, it was fun and then it was over.

Leaving Shea Stadium

Shea Rocks

As we drove away, the continuous screaming of the crowd ringing in our ears, the four boys expressed complete satisfaction with the show, something that rarely happened on tour. Even the sound system got a thumbs-up. As we travelled along in the claustrophobic truck I was already re-living highlight moments of an evening that would stand forever as the most vivid memory of my six years with them. Shea Stadium '65 was in a class of its own. This was the ultimate pinnacle of Beatlemania. This was the group's brightly-shining summer solstice, after which all The Beatles' days would insidiously grow a little darker.
- Tony Barrow (30)

Cousin Bruce Morrow

Now, the postscript of all this is that nothing bad happened that day. The kids, once again with all that energy and spirit and rock'n roll excitement, nothing bad happened. Nobody got hurt. Nobody had any fights.

Scott Ross

I split before the concert was over. I wanted to hear them but couldn't. The whole thing was too much. The Beatles came off stage and I got outside and there were thousands of fans waiting. The Ronettes and I signed autographs. It started to get rough. We ran for the car and just made it.

My manager at that time was a guy named Jerry Shatzberg. He went on to become a movie director and did *Panic in Needle Park*, *Scarecrow* and a lot of other films. Shatzberg had a Bentley. You know, it looks like a Rolls and he was taking me out of Shea with two of The Ronettes. Nedra was not in our car.

Nedra Talley-Ross

Afterwards they were going to go someplace for a party or something. I didn't go because I was going to go talk to my mom. I had brought my car to Shea. That's why I wasn't in the car at the end of the show with Scott and my cousin Estelle.

I went to talk to my mom and that night I agreed to delay marrying Scott for a year. So I was sort of caught up in the reality of what was going on in my life and not so much going, oh *my gosh! Here I am at Shea Stadium!*

Scott Ross

The Beatles had left. Jerry was driving and we were in this car and the kids saw us. They saw me with the hair and stuff and saw the Ronettes, so they jumped the car. It was one of the most frightening experiences of my life because we were mobbed. And I'm telling you, if it had been a Chevrolet, I'd probably be dead because they were all over the car. We were trapped for an hour and fifteen minutes before the police rescued us. Estelle, one of the Ronettes and Nedra's cousin, was in the backseat screaming, "We're gonna die! We're gonna die!" It was really intense.

The end result was $2,000 worth of damage to the Bentley, a court suit because a girl had her leg broken, and fear. I really thought I was going to die.

> **"The postscript of all this is that nothing bad happened that day."**
> **- Cousin Bruce Morrow**

Shaun Weiss

Because of where I was sitting I never even bought a program. I got ushered down into the dugout and there was nobody walking in selling Beatles programs. But I did get a souvenir. I got a record from Murray the K that he was handing out. It's a black and white thing and I got him to sign the top of it for me. It says *Murray the K and The Beatles.* That's what I walked away with as a present. You know, that was my gift.

As I was leaving, honestly without exaggerating, the girls that were around the dugout who knew I was there waited for me to walk out. Then it was like, "Let me touch you." They were touching my hair and I felt really important. But why? Because the Beatles ran by me? It was a big deal to those girls because I was someplace they couldn't be.

It was unbelievable how the audience wanted stuff. The girls wanted anything. They wanted me to take the signs off the dugout. One girl was screaming, "Give me dirt! Give me dirt!" So I just scooped a handful of dirt and handed it to her. And then she's pulling my arm. I thought my arm was gonna come off.

> **"It was one of the most frightening experiences of my life because we were mobbed."**
> **- Scott Ross**

Judith Kristen

When we left I remember singing *I'm Down* the whole way out of the stadium. The acoustics in Shea were really very good and there was a lot of echo stuff going on. It was almost as if I could carry a piece of the concert with me. I sang it probably much to the chagrin of a few thousand other girls who had to put up with me singing at the top of my lungs.

George Orsino

The show was over. The Beatles had disappeared and I was left there. When I got back on the bus these teenagers attacked me because they found out I was with the Beatles. They were grabbing at me and wanted to sit on my lap. "I want to touch you!" I had to get off that bus and look for the next bus.

Then the word got out there that George Orsino was with the Beatles and the kids started crying. They were saying, "Why didn't you tell us? You could've told me. I would've given them this or that…"

Ann Wix was a chaperone on the bus. Her daughter, I think she was twelve years old, was one of the girls that was crying, "Why couldn't you have told me? I could've given them a letter or a note." So I took out a ballpoint pen and said, "This is the pen that Ringo Starr signed the autographs with." And Ann saw me hand it to her daughter and she kind'a flipped. I did this for her because Ann did a lot. So I gave it to her daughter. It was the pen Ringo had used to sign the autographs.

The Fans Leaving Shea Stadium

Dotty Poirier

Unfortunately they were only on for a short time. It seemed like about thirty minutes. Like anything else, when you wait to see the best band in the world, when it is over there is disappointment. My ears were buzzing for several hours after the concert due to the extreme noise level there, but I didn't care. I will always have the video of this in my mind. And to this day, other than getting married and having a child whose name is Michelle, this is one of the most exciting days in my life and I feel blessed to have been there. Who knew that this would be so significant in the lives of so many people?

Steve Zisk

I didn't know how long a concert should be, but I think we were very surprised at how short it was. Now that I think about it. Because it was such a big, major build up and it was such a tremendous event.

Debbie Stern

Over but not forgotten! We excitedly relived the concert second by second during the ride home – totally in awe and partly in shock, that we had indeed just seen The Beatles live in concert.

Joyce Shelfo

As we piled out of the stadium after the concert, I could barely speak. I didn't want to. Instead, I wanted to bask in the aura of pure joy and satisfaction. If I died then and there at the ripe age of twelve it would have been okay. My life was complete.

Pattie Noah

When we got home, I was completely voice-less from screaming. My brother told my parents about it and I remember my mom saying if she'd had any idea it would be like that, she never would have let me go. But she admitted she'd never seen me that happy.

I hold that memory of the hottest night of 1965 close to my heart. I still tear up when I watch the footage. I witnessed history in the making and that will always be one of the most important nights of my life.

Arlene Levine

We must have been on a high. We couldn't stop talking about it. We were laughing. We were exhausted.

Eve Hoffman

When it was over my friend Neli and I slowly made our way down to the parking lot where there were what looked like hundreds of vendor booths set up with banners, t-shirts and other Beatles merchandise for sale. After not eating all day and now voiceless, I spent the entire five dollars my mom had sent with me for a meal on Beatles souvenirs.

I actually don't remember how Neli's father found us in such a crowd of girls, but I do remember the ride back up to the Catskills that night. Neli and I tried to speak to one another in the back seat but we were squeaking due to barely having a voice after all the screaming we did.

Maxine Ascher

I came out of there just loving The Beatles. I loved them going in, but it was just a different feeling after you see them. That is a highlight of my life, especially now when people talk about The Beatles.

We sat in Row J at Shea Stadium. I had the original ticket stubs. I gave them to my framing lady to frame and her son stole them. She had to replace them for me so now I have two new ones. Not the same thing, but she did replace them. She was honorable about it.

Marc Catone

It was normally about a two hour drive home, but with all the traffic and everything it probably took our bus about three hours. And my parents were on the bus as chaperones. So what I remember is sitting next to this girl and trying to talk to her because I'm a fifteen year old guy. And my parents were sitting in the seat in front of me. You know, it wasn't conducive to having a conversation with this girl about the Beatles.

Doug Fernandez

Getting home proved far more difficult than getting there. The trains took me to the bus, but the bus had stopped running. So I began to walk and it was a distance of about ten miles. It was late and I went into a gas station to ask directions and a guy offered me a ride which I took right to my front door.

Janice Bartel

I feel so fortunate to have witnessed the greatest rock and roll band of all time, The Beatles playing at what turned out to be one of the most famous stadium concerts in rock history. And hey, it was especially special to me because it was in my ole hometown of Flushing, Queens, New York.

MAKING THE TELEVISION SPECIAL

Not Ready for Prime Time

Encompassing eleven shows in ten cities, the 1965 North American tour ended with a performance at San Francisco's Cow Palace on August 31st. The Beatles returned to England and before the year was over had recorded and released the album *Rubber Soul* and the double-A sided single *Day Tripper* and *We Can Work It Out*. On October 16th they were presented with MBE Awards at Buckingham Palace and by mid-December had finished their final concert tour of Britain.

Brian Epstein was mapping out 1966 to be another banner year for the group. The next series of recording sessions would result in the album *Revolver* and the single *Paperback Writer* and *Rain*. In June and July they would perform in Germany, Japan and the Philippines, and in August make another triumphant return to North America and a second concert produced by Sid Bernstein at Shea Stadium.

The process might have been a continuous annual cycle, but it didn't turn out that way. Protests in Tokyo surrounding their concerts at Nippon Budokan, which was meant to be an arena strictly for martial arts, and in Manila over their assumed snub of First Lady Imelda Marcos, the infamous *Butcher Cover* for the U.S. album *Yesterday... and Today*, and the uproar over Lennon's remarks about Christianity and comparing the Beatles to Jesus resulting in more protests and death threats, the group's touring juggernaut came to a screeching halt. Their last official concert would also take place in a stadium, but this time at San Francisco's Candlestick Park on August 29th. From that point on Beatlemania would be relegated to studio recordings, rare television appearances and music videos.

With these events still in the unforeseen future, Epstein had another pressing matter to deal with. The special documenting the Shea Stadium concert still needed to be edited for television. Broadcasting their historic performance in primetime during the 1965 holiday season was certainly in his plans to keep The Beatles in the public eye and continue building fan interest in the upcoming records and summer tours.

As it turned out, this project also presented unexpected complications. When the program finally aired in England and later in North America, it wasn't necessarily what the fans, or even The Beatles, had heard at Shea Stadium.

Produced by Bob Precht, who also produced *The Ed Sullivan Show*, the television special would be presented by Sullivan Productions in association with Epstein's NEMS Enterprises and the Beatles' company Subafilms. Thirteen cameras from Clayco Films, including one in the Beatles' helicopter and dressing room, had captured the entire concert and fan reaction throughout the stadium.

But the original concept for the television special was to follow the Beatles throughout their stay in New York. Pre-production notes show filming started on Friday, August 13th when they landed at Kennedy Airport and continued through their arrival at The Warwick Hotel, afternoon press conference, and later that evening in the hotel.

On Saturday, August 14th the Beatles were filmed leaving the hotel. Another camera crew shot their arrival at CBS Studio 50 for *The Ed Sullivan Show*, rehearsal and show taping, and exit through the studio front lobby into a waiting car. They were again filmed returning to The Warwick Hotel and during the early evening until leaving for Rockefeller Center and dinner at The Rainbow Room.

On the day of the concert a 16mm camera stayed with the Beatles while twelve 35mm cameras documented the pre-concert activities and performances at Shea Stadium. On Monday, August 16th there was more filming at the hotel and on Tuesday they were filmed in their car traveling from the hotel to the airport and their departure for Toronto.

Ron Furmanek

Ed Sullivan was a real professional and hired M. Clay Adams and Clayco Films. Almost everything Clay Adams did was shot with 35mm film. A great example of this is the famous *Victory at Sea* television series from the 1950's. Clay worked on a lot of projects and has a great history in the business.

Shea Stadium is probably the most professionally filmed concert from that era because it's filmed in 35mm. Everything else that came after was shot in 16mm, like *Woodstock* and *Gimme Shelter*.

Using 35mm film explains the outstanding quality and the television special really was a first of its kind. Clayco still used some 16mm footage from hand carried cameras in *The Beatles At Shea Stadium*, for instance during the helicopter ride and in the limo. They also had footage from

The Ed Sullivan Show rehearsal and taping, which would be fantastic if it still existed.

•

Copies of the original pre-production notes are shown here, but it is obvious age has taken a toll on the quality of these pages. In addition to listing the above schedule with number and types of cameras, selected handwritten notes from (assuming) either Precht or M. Clay Adams from Clayco Films give insights into why footage not directly related to the Shea Stadium concert was cut from all edits of the television special. Also shown is the contract between Clayco Films and Sullivan Prods that was not signed until after the concert was filmed, and a letter from Precht to Clayco with his editing suggestions.

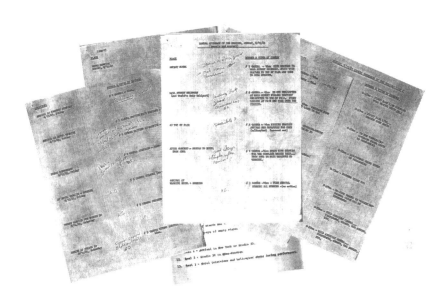

Original Pre-Production Notes
August 13 - 17, 1965

Location	Handwritten Notes
Kennedy Airport 8/13/65	Ordinary - dull
Arrival At Hotel Warwick	Good material - crowds, police, etc.
Press Conference 8/13/65	Fair - good reverse shot, check CBS
At Hotel Warwick - Evening 8/14/65	N.G. (no good)
Depart Warwick for Studio 50	N.G.
Arrive At Studio 50	Good crowd shots outside 50
At Studio 50 8/14/65	Some useable shots on stage
Depart Studio 50	N.G.
Arrive Warwick	N.G.
At Warwick Sat Evening	N.G.
Depart Hotel 8/15/65	Interior helicopter good & shot down at stadium
World's Fair Heliport	Landing shot good armored car N.G.
Hotel Warwick 8/16/65	N.G.
Hotel to Airport 8/17/65	Possible, first pass down 5th Ave.

Contract - Clayco Films, Inc.
& Sullivan Productions, Inc.

Clayco Films, Inc.

105 East 106th Street, New York 29, New York

LEhigh 4-1200

August 23, 1965

Sullivan Productions, Inc.
524 West 57th Street
New York, New York 10019

Att: Mr. Robert Precht

Gentlemen:

This is to acknowledge receipt, as of this date, of $40,000 from Sullivan Productions, Inc. by checks dated August 10, 1965, and August 16, 1965, in the amount of $25,000 and $15,000 respectively as an advance to be accounted for by Clayco Films, Inc. against expenses incurred in providing film production services in connection with the contemplated television show tentatively entitled, THE BEATLES FILM SPECIAL. To enable Clayco to promptly meet all expenditures committed in your behalf, Sullivan Productions, Inc. agrees to make further advances to Clayco from time to time as required in the normal course of producing the above mentioned film.

It is understood that Clayco will at all times obtain the approval of Mr. Precht prior to making financial committments for the major elements of this production and will endeavor to keep Mr. Precht further informed as to the extent of other expenditures deemed necessary for the orderly completion of the production. It is further understood that Clayco will submit to Sullivan Productions, Inc., from time to time during the course of production, accurate and detailed statements of expenditures incurred to date. As required, Clayco will also make available for your scrutiny, all paid invoices, petty cash vouchers, payroll records, etc., as evidence of expenditures made in your behalf.

For providing production services as outlined above and as required for this production, Sullivan Productions, Inc. agrees to reimburse Clayco for all out-of-pocket expenses, charges and other direct expenses in connection with THE BEATLES FILM SPECIAL, plus an overhead charge of 5% on materials, services and facilities not furnished directly by Clayco, and 10% as a profit and production fee. Prior to completion of the production, Sullivan Productions, Inc. will notify Clayco in writing as to the delivery of all final production elements. If such delivery causes the production to be subject to sales and/or any other taxes, such taxes will be billable by Clayco as an additional cost of production.

It is understood that we are acting as an independent contractor. We shall have the entire responsibility as employer with respect to all persons

Sullivan Productions, Inc.   -2-   August 23, 1965

employed by us in connection with our services. We will comply with all
applicable provisions of any codes, rules, or regulations of any Union
having jurisdiction over any such persons.

As between us, you should have all rights, title and interest in and to
the results and product of our services, and you shall have the right to
use, publish and exhibit the results and product of our services with the
understanding that any claim arising out of such use, publication or
exhibition shall be solely your responsibility, and you agree to indemnify
us and hold us harmless against any claims, damages, liabilities, costs
and expenses, including reasonable counsel fees, arising out of the use,
exhibition or publication of the product of our services.

We shall at all times indemnify you and hold you harmless from and against
any and all claims, damages, liabilities, costs and expenses, including
reasonable counsel fees, attributable to our services hereunder or arising
out of any breach of any of our obligations or representations hereunder,
but this indemnification shall not extend to any claims arising out of the
use, exhibition or publication of the product of our services.

I trust the above is in accordance with our mutual understanding. If so,
please sign the attached copy of this letter in the place designated,
indicating acceptance of this agreement.

                                        Very truly yours,

                                        CLAXCO FILMS, INC.

                                        M. Clay Adams, Pres.

SULLIVAN PRODUCTIONS, INC.

By

Letter from Bob Precht
To Sid Katz & Clayco Films

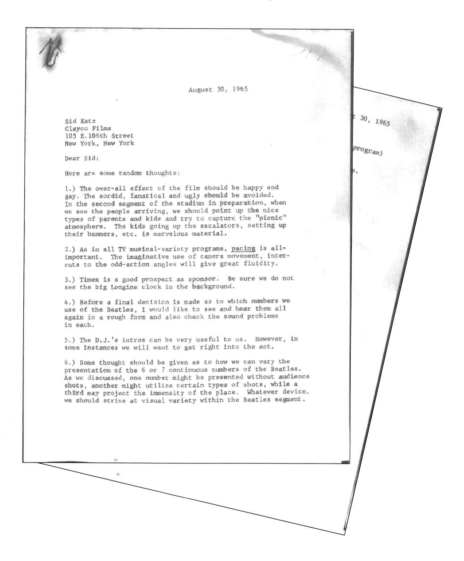

August 30, 1965

Sid Katz
Clayco Films
105 E.186th Street
New York, New York

Dear Sid:

Here are some random thoughts:

1.) The over-all effect of the film should be happy and gay. The sordid, fanatical and ugly should be avoided. In the second segment of the stadium in preparation, when we see the people arriving, we should point up the nice types of parents and kids and try to capture the "picnic" atmosphere. The kids going up the escalators, setting up their banners, etc. is marvelous material.

2.) As in all TV musical-variety programs, pacing is all-important. The imaginative use of camera movement, inter-cuts to the odd-action angles will give great fluidity.

3.) Timex is a good prospect as sponsor. Be sure we do not see the big Longine clock in the background.

4.) Before a final decision is made as to which numbers we use of the Beatles, I would like to see and hear them all again in a rough form and also check the sound problems in each.

5.) The D.J.'s intros can be very useful to us. However, in some instances we will want to get right into the act.

6.) Some thought should be given as to how we can vary the presentation of the 6 or 7 continuous numbers of the Beatles. As we discussed, one number might be presented without audience shots, another might utilize certain types of shots, while a third may project the immensity of the place. Whatever device, we should strive at visual variety within the Beatles segment.

August 30, 1965
Dear Sid:
Here are some random thoughts:

1.) The over-all effect of the film should be happy and gay. The sordid, fanatical and ugly should be avoided. In the second segment of the stadium in preparation, when we see the people arriving, we should point up the nice types of parents and kids and try to capture the "picnic" atmosphere. The kids going up the escalators, setting up their banners, etc. is marvelous material.

2.) As in all musical-variety programs, <u>pacing</u> is all-important. The imaginative use of camera movement, inter-cuts to the odd-action angles will give great fluidity.

3.) Timex is a good prospect as sponsor. Be sure we do not see the big Longine clock in the background.

4.) Before a final decision is made as to which numbers we use of the Beatles, I would like to see and hear them all again in a rough form and also check the sound problems in each.

5.) The D.J.'s intros can be very useful to us. However, in some instances we will want to get right into the act.

6.) Some thought should be given as to how we can vary the presentation of the 6 or 7 continuous numbers of the Beatles. As we discussed, one number might be presented without audience shots, another might utilize certain types of shots, while a third may project the immensity of the place. Whatever device, we should strive at visual variety within the Beatles segment.

7.) The number at the top (i.e. the last number of the program) should be as mad and exciting as possible.

Best,
Bob Precht

rhp

BEATLES SPECIAL
(TENTATIVE RUNNING ORDER)

a/o 8/30/65

1. OPENING - SHEA STADIUM
   Empty segue to Beatles & Paul intro last number,
   BEATLES number

2. TITLES - BILLBOARDS
   /1ST COMML/

3. STADIUM - day - in preparation for Concert

4. MURRAY THE K - intro into Discoteque Dancers

5. STADIUM - later preparation - people coming in stands,
   filling in banners, etc.

6. KING CURTIS

7. /2ND COMML/

8. CANNIBAL & HEADHUNTERS

9. HELICOPTER SEQUENCE - departure N.Y. - arrival Shea.

10. BRENDA HOLLOWAY

11. SOUNDS, INC.

12. /3RD COMML/

13. TEASE ?

14. /MIDDLE BREAK/

15. SOUNDS, INC.

16. DRESSING ROOM - BEATLES

17. ED SULLIVAN INTRO & BEATLES ENTRANCE

18. 1ST BEATLES NUMBER

19. /4TH COMML/

20. BEATLES   (note: Epstein comment to be
                          included in Beatles segment)

Initialed "rhp" - Robert Henry Precht

BEATLES SPECIAL
(TENTATIVE RUNNING ORDER - CONT'D:)   (2)

21. /5TH COMML/

22. BEATLES

23. /6TH COMML/

24. PAUL GOODNIGHT into last number

25. CLOSING CREDITS

Based on Precht's post-concert suggestions and tentative running order for sequences and commercial breaks in the August 30th letter to film editor Sid Katz, Clayco Films company head and manager of production operations for the special, M. Clay Adams, worked with thousands of feet of film from all thirteen cameras to piece together a rough fifty two minute edit of the film by September 23rd. Segments included 16mm footage taken during the helicopter ride to Shea Stadium and backstage, while the majority of the special in 35mm showed fans arriving, the opening acts, on stage MC's, fans reacting in the stands, and the Beatles performance. Film shot on the previous Friday and Saturday, and the Monday and Tuesday following the concert was not used.

The 35mm cameras on the field were synchronized for the editing process by using five clocks placed at various locations near the stage. A number of cameras focused on the Beatles had simultaneously run out of film and had to be reloaded during *She's A Woman*, so Adams used footage of the audience and brief shots from other songs to create a usable version. As mentioned earlier, because of time restraints and possibly the lack of a Beatles residual-earning writing credit, *Everybody's Trying To Be My Baby* was not considered for inclusion.

On the following pages are the original notes from Clayco Films mapping out the entire concert as timed by the synchronized clocks. These clocks were set approximately fifteen minutes ahead of the actual time and show the 7:30 pm concert was only five minutes late in starting.

Author's note: Efforts were made to lighten and sharpen the next four pages of aged notes from Clayco Films, but failed to improve the quality. We've decided to include them as they appear for Beatles historians and fans interested in viewing these documents.

1.

THE BEATLES CONCERT at Shea Stadium
August 15, 1965

(Note: The times noted are for the five SYNCHRONIZED CLOCKS used
by the film cameras; the actual time of night was appx.
15 minutes later.)

7:50:10   Announcer (?) introduces National Anthem.
7:50:35   Singing of National Anthem. (King Curtis Orch. plays)
7:52:30   Announcer (Bruce Morrow) introduces Murray The K.
7:53:10   Murray The K. gives "greetings" and introduces
              The Discotheque Dancers.
7:54:40   THE DISCOTHEQUE DANCERS (King Curtis Orch. plays)
              5 Girls and 1 Boy - various dances: Frug, Watusi, etc.
7:58:45   An Announcer (?) introduces the King Curtis Orch.
8:00:00   THE KING CURTIS ORCHESTRA
              starts with full band; then solo guitar;..... 8:01:35
       8:03:   King Curtis sings solo
       8:04:55   Band continues, then King Curtis' Tenor Sax solo.
8:06:50   Announcer (Bruce Morrow) introduces Frank Siokle (?)
              who then introduces WMCA Good Guys.
8:07:35   The Six WMCA GOOD GUYS sing a Jingle for the occasion,
              to introduce themselves individually, & WMCA Radio.
8:08:00   One of the Good Guys introduces Cannibal & The Headhunters.
       "   CANNIBAL & THE HEADHUNTERS (Four Boys...Guitars)
              "Out Of Sight" - Leader sings, all dance.   8:10:35
       8:11:00   "Nan Niany Nan" - Lead er sings, 3 Others BG;
                  then Leader uses Hand Mike. & Others dance;
                  then all 4 sing.
       8:13:30   "Mickey's Monkey" - same routine...
       8:15:20   they take their jackets off & dance
       8:18:40   "The Way You Do It" - all 4 sing.
       8:20:15   they dance.
       8:21:40   "Land Of 1,000 Dancers".
       8:25:10   Their Goodbye song.
8:25:35   Announcer (Bruce Morrow) sends off Cannibal...
              talks about WABC & introduces Hal Jackson.
8:26:30   Hal Jackson introduces Marvin Gay.
8:26:45   Marvin Gay introduces Brenda Holloway.
       "   BRENDA HOLLOWAY - solo Girl singer (King Curtis Orch. BG)
              "Shake"
       8:27:55   "I Can't Get No Satisfaction"
       8:29:40   "I Can't Help Myself" (King Curtis Sax solo)
       8:32:10   "Put Your Head On My Shoulder"
       8:35:46   "When I'm Gone"
       8:37:50   Send-off and bows.

......THE BEATLES Concert   8-15-65

8:30:30	Announcer, BRUCE MORROW of WABC - a few remarks, then asks, "Are you ready?" (for Beatles) Kids scream! Bruce Morrow introduces Charlie Greer of WABC.
8:34:30	Big scream as Sounds, Inc. walk across field.
8:35:15	Bruce Morrow, still chatting, reads off a few of the fans' signs hanging around stadium, as Kids CHANT "We love you", "We want The Beatles".
8:36:00	Bruce Morrow introduces Sounds, Inc. as THEY set up instruments, etc. (come ??)
8:37:00	SOUNDS, INC. (instrumental group) start with 8 bars of "America" from West Side St.. & into a rumba with things like "everybody clap" shout "Yeah!"Yeah!", etc. + some dancing.
8:45:??	"William Tell Overture" starts with 3 Saxes grouped in front of Electric ...
8:47:15	" " with a long DRUM SOLO (8:48:20 to 8:50:45)
8:51:15	"Maria" from West Side Story (w/ flute solo)
8:54:40	"In The Hall Of The Mountain King"
8:55:00	Big scream from Kids as 4 Guitars are brought across field toward stage.
8:56:??	Sounds, Inc. finish and Stage is cleared and re-... while KIDS chant.
9:00:00	Murray The K. orders field and KIDS cheer.
9:00:30	Bruce Morrow introduces Sid Bernstein.
9:00:55	Sid Bernstein introduces Ed Sullivan.
9:01:20	ED SULLIVAN - brief remark.. - long cheer as he talks..
9:01:45	THE BEATLES !! cross the Field from Visitors' Dugout, along Third Base line to Stage at Second Base. Bedlam in the stands with thousands of ... Flash Bulbs popping & a continuous roar of sound, as The Beatles tune-up.
9:03:10	The Beatles on mike., Kibitizing and "barking" to test mikes., etc.
9:03:30	"TWIST AND SHOUT" Kids screaming continue throughout song. Kids screaming continues throughout rest of entire program, pitched at a constant roar and rising to crescendos at salient points like the end of a chorus and the beginning of an instrumental break or a bit of choreography or a familiar turn of phrase or...anything!! The Crescendos of sound also introduce bursts of action in the stands or on the field.

```
                    ......THE BEATLES Concert      8-15-65                    3.

     9:04:50          .     "SHE'S A WOMAN"
              9:0 6:30         GIANT ROAR from KIDS as COPS chase 2 GIRLS racing
                              around center field behind stage.
     9:07:30             PAUL says Thank you after number & introduces:
     9:08:00             "I FEEL FINE"
     9:10:05             JOHN says Thank you after number, and says to Kids,
                              "Can you hear me?", and a Giant Roar drowns
     9:10:45             "DIZZY MISS LIZZY"
                                         John does a solo.
     9        9:13:20        COPS catch GIRL.
     9:13:30             number ends and PAUL introduces:
     9:1 :05             "TICKET TO RIDE"
                                        with - JOHN & PAUL just @ camera left
     9:16:15             GEORGE introduces:
     9:16:45             "TRYIN' TO BE MY BABY"
                                         with a GEORGE solo.
              9:17:20        COPS run to Center Field (???)
              9:18:40        GIRL fights with COPS along Right Field line. (
     9:19:00             PAUL says Thank you after number & asks that "everybody
                                         join in" for:
     9:19:45             "CAN'T BUY ME LOVE"
                                     with a PAUL solo.
     9:21:55             JOHN says Thank you and introduces:
     9:22:30             "BABY'S IN BLACK"
                                        with a JOHN & PAUL duet @ camera right of stage.
              9:23:15        GIRL FAINTED, carried along 1st Base line to Mets Dugout.
     9:24:40             RINGO says Thank you and his own special "Hello" to fans,
                              then PAUL introduces:
     9:25:               "ACT NATURALLY"
              9:25:40        GIRL FAINTED, carried along 1st Base line to Mets Dugout.
       :27:40             JOHN says Thank you to Ringo, then does some Gibberish like
                              a Double-talk routine with a gesture to The Heavens, &
                              much delighted response from The Kids, then introduces:
     9:28:20             "A HARD DAY'S NIGHT"
              9:28:30                       greeted with the biggest, long full cheer.
                              big cheer as they continue into last chorus
```

```
......THE BEATLES Concert      8-15-65

9:30:50      PAUL says Thank you after number  as all attention goes
             to center field behind stage where GIRL in white is
             chased & caught by COPS.  PAUL boos COPS & comments;
             KIDS echo Paul's Boos & comments; then Paul introduces:

9:31:30      "HELP!"  from The Beatles' new movie; gets biggest, sustained
                      cheer of the night.

     9:33:25      Giant cheer for last chorus

9:33:50      PAUL says Thank you, then asks that everybody clap hands
             on next number, which is to be the last of the evening;
             he says Thank you, and good night, then introduces:

9:34:45      "I'M DOWN"
                      GEORGE plays Electric Organ...
                      PAUL shouts out the title words...

     9:36:00      GIRL struggles with COPS near 3rd Base Dugout.

9:36:50      THE BEATLES finish last number...

9:37:00      THE BEATLES wave goodbyes to Kids, scurry into Station
             Wagon waiting @ edge of stage, & scoot across  Left
             Field & out gate to waiting Armored Car.

9:37:20      Several GIRLS break through Police Barriers & start out
             on to Field, but all are stopped by COPS who must
             tackle them & carry them bodily off Field.  Numerous
             such little skirmishes occur throughout the Stands
             at the edge of the Field and seem for a moment
             precipitous, but the POLICE contain them and a
             possible riot is averted...

     9:37:45      COPS carry a COUPLE OF GIRLS out along Left Field line.

     9:38:30      ONE or TWO GIRLS fight COPS @ Left Field Boxes.

             ...and so it goes - as the crowd lingers, fretfully;...
             the tears go on; eyes and noses are red and the
             girls are blue... The Beatles are gone.
```

Note: At 9:34:45 - *I'm Down* reads, "George plays Electric Organ."

The September 23rd edit with scene and time listings from Clayco Films shows *She's A Woman* had already been cut. Following more correspondence between Precht and Adams an additional one minute and six seconds was deleted, bringing the final running time down to fifty minutes and forty eight seconds.

Ron Furmanek

The concert audio was recorded using two quarter inch stereo tapes running in sync. Technically that would be a four track recording, which was rather odd because using half inch three or four track machines was pretty much the industry standard at that time. There were also one inch eight track machines around in 1965.

Bob Fine from the legendary Fine Recording Studios produced the audio for the concert, so I was a bit surprised when restoring the film that it wasn't recorded on three or four track tape. It might have been because of the size. My guess is that they didn't want to have a lot of big recording equipment there.

Michael Adams

The equipment was definitely state of the art, but nothing on that scale had been tried before so no one really knew how it would turn out. All the screaming and all the noise in the background... And there were a few songs where the Beatles kind of lost the plot and some of the sound. And toward the end it got a little sloppy. Especially *I'm Down*. They were kind of nuts by that point. You could tell. Especially John and you could see he was just... well, *go for it*. But it really didn't sound that bad.

•

On November 9th the film was ready to be copied and sent to London for approval by Epstein and the Beatles. But once again, there would be unexpected complications...

Bob Precht

THE BEATLES AT SHEA STADIUM
(Running Order as of 9/23/65)

	Estimated Footage	Time
Opening tease to end of titles	333	3:45

1st Commercial

Stadium (first sequence)	113	1:15
Murray the "K"	91	1:00
Discotheque Dancers	230	2:34
Stadium (second sequence)	198	2:12
King Curtis	90	1:00

2nd Commercial

Cars on East River Drive to Helicopter Take-off	398	4:25
Brenda Holloway	180	2:00
Helicopter over N.Y. to Shea	(included above)	
Sounds, Inc.	300	3:20

3rd Commercial

Ringo teaser	42	:28

Middle Break

Sounds, Inc.	222	2:28
Dressing Room	121	1:20
Ed Sullivan entrance to Stadium	170	1:53
Beatles "Twist and Shout"	130	1:27

4th Commercial

Beatles - "I Feel Fine"	225	2:30
"Dizzy Miss Lizzy"	290	3:10
"Ticket to Ride"	228	2:32

5th Commercial

Beatles - "Can't Buy Me Love"	235	2:37
"Baby's Inc."	238	2:35
"Hard Days Night" (v.o.)	269	3:00
"Help"	264	2:56

6th Commercial

Beatles - "I'm Down" Repeat	180	2:00
	4,666'	51:54

11/9/65

THE BEATLES AT SHEA STADIUM

(Running Order as of Nov. 9, 1965)

		Time
Opening Tease to end of Titles	4:55	4:55

1st Commercial Break

Stadium (first sequence)	1:10	
Murray The "K"	1:15	
Discotheque Dancers	1:50	
Stadium (second sequence)	2:20	
King Curtis	1:10	7:45

2nd Commercial Break

Cars on East River Drive to Helicopter Take-Off	1:15	
Brenda Holloway	2:35	
Helicopter Over N.Y. to Shea Air View	1:48	
Sounds, Inc. (Drum bit)	1:05	
Announcement & William Tell Overture	2:21	9:04

3rd Commercial Break

| Ringo Tease | :33 | :33 |
| | | 22:17 |

Middle Break

Sounds, Inc. (Everybody Shout Yeah!)	2:30	
Dressing Room	1:20	
Ed Sullivan Intro. and Beatles On Stand	1:55	
Beatles - "Twist And Shout"	1:23	7:08

4th Commercial Break

Beatles - "I Feel Fine"	2:28	
- "Dizzy Miss Lizzy"	3:18	
- "Ticket To Ride"	2:37	8:23

5th Commercial Break

Beatles - "Can't Buy My Love"	2:39	
- "Baby's In Black"	2:40	
- "Hard Day's Night"	3:00	
- "Help"	2:45	11:04

6th Commercial Break

| Beatles - "I'm Down" (Repeat) to end of Titles | 1:56 | 1:56 |

| | Second Half | 28:31 |
| | Full Show | 50:48 |

Card # 1A   THE BEATLES AT SHEA STADIUM

Card # 1   Produced by
BOB PRECHT

Card # 2   Continuity by
BUZZ KOHAN
BILL ANGELOS

Card # 3   Associate Producer
TONY JORDAN

Card # 4   Film Editors
SIDNEY KATZ
ARLINE GARSON

Card # 5   Production Associate
BRIAN EPSTEIN

Card # 6   Manager of Production Operations
M. CLAY ADAMS

Card # 7   Director of Photography
ANDREW LASZLO

Card # 8   Cameramen

BERNARD M. DRESNER   FRED PORRETTE
FRANCOIS FARCAS   MICHAEL RAYHACK
PETER GABARINI   WARREN ROTHENBERGER
HARVEY GENKINS   GORDON WILLIS
JACK HORTON   JOHN WING
EDWARD HUGHES   RAYMOND ZIESSE

Card # 9.   Sound Engineer   FRED BOSCH
Assistant to the Producer   VINCENT CALANDRA
Sound Mixer   BOB FINE
Beatle Comments Recorded by   LARRY KANE

9A→

Card # 10   →   A Presentation of
SULLIVAN PRODUCTIONS, INC.
In Association with
NEMS ENTERPRISES LTD.
and
SUBAFILMS, LTD.

Card # 11   The Beatles at Shea Stadium
c MCMLXV - Nems Enterprises Ltd.
All Rights Reserved

Apparently satisfied with the November 9th edit, Adams sent a letter to Tony Jordan, an associate producer for the special at Sullivan Productions, on December 8th listing the number of copies made of this edit and who had possession of the prints. Mentioning a problem with sales tax could point to a delay in sending a copy of the film to Epstein and the Beatles in London since they are not listed in this letter as having a print.

Another clue this was considered the final edit were Adams' instructions on what to do with the film negatives and master prints. In case revisions and additional prints were needed, Clayco Films would hold the negatives and master print. After broadcast these would be delivered to Epstein in England.

Ron Furmanek

Brian Epstein was very smart in that regard because he made sure he kept important items pertaining to the Beatles. As you can see in the letter he made sure he received the film negatives, the IP's; (the inter-positives), and the track negatives. The film negatives are the original camera-cut negatives using film that was actually in the cameras at Shea Stadium. An inter-positive is made from the camera negatives that could be used to make additional negatives. And finally, a track negative is the audio from the original television negative.

No one from NEMS or Sullivan Productions ever asked for anything else, such as the film outtakes or unenhanced audio recordings of the concert. Clay held onto the original audio tapes from the on sight recording machines. Wilma Cozart Fine, Bob Fine's wife, told me that he's probably the one that ran out of the stadium with those tapes that night. I'm pretty sure Clay might have told me that also.

•

Unfortunately, there were additional instructions in Adams' letter concerning what to do with any prints or negatives not in Epstein's possession six months after television broadcast. All remaining film shot at Shea Stadium and additional footage of the Beatles in New York from their arrival on August 13th until their departure on August 17th would be destroyed.

Letter from M. Clay Adams
To Tony Jordan at Sullivan Prods.

Clayco Films, Inc.   *Fred Bosch*

105 East 106th Street, New York 29, New York

LEhigh 4-1200

December 8, 1965

Mr. Tony Jordan
Sullivan Productions, Inc.
524 West 57th Street
New York, N. Y. 10019

Dear Tony,

As you suggested, I tried to speak to Bernie Stebel yesterday with regard to deliveries of THE BEATLES AT SHEA STADIUM film elements to avoid having them subject to sales taxes. He was unavailable, however, so the problem is not yet resolved as of this moment.

For your information, here is the status of prints as of this date:

```
    35mm Original version answer print -- At Clayco (NG for screening)
    35mm Revised Version - Corrected Print #1 -- Norman Weiss 12/7/65
      "    "        "      -     "      "   #2 -- Norman Weiss 11/29/65
      "    "        "      -     "      "   #3 -- Bob Precht 12/9/65
    16mm  "         "      - Answer Print -- Tony Jordan 12/7/65
      "    "        "      - Corrected Print #1 -- Norman Weiss 12/7/65
      "    "        "      -     "      "   #2 -- Norman Weiss 12/8/65
      "    "        "      -     "      "   #3 -- Bob Precht 12/9/65
```

As I mentioned yesterday, I would appreciate it if you will give me instructions for final disposition of all residual elements of the show. My suggestion for each element is as follows:

(a) 35mm and 16mm Picture and Track negatives to be left at Lab for possible additional prints for use on air. After broadcast date deliver to Brian Epstein in England.

(b) 35mm Interpositive Master (Picture Only) -- Same as (a) above.

(c) 35mm Magnetic Tracks of final Mix -- Now at Fine recording. After broadcast, deliver to Brian Epstein in England.

(d) 35mm Picture Work Prints and Magnetic Work Tracks -- Store here for six months, then destroy.

(e) 35mm Negative, Prints and Original Sound Tracks of all "trims" and "out-takes" -- Hold for broadcast revisions, if any, then destroy immediately after air date.

Please try to let me have a final determination on these points as soon as you can so I can get myself organized accordingly.

My best regards,

M. Clay Adams

Note: (d) and (e) instruct to destroy the film

Author's Note: Norman Weiss was an executive at General Artists Corp (GAC), the talent agency responsible for booking the Beatles' North American tours.

•

December 8, 1965
Dear Tony,

As you suggested, I tried to speak to Bernie Stebel yesterday with regard to deliveries of THE BEATLES AT SHEA STADIUM film elements to avoid having them subject to sales taxes. He was unavailable, however, so the problem is not yet resolved as of this moment.

For your information, here is the status of prints as of this date:

```
35mm Original version answer print - At Clayco (NG for screening)
35mm Revised Version Corrected Print #1 - Norman Weiss 12/7/65
  "       "       "        #2 - Norman Weiss 11/29/65
  "       "       "        #3 - Bob Precht 12/9/65
16mm   "      " - Answer Print - Tony Jordan 12/7/65
  "       "       " - Corrected Print - #1 - Norman Weiss 12/7/65
  "       "       "        #2 - Norman Weiss 12/8/65
  "       "       "        #3 - Bob Precht 12/9/65
```

As I mentioned yesterday, I would appreciate it if you will give me instructions for final disposition of all residual elements of the show. My suggestion for each element is as follows:

(a) 35mm and 16mm Picture and Track negatives to be left at Lab for possible additional prints for use on air. After broadcast date deliver to Brian Epstein in England.

(b) 35mm Interpositive Master (Picture Only) - Same as (a) above.

(c) 35mm Magnetic Tracks of final MIX - Now at Fine Recording. After broadcast, deliver to Brian Epstein in England.

(d) 35mm Picture Work Prints and Magnetic Word Tracks - Store here for six months, then destroy.

(e) 35mm Negative, Prints and Original Sound Tracks of all

"trims" and "out-takes" - Hold for broadcast revisions, if any, then destroy immediately after air date.

Please try to let me have a final determination on these points as soon as you can so I can get myself organized accordingly.

My best regards,

Clay Adams

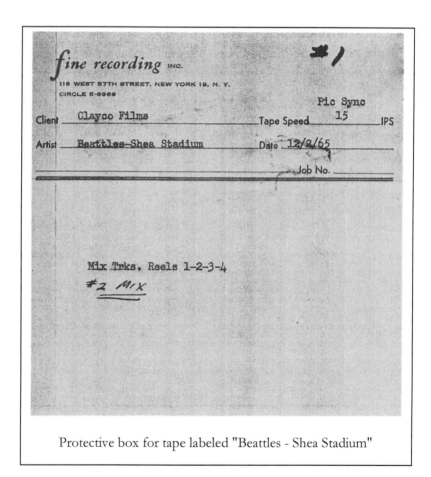

Protective box for tape labeled "Beattles - Shea Stadium"

Ron Furmanek

People are going to be really sad when they learn that the outtakes and footage not used in the television special were ordered to be destroyed. Clay recommended that all the unused film be destroyed six months after the broadcast. It's the news that no one will ever want to believe almost fifty years later.

Everyone has always wanted to know why there are no outtakes. It was just basically a sentence or two in the letter from Clay to Sullivan Productions about what to do with all the leftover footage. They were instructions to destroy everything that had been left on the cutting room floor. When considering all the cameras used at the concert and different locations they filmed the Beatles when they were in New York, I can only imagine how many feet of film was destroyed.

Clayco held it in case they needed to make any revisions to the final edit of the television special. That meant they could pull a song out or put another in if they wanted to. But after it was broadcast, they destroyed it. That includes all the outtakes and *Everybody's Trying To Be My Baby*, the song that was shot and not used in the finished film.

The only footage we still have is what you see in the television special. That's it and nothing else has ever turned up. Not even a work print or a scratch print that Clay might have used while editing.

•

Within a week the four prints of this edit assigned to Norman Weiss at GAC, two 35mm and two 16mm, were delivered to Epstein in London. Based on his initial response, he had watched the film and made an opinion about the quality before consulting the Beatles.

In a telegram dated December 13th to Precht, Epstein expressed his "delight" and "absolute approval" for this version of the television special. But within days that attitude would change dramatically.

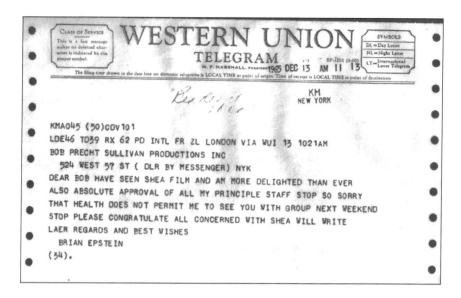

Acknowledging Epstein's confirmation he had received and approved the November edit of the special, Precht sent a letter on December 15th reiterating contract terms and money due. As far as Sullivan Productions and Clayco Films were concerned, their work was complete and the special ready for broadcast.

December 15 letter from Bob Precht to Brian Epstein

December 15, 1965
Dear Brian,

As you requested, and in order to expedite the project, I have delivered to you via Norman Weiss of G.A.C. two (2) 35 mm. and two (2) 16mm. color-corrected prints of the completed film. I consider this delivery to comply with Paragraph (3) of our agreement. For our convenience, with respect to any necessary revisions required by the U.S. network and any further editing necessary for foreign distribution in the U.K. or elsewhere, I will hold all 35 and 16 picture and track negatives plus all magnetic tracks, work prints, "trims" and "out-takes". All this material, of course, will be delivered to you at appropriate future times.

There is due to us our production fee of $7500, plus the sum of $27,832.99, being the difference between our actual out-of-pocket costs to date and the $75,000 which you have advanced. I have enclosed an itemization of our costs and will of course furnish such other available substantiation as you may request. We have provided in our accounting for amounts which we may have to expend in connection with Screen Actors Guild minimum regulations for U.S. television exposure. Of course, if we are not required to expend said sums we will refund them to you. In the event that our allowance does not cover all contingent expenses in connection with foreign distribution, theatrical release, or any other additional costs, we will expect to be reimbursed by you or request that you pay such amounts directly.

If and to the extent there are sales and similar taxes payable in connection with our production and delivery of the Film, these will also be payable by you.

Finally, I have enclosed the compensation portion of our arrangement with Buzz Kohan and Bill Angelos who handled the continuity. We have already made the initial payment of $6000 and this is of course included above as an out-of-pocket expense. However, you will see that there are possible residual obligations for reruns, foreign, theatrical use, etc. Since we are to be reimbursed for all costs, your attorneys and ours have suggested that the best way of handling the contingent obligations to Kohan and Angelos is for you to expressly assume the same.

I would therefore appreciate your signing and returning a copy of this letter, thereby acknowledging our delivery as aforesaid, your agreement to the handling of contingent expenses as aforesaid (including your assumption of the future obligations to Kohan and Angelos), as well as your agreement to pay and to hold us harmless from possible sales and other taxes referred to above.

Sincerely,
Robert H. Precht

•

However, after viewing the film, the Beatles and their record producer George Martin were unhappy with the soundtrack. The audio had been wired into Bob Fine's sound equipment directly from the stage with the Beatles' vocals recorded by smaller microphones placed underneath the microphones used to carry their voices through the stadium's public address system. Commentary from the Beatles and Brian Epstein was taken from interviews by journalist Larry Kane.

As explained to Adams (and in a letter to Precht dated February 16th) the Beatles and Martin claimed the music was "generally lacking in bottom" (bass guitar) and drums. It was understood the live performance would not sound as polished as their studio recordings, but bass and drums were vital to the Beatles' sound. A decision was made and related to Epstein that the group, along with Martin, would go into the studio and enhance the live soundtrack.

In response to a message from Epstein concerning this news, Precht sent a letter on December 17th asking him to speak with John, Paul, George and Ringo about reconsidering and allowing him to sell the program for broadcast "as it happened." But the Beatles and Martin were already making arrangements to fix their performance. As they also reported to Adams, if it didn't work, "they were quite satisfied to let it go as it was."

Letter from Bob Precht
To Brian Epstein

SULLIVAN PRODUCTIONS, INC.

124 WEST 57TH STREET, NEW YORK, N. Y. 10019 · 765-4321

December 17, 1965

Brian Epstein
15 Whaddon House
William Muse S.W. 1
England

Dear Brian:

I am deeply troubled about the plan to post-record the Shea film.

There is no doubt that the sound can be improved by going into a studio under controlled conditions and an acceptable lip syc might be possible after careful rehearsal. However, I feel strongly that the result will mean an enormous compromise in the over-all concept of the film. We will get excellent sound, but it will not be related to the picture.

Whatever the film's merit may be, it rests largely on the fact that the audience views the Beatles in a new and very real situation. Everything -- the crude stage, the improbable setting and, indeed, the imperfect sound -- gives an audience the joy of experiencing this phenomenon as it happened. There are no tricks or masquerades -- the Beatles work hard -- we see it by their perspiration. The fans are wild and uninhibited -- the camera catches it. The boys go out, plug in and play -- there are no sound baffels, no engineers, we hear imperfections. This singular fantastic performance at Shea Stadium must not be confused with any future performances or any attempt at recreation.

The Beatles' fans know the Beatles' sound from their records; they know how they sound on television, (we did better this last time). I don't think they will object if our sound at Shea does not equal what they are accustomed to hearing on their stereo hi fi recordings. On the contrary, they will have a right to object if we resort to a synthetic sound track. Incidentally, if this is done here on U.S. television, a disclaimer will have to be made to the effect that the Beatles music was pre-recorded.

December 17, 1965
Dear Brian:

I am deeply troubled about the plan to post-record the Shea Film.
There is no doubt that the sound can be improved by going into a studio under controlled conditions and an acceptable lip sync might be possible after careful rehearsal. However, I feel strongly that the result will mean an enormous compromise in the over-all concept of the film. We will get excellent sound, but it will not be related to the picture.

Whatever the film's merit may be, it rests largely on the fact that the audience views the Beatles in a new and very real situation. Everything -- the crude stage, the improbable setting and, indeed, the imperfect sound -- gives an audience the joy of experiencing this phenomenon <u>as it happened</u>. There are no tricks or masquerades -- the Beatles work hard -- we see it by their perspiration. The fans are wild and uninhibited -- the camera catches it. The boys go out, plug in and play -- there are no sound baffles, no engineers, we hear imperfections. This singular fantastic performance at Shea Stadium must not be confused with any future performance or any attempt at recreation.

The Beatles' fans know the Beatles' sound from their records; they know how they sound on television, (we did better this last time). I don't think they will object if our sound at Shea does not equal what they are accustomed to hearing on their stereo hi fi recordings. On the contrary, they will have a right to object if we resort to a synthetic sound track. Incidentally, if this is done here on U.S. television, a disclaimer will have to be made to the effect that the Beatles music was pre-recorded.

We have atmosphere at Shea. When John says, "Hello! Hello! Can you hear me?" it is meaningful. To follow this moment of real recognition of adverse sound conditions with a technically balanced number would be wrong. And how can we possibly recapture the good fun and abandon of "I'm Down" in the sterile and mechanical surroundings of a recording studio?

Brian, I sincerely believe that sound is all-important in the presentation of the Beatles. If this film of ours were anything but the honest documentary that it is, I would do everything to achieve absolute perfection of sound balance. At Shea, the occasional imperfections became an integral part of the film itself.

I believe we are obliged to make a very basic choice. We either set about to make a film with script, sets, lines and direction with the polish and sophistication of the very best available in cinematography and audio recording, or we do what we did -- set down simply and directly what happened at Shea. If I can improve what was legitimately recorded, I will go back and try, but let us not compromise in an effort to achieve studio quality and sacrifice the real values.

Please speak to John, Paul, George and Ringo and let us discuss this matter further before you schedule a post-recording session.

Warmest personal regards,
Robert H. Precht
Sullivan Productions, Inc.

•

The Beatles and George Martin won the battle of nerves and words and through Epstein, notified Precht they would continue with plans to over-dub the film. On December 22nd Precht relented and sent Epstein a telegram (viewed by author but not shown due to dark quality) at NEMS Enterprises:

"Clay Adams Production Manager and Bob Fine Sound Mixer will be available London for post record session December 29 STOP Adams telephoning George Martin to coordinate details Regards Bob"

•

Michael Adams

My dad had put together a first edit of the film and sent it to Brian Epstein. This had to be sometime in late November or early December. The Beatles hadn't played bad, but they said no. It was not going out that way. It was a judgment call and of course, it was their call. They said no and that stopped it right there.

However the film footage definitely had excitement. They weren't happy because of what happened with the sound.

--------------------- Shea Rocks ---------------------

Shea Stadium was different from other gigs because of the size at the time and the sound was hopeless. The screaming was ear splitting and the mop-tops were more animated than normal to make themselves seen from such a distance. The film turned out great but the sound was atrocious and we had to carefully overdub it all in the studio later. - Tony Bramwell (31)

Ken Mansfield

They were a good band. I was on the Apple rooftop in 1969 when they played up there. When you listen to the (rooftop) raw tapes and think about it, they hadn't played live for so many years, they were having all this dissention among themselves, and it was freezing cold up there. It almost made you inoperable. If you listen to those raw tapes you realize just how good this band was even under those circumstances.

I sat in the studio during the *Let It Be* sessions. I was just sitting on the floor leaning against the wall next to Billy Preston, who was an old friend of mine. And Billy and I kept looking at each other because we both were just amazed at what a good band they were. They were just good musicians. It was just the way they gelled and the way they did things and the way played. He and I were both just amazed at what a good band they were.

Ringo also told me that when I represented him in the '90s. We sat down for dinner and to plan the *Time Takes Time* album and he said, "The reason I want to make this album is because I want to put together a really good band. That's why we were famous. We were a good band."

That was Ringo's final analysis of the Beatles. You can hear that on the raw tapes from Shea. I saw that sitting on the floor in the Apple Studios and I saw it on the rooftop. That's the overriding thing. They were a great band whether it was in a little room or in Shea Stadium.

Michael Adams

My dad flew to London at the beginning of January 1966 with Bob Fine, who was a well respected and innovative sound engineer from New York City. Bob was the sound guy at the concert. They went over to work with George Martin and the Beatles. On a big sound stage they dubbed in what they needed. It just sounds great.

A recording session was scheduled for January 5, 1966 to enhance the audio where needed and in some cases, completely re-record the songs. Word of this session was kept secret to avoid Precht's earlier warning of a required disclaimer needed for U.S. television if any Beatles music was rerecorded. The special would be sold to broadcasting networks and sponsors, and advertised to viewers as a live, "as it happened," concert by The Beatles. There were also worries EMI, the company that owned their recording contact, could delay or stop the project for legal reasons.

Instead of using EMI Studios where they normally recorded, the overdubs were performed at Cine Tele Sound (CTS) Studios in London's Bayswater District. The large studios were used primarily for recording audio and soundtrack for films. In addition to hosting sessions by Henry Mancini, John Barry and Frank Sinatra, CTS is probably best known for recording music used in the James Bond movies.

M. Clay Adams, Bob Fine and George Martin arrived early and were joined by Mal Evans and Beatles assistant and friend, Tony Bramwell. According to Bramwell's book, *Magical Mystery Tour*, when the Beatles arrived even they were unaware of what the secretive recording session was about.

———————————— Shea Rocks ————————————

"So what's this all about?" Ringo asked.
"You have to lay down a new soundtrack, sound to picture," I said. I explained the problems and they were quick to grasp what had to be done, and why it had to be secret. "If anyone asks, the story is that the soundtrack has been sweetened," I said, adding, "Think 'Honey Pie.'"
"Sounds like 'money pie' to me," said John. - Tony Bramwell (32)

224 - The Beatles At Shea Stadium

Michael Adams

I was in school when my dad was doing that and he sent me a letter about it that's pretty well detailed. He was there and his memories were pretty fresh. It might have been a few days at the most when he jotted that letter down and sent it to me.

It's a great fly on the wall for sure. My dad was a great one for detail and it's all in the letter. It should be public domain because it's a great story and it hadn't come out before. I mean that stuff has been written about by some of the Beatles experts and whatever, but they're second hand and don't beat his first hand recollections. Here's the guy who was actually there with them and not somebody just talking about what they thought happened. He's somebody who could tell you and his memories are in the letter verbatim. He wrote it before he would get busy again and would forget about it.

> **"They were a great band whether it was in a little room or in Shea Stadium."**
> **- Ken Mansfield**

I have the letter. He made a typewriter paper copy and saved it. He saved everything. You should see the stuff I've got...

Letter from M. Clay Adams
To son Michael Adams

Clayco Films, Inc.

105 East 106th Street, New York 29, New York

LEhigh 4-1200

January 10, 1966

Dear Mike,

Well, here I am back home from London and back at the old grind. I sent you a post card from there which I hope you received.

I suppose you would like to hear all about the trip -- so here goes:

The flight over the Atlantic via Pan American Airways was uneventful. Only about five a one half hours in the air and we landed right on the button at London Airport last Tuesday night with the wheels on the blocks within a minute or two of schedule at about 9:30. Taxied into town to the London Hilton Hotel in one of these quaint little British taxis that scared the life out of me going like sixty on the "wrong" (left) side of the expressway for the full half hour or so that it takes from the airport.

After a good night's sleep on the 24th floor of the Hilton with a picture window in my room that overlooks the whole East side of London, including Buckingham Palace, Westminster, The House of Parliament, Big Ben, etc., got up early Wednesday morning, had breakfast and then got in touch with George Martin who was waiting for my call. George turned out to be a fine person -- very thoughtful, cooperative, and very "giving" of himself. He has been recording The Beatles as their A & R man ever since the beginning. As a matter of fact, from what he told me, it was George who kicked out Peter Best when the boys were rehearsing for their first album. He just didn't think he was a good enough drummer. Apparently he didn't know too much about Ringo at that time, even though Ringo was a friend of the boys. But George didn't want to take a chance with an unknown quantity and had a drummer he knew well do the first album with Paul, George and John. By the way, I could see very clearly later when we were working with the boys that they really look up to George Martin. Whenever they are recording, they do exactly what he tells them and they take his criticisms to the letter. Did you also know that George produces the records for many of the other top groups like Gerry and the Pacemakers, Cilla Black, David & Jonathon, etc.? He told me that in 1964, I think it was, he produced the Number 1 releases for 37 out of the 52 weeks that year. Some record!

Getting back to us -- George picked me up at the hotel in his Triumph Wednesday morning and after a nice get-to-gather lunch, we went over to the E.M.I. recording studios so I could play my tape of the Shea Stadium sound track for him. We all discussed these and made decisions on what we were going to do with each song in our over-dubbing session scheduled for Thursday morning. Later in the afternoon, we all went up to George's office to telephone each of the boys and talk over the plans for the next day. Incidently, George had a lot of English music magazines and papers around the office which he gave me to give to you as souvenirs. He also gave me BEATLES FOR SALE and RUBBER SOUL on the English Parlophone albums for you. Apparently, they put more songs on the English albums than the American.

...this was nothing much after the recording session that was eventful. We went back to his office with George Martin and spent the rest of the day with him discussing some ideas that we might work on together. He plans to come to New York next month and we'll talk about them further then. Mr Bob Fine and I saw a movie in London that night and then right after breakfast Friday morning got the 1100 A.M. flight back to New York. Got in here in the middle of the afternoon, picked up Mary at her office and got back to Goldens Bridge in time for dinner. The only thing interesting on the flight is the "In Flight" movies they show. You have an ear phone that tunes into 10 different channels of music of different types and one is on the movie they show on TV monitors placed in different positions in the plane.

That's it for now. I trust you are hard at work preparing for your mid-term exams which I am confident you will successfully hurdle with flying colors. Write to me soon -- being sure to include some insight on your school activities as well as r & r news.

My best love to you. bov.

Author's Note: In the letter to Michael Adams, *Baby's In Black* was
spelled as "Babies."

•

January 10, 1966
Dear Mike,

Well, here I am back home from London and back at the old grind. I
sent you a postcard from there which I hope you received.

I suppose you would like to hear all about the trip – so here goes:

The flight over the Atlantic via Pan American Airways was
uneventful. Only about five and one half hours in the air and we landed
right on the button at London Airport last Tuesday night with the
wheels on the blocks within a minute or two of schedule at about 9:30.
Taxied into town to the London Hilton Hotel in one of those quaint
little British taxis that scared the life out of me going like 60 on the
"wrong" (left) side of the expressway for the full half hour or so that it
takes from the airport.

After a good night's sleep on the 24th floor of the Hilton with a
picture window in my room that overlooks the whole East side of
London, including Buckingham Palace, Westminster, The House of
Parliament, Big Ben, etc., got up early Wednesday morning, had
breakfast and then got in touch with George Martin who was waiting for
my call. George turned out to be a fine person – very thoughtful,
cooperative, and very "giving" of himself. He has been recording The
Beatles as their A&R man ever since the beginning. As a matter of fact,
from what he told me, it was George who kicked out Peter Best when
the boys were rehearsing for their first album (sic) [single]. He just didn't
think he was a good enough drummer. Apparently he didn't know too
much about Ringo at that time, even though Ringo was a friend of the
boys. But George didn't want to take a chance with an unknown
quantity and had a drummer he knew well do the first album (sic)
[single] with Paul, George and John. By the way, I could see very clearly
later when we were working with the boys that they really look up to
George Martin. Whenever they are recording, they do exactly what he
tells them and they take his criticisms to the letter. Did you also know

that George produces the records for many of the other top groups like Gerry and the Pacemakers, Cilla Black, David & Jonathan, etc.? He told me that in 1964, I think it was, he produced the Number 1 releases for 37 out of the 52 weeks that year. Some record!

Getting back to us --George [Martin] picked us up at the hotel in his Triumph Wednesday morning and after a nice get-together lunch, we went over to the EMI recording studios so I could play my tape of the Shea Stadium soundtrack for him. We all discussed these and made decisions on what we were going to do with each song in our over-dubbing session scheduled for Thursday morning. Later in the afternoon, we all went up to George's office to telephone each of the boys and talk over the plans for the next day. Incidentally, George had a lot of English music magazines and papers around the office which he gave me to give to you as souvenirs. He also gave me BEATLES FOR SALE and RUBBER SOUL on the English Parlophone albums for you. Apparently, they put more songs on the English albums than the American.

I'll send you the magazines and stuff today but I'm afraid to send the records through the mail. You don't seem to get packages when I send them.

Recently, George [Martin] quit his job with EMI where he has worked ever since starting The Beatles down the road to fame, and has formed a new company with three other fellows, all of whom produce English records with various famous groups. Their office is on the top floor of a quaint old-fashioned English building where you get up there in one of those ancient open-cage type elevators. They all seemed very nice – Ron Richards, John Burges and Peter Sullivan. I don't know whether you have heard of any of them but between the four of them, they do just about every big English group. Their new company is called "AIR (Associated Independent Recording) LONDON, LTD." on Baker Street which is the same street Sherlock Holmes lived on. I imagine we'll all be hearing a lot from these AIR London fellows.

Wednesday night Bob Fine (my recording engineer who I brought with me) and I went over to Cine Tele Studios which is the studio

George Martin had engaged to do our new recordings. We worked there with the technicians getting things ready for the next day, until about 8:00 P.M. Bob and I were supposed to go to the theatre later to see a Bernard Shaw play with George [Martin] but at the last minute we decided we would rather do some sightseeing around London. We did just that and had a very interesting evening. We wound up at the "007 Club" which is on the 2nd floor of the Hilton. On display around the Club are souvenirs from "Thunderball" like the motorcycle that shoots rockets, some trick guns, secret radio transmitters, etc. Playing for dancing is a young new English group who call themselves The Untamed. I told George Martin about them the next day and he is going to look them up.

The next morning, Thursday, after an early breakfast, Bob Fine and I went out to the recording studio with George and got things set up before the boys arrived. We wanted to do all the over-dubbing to the film which I brought with me. Paul was the first one to get there, right on the dot of 9:30. He came in with a short black fur coat and needing a shave. But he was full of fun and ready to get down to work right away. Actually what the boys and George Martin really felt was wrong with the Shea soundtrack was only that it was lacking in the "low end" and drums in some places. The bass guitar was not as loud as on their records. So while we were waiting for the other boys to arrive, we over-dubbed "I'm Down", "Dizzy Miss Lizzy", "Can't Buy Me Love", and "Babies in Black" with Paul only.

Paul was quite a lot of fun. The boys have a fellow by the name of Malcolm who takes care of their instruments and sets them up, etc. Mal had set up Paul's bass amplifier but while Paul was tuning up and playing around he couldn't get the volume high enough. He started to kid Mal in his "way out" way by saying, "Where are the sounds, Mal – can't hear the sounds." Eventually Mal brought out another amplifier and Paul was happy playing bass notes so loud they felt like they were loosening the fillings in your teeth. We then got going with the recordings and in the next hour knocked off all of the songs that we only needed Paul for. Meanwhile nobody seemed to know where the rest of the boys were. Every time I'd ask what has happened to John, George and Ringo – George Martin would say he hadn't the slightest idea except that Paul was living in the city nearby while the other boys had to come from out of town.

Finally at about 10:30 in bounced the other three, all laughing and quite unaware that they had been keeping us in suspense. You should have gotten a load of Ringo. He had on brown suede pants, brown suede jacket and the same in a Civil War type hat. He was wearing glasses like the ones you bought in New York and is now sporting a mustache and full beard including "Mutton Chops" all the way down the sides of his face. When the introductions were over, I said we'd better get going because we only had the studio until 2:30 P.M. and asked the boys to get out their guitars. All of a sudden it developed that someone had forgotten the guitars. John was quite unconcerned over the turn of events and went off on a kick saying, "Maybe it's good we didn't bring them — maybe they might have got smashed!" When I reminded them that we couldn't do our session without them, John persisted with his kidding, "Well at least they didn't get here all smashed. They wouldn't be any good to us if they arrived smashed, would they now?"

Anyway, Malcolm and their driver, Alf Bicknell had already left to retrieve the guitars and soon arrived with them. From then on things went great. All four of the boys were really great. They worked hard, did anything we asked them to and cooperated in every way. Also, they are such great "pros" and know their own arrangements so well that the recording session went much easier and faster than I ever anticipated. John was quite anxious to do "Ticket to Ride" better so we did that completely over and our track of "Help!" had a big drop-out in it which we had tried to fix up in New York — so we did that one all over. The rest were merely fixed here and there to fortify the Shea track. Paul loved my word "fortify" and whenever there was a lull he would say to me, "How are we doing Clay — did we fortify that one okay?" It was fun between recording sessions. Almost invariably Paul and John would immediately start tinkering around with some new musical ideas for new songs on their guitars. As soon as one would play a few notes, the other would pick up an accompaniment no matter how complex the arrangement. Meanwhile, George Harrison — who I called a frustrated drummer — would be trying to teach Ringo some new trick beat that he had thought up. They are all constantly fooling around with the other's instruments. Ringo fooling with a guitar or the piano. George on the drums, etc. I thought Paul was the most musical though. When we had finished the over-dubbing I sat with him at the piano while he improvised. He has a great sense of harmony and phrasing. You should have heard his improvised chords fooling around with that song that's my favorite from "Oliver" -- I can't think of the title.

Well, to bring this long letter to a close. I'm overdue downtown right now. There was nothing much after the recording session that was eventful. We went back to his office with George Martin and spent the rest of the day with him discussing some ideas that we might work on together. He plans to come to New York next month and we'll talk about them further then. Bob Fine and I saw a movie in London that night and then right after breakfast Friday morning got the 11:00 A.M. flight back to New York. The only thing interesting on the flight is the "In Flight" movies they show. You have an earphone that tunes into 10 different channels of music of different types and one is on the movie they show on TV monitors placed in different positions in the plane.

That's it for now. I trust you are hard at work preparing for your mid-term exams which I am confident you will successfully hurdle with flying colors. Write to me soon – being sure to include some insight on your school activities as well as R & R news.

My best love to you, boy.

•

In comparing the original concert audio recording by Clayco Films to the television soundtrack, it is apparent the Beatles also recorded a new version of *I Feel Fine* at CTS Studios. For *Act Naturally* they used the studio recording from the *Help!* album and synced it over edited film footage. This resulted in a brief segment where Ringo is heard singing, but not seen moving his mouth.

A Hard Day's Night was left as it was performed at Shea Stadium but lowered in volume since comments from all four Beatles and Brian Epstein would be overdubbed on top of the song. George Martin had also planned a remake of *Twist and Shout*, but with the session ending at 2:30 p.m. they ran out of time.

Fortunately during the same tour, Martin had recorded two shows at The Hollywood Bowl for a possible live album. His solution was to take the recording of *Twist and Shout* made on August 30th and sync it over the Shea Stadium footage.

Ron Furmanek

During the restoration of the film, I used the material that they rerecorded in the studio that was inserted into the final film mix. The reason was that the sound wasn't as good from the original concert. There were a lot of problems, for instance a microphone would go out in the middle of a song or something else similar would happen.

I also noticed the screaming was very loud in the movie and found it had been sweetened. What I did for the restoration of the majority of the film was use the original audio recordings from Clay Adams, so the screaming is now more subdued. But it was a nightmare and a lot of work to mix the sound and sync it to the film.

•

In a February 16th letter to Precht, Adams reported song by song details from the secret recording session. At the end was a special request from "the boys."

Letter from M. Clay Adams
To Bob Precht

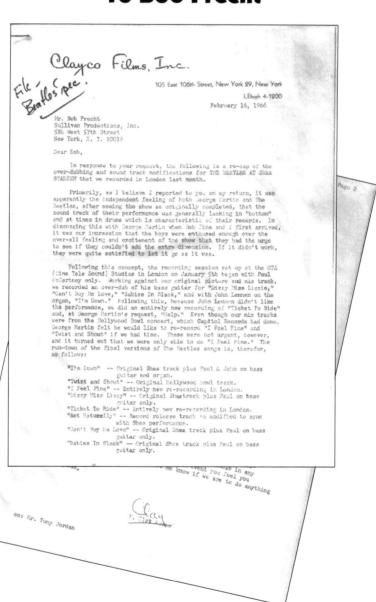

Clayco Films, Inc.

File -
Beatles Spec.

105 East 106th Street, New York 29, New York

LEhigh 4-1200

February 16, 1966

Mr. Bob Precht
Sullivan Productions, Inc.
524 West 57th Street
New York, N. Y. 10019

Dear Bob,

In response to your request, the following is a re-cap of the over-dubbing and sound track modifications for THE BEATLES AT SHEA STADIUM that we recorded in London last month.

Primarily, as I believe I reported to you on my return, it was apparently the independent feeling of both George Martin and The Beatles, after seeing the show as originally completed, that the sound track of their performance was generally lacking in "bottom" and at times in drums which is characteristic of their records. In discussing this with George Martin when Bob Fine and I first arrived, it was our impression that the boys were enthused enough over the over-all feeling and excitement of the show that they had the urge to see if they couldn't add the extra dimension. If it didn't work, they were quite satisfied to let it go as it was.

Following this concept, the recording session set up at the GTS (Cine Tele Sound) Studios in London on January 5th began with Paul McCartney only. Working against our original picture and mix track, we recorded an over-dub of his bass guitar for "Dizzy Miss Lizzie," "Can't Buy Me Love," "Babies In Black," and with John Lennon on the organ, "I'm Down." Following this, because John Lennon didn't like the performance, we did an entirely new recording of "Ticket To Ride" and, at George Martin's request, "Help." Even though our mix tracks were from the Hollywood Bowl concert, which Capitol Records had done, George Martin felt he would like to re-record "I Feel Fine" and "Twist and Shout" if we had time. These were not urgent, however, and it turned out that we were only able to do "I Feel Fine." The run-down of the final versions of The Beatles songs is, therefor, as follows:

"I'm Down" -- Original Shea track plus Paul & John on bass
        guitar and organ.
"Twist and Shout" -- Original Hollywood Bowl track.
"I Feel Fine" -- Entirely new re-recording in London.
"Dizzy Miss Lizzy" -- Original Shea track plus Paul on bass
        guitar only.
"Ticket To Ride" -- Entirely new re-recording in London.
"Act Naturally" -- Record release track as modified to sync
        with Shea performance.
"Can't Buy Me Love" -- Original Shea track plus Paul on bass
        guitar only.
"Babies In Black" -- Original Shea track plus Paul on bass
        guitar only.

Page 2

me know if we feel you
event you are in any
to do anything

Clay
M. Clay Adams

cc: Mr. Tony Jordan

Author's Note: In the letter to Bob Precht, John Lennon's name was spelled "Lennen" and *Baby's In Black* as "Babies." Geoffrey Ellis was Chief Executive of NEMS Enterprises.

•

February 16, 1966
Dear Bob,

In response to your request, the following is a re-cap of the over-dubbing and sound track modifications for THE BEATLES AT SHEA STADIUM that we recorded in London last month.

Primarily, as I believe I reported to you on my return, it was apparently the independent feeling of both George Martin and The Beatles, after seeing the show as originally completed, that the sound track of their performance was generally lacking in "bottom" and at times in drums which is characteristic of their records. In discussing this with George Martin when Bob Fine and I first arrived, it was our impression that the boys were enthused enough over the over-all feeling and excitement of the show that they had the urge to see if they couldn't add the extra dimension. If it didn't work, they were quite satisfied to let it go as it was.

Following this concept, the recording session set up at the CTS (Cine Tele Sound) Studios in London on January 5th began with Paul McCartney only. Working against our original picture and mix track, we recorded an over-dub of his bass guitar for "Dizzy Miss Lizzy," "Can't Buy Me Love," "Babies In Black," and with John Lennen the organ, "I'm Down." Following this, because John Lennen didn't like the performance, we did an entirely new recording of "Ticket To Ride" and, at George Martin's request, "Help." Even though our mix tracks were from the Hollywood Bowl concert, which Capitol Records had done, George Martin felt he would like to re-record "I Feel Fine" and "Twist and Shout" if we had time. These were not urgent, however, and it turned out that we were only able to do "I Feel Fine." The run-down of the final versions of The Beatles songs is, therefore, as follows:

"I'm Down" -- Original Shea track plus Paul & John on bass guitar
and organ.

"Twist and Shout" -- Original Hollywood Bowl track.

"I Feel Fine" -- Entirely new re-recording in London.

"Dizzy Miss Lizzy" -- Original Shea track, plus Paul on bass guitar
              only.

"Ticket To Ride" -- Entirely new re-recording in London.

"Act Naturally" -- Record release track as modified to sync with Shea
              performance.

"Can't Buy Me Love" -- Original Shea track plus Paul on bass guitar
              only.

"Babies In Black" -- Original Shea track plus Paul on bass guitar only.

"Hard Day's Night" -- Original Shea track.

"Help" -- Entirely new re-recording in London.

I believe that about sums it up. If you need any further details please let me know.

To bring you up to date on the release print situation, here is a re-cap on that:

ORIGINAL MIX PRINTS

35mm Print	#1 - Brought back from London by Clay Adams and is now used as replacement for original work print.
" "	#2 - Returned by Norman Weiss and being held at Clayco.
" "	#3 - Originally Sullivan office print - Shipped to Brian Epstein and still held by him.
16MM Print	#1 & 2 - Shipped to Brian Epstein by Norman Weiss and still held by him.
" "	#3 - Originally Sullivan office print - Shipped to California by GAC - Tony Ford's secretary is to recall and return to Clayco.
"	Answer Print - Damaged by Sid Katz -- Now held at Clayco.

NEW MIX PRINTS

35mm Print	#4 - Delivered to Norman Weiss 2/1/66
" "	#5 & 6 - Shipped to Geoffrey Ellis, London 2/2/66
" "	#7 - Delivered to Sullivan office 2/2/66
16 mm Print	#4 - To be delivered to Sullivan office

"   "   #5 - Delivered to Tony Ford, GAC 2/15/66
"   "   #6 & 7 - Shipped to Geoffrey Ellis, London 2/15/66

One final matter:

When I was in London, all of the boys asked me several times about getting each of them 16mm prints of the show. Naturally, I indicated that could be done when it was re-mixed and finished. Also I happened to mention the unused 16mm material that we shot to John Lennen (their arrival, at the Warwick, at the Sullivan Show, etc.). He asked me if he could have it for home movie use. Actually right now it's a cut up mess of dis-organized small rolls which I would hate to have to reassemble in any order. However, I bring up these requests in the event you feel you should mention them to Brian Epstein. Let me know if we are to do anything about them.

Best regards,
M. Clay Adams

•

Ron Furmanek

The Beatles were really into the film at that time, especially John. You can see in the letter from Clay that John had asked for a copy of the trims. But the footage not used in the film was all cut up in little rolls and on the cutting room floor.

If any of that film was ever given to John or any of the Beatles, we have no idea where it is today. I've never seen any evidence of that material in any of the Beatles' film vaults, and I was the Beatles first film archivist.

Michael Adams

My dad got to spend the full day with The Beatles and with George Martin. I remember him saying there was just so much film left on the floor. He should've grabbed it up, but it just got lost by the wayside. Everything got thrown away and none of it has ever shown up.

That's a tragedy, but also how they did it back then. Look at what the BBC did with their Beatles footage and stuff from other groups. Same thing. And if you were in New York you remember *The Clay Cole Show*.

Where's all that? I saw The Rolling Stones do their whole second album live from start to finish on that show back in early '65. A lot of The British Invasion acts would come on and he would just let them roll. It wasn't like they did two songs and then they were gone. He'd let them get on there and play a set and it was great. And the station erased everything. That's a crime. We're very fortunate to have the Shea Stadium concert on film.

•

The delays caused by film editing and over-dubbing the soundtrack cancelled the goal set by Epstein and Precht for broadcasting *The Beatles At Shea Stadium* during the 1965 Christmas Season. But even if the production had gone as planned, there was another glaring problem.

With the involvement of Sullivan Productions and Precht, it was assumed CBS Television, the network home for *The Ed Sullivan Show*, would broadcast the special. As reported in the *Journal-American* (New York City) on August 16th, the day after the concert:

"If local channels other than CBS barely covered last night's Beatle bash at Shea Stadium on the late news, it was because Ed Sullivan's Productions and the network have the Moptops sewed up for a forthcoming spec. Yesterday's show at Shea was covered by CBS from stage close-ups to helicopter shots. The opposition had a hard time."

•

This CBS-Sullivan connection was also repeated by many other news outlets throughout the country. On August 18th the *Vindicator* in Youngstown, Ohio reported:

"Plans are to present 'The Beatles At Shea Stadium' program as a CBS-TV attraction in December."

•

Although Ed Sullivan was one of the most influential and popular personalities on television in 1965, the network heads at CBS had no commitment or plans to broadcast *The Beatles At Shea Stadium*. As early as August 14th, the day before the concert, the *Times* in New York reported:

"It has not yet been determined which network will televise the special program. Although the Columbia Broadcasting System televises Mr. Sullivan's Sunday evening show, it was reported that CBS did not plan to present the Beatles' special. Last November both CBS and the American Broadcasting Company presented special shows starring the Beatles. Both shows failed to fulfill rating expectations."

•

On August 20th, the *Star* in Washington, D.C. printed the following update:

"Yes, there was a TV special taped of the Beatles during their Shea Stadium concert, by Bob Precht, Ed Sullivan's producer - but Variety says CBS is 'reportedly not the least interested...' Could be the Capitol Hill criticism over Murray the K's 90-minute rock special has something to do with the turndown, but the Beatle special pre-empting 'The Entertainers' last season was a ratings flop."

•

The programs referred to as ratings failures for CBS demonstrate the generation gap was alive and well on network television. The Beatles' first appearance on *The Ed Sullivan Show* in February 1964 had drawn a record breaking number of viewers that included not only teenagers, but also most likely out of curiosity, their parents, grandparents and siblings. But during normal primetime family viewing hours in 1965, long-haired pop singers and out of control teenagers didn't always have parental approval. As another example of morals on network television, only a month after the Shea Stadium concert NBC made sure Barbara Eden's genie costume covered her navel in *I Dream of Jeannie*.

The Entertainers was a CBS variety series that ran for one season in 1964 starring an ensemble of singers, dancers and comedians. The hosts were Carol Burnett and Bob Newhart. On November 13th, instead of the usual song and dance routines, spiced up with family friendly jokes, the show dedicated its full hour to a documentary about the Beatles' 1964 North American tour.

Murray the K's *It's What's Happening, Baby!* aired Monday, June 28, 1965 on CBS from 9:30 to 11:00 pm. To be fair, it did not include an appearance by the Beatles. It featured a mix of white, black and Latino performers lip-syncing their latest hits in various locations, much like MTV videos fifteen years later. The line-up included Jan & Dean, Mary Wells, The Dave Clark Five, Cannibal and the Headhunters and others. According to a promotional release from CBS, it was produced "in conjunction with the U.S. Office of Economic Opportunity and dedicated to the needs and interests of out-of-school teenagers." As referred to in the *Washington Star* article, it was reported the program "outraged the U.S. Congress."

•

The Beatles At Shea Stadium was broadcast in black and white on BBC Television in England on Tuesday, March 1, 1966. But when the ABC Network in North America finally aired the special in color on Tuesday, January 10, 1967, it was already a piece of pop culture history. Musically The Beatles had progressed at a rapid pace and none of the songs from their last two albums, *Rubber Soul* and *Revolver,* had been included in the concert. They had stopped touring, matured their public image by growing mustaches and discarding matching suits for colorful and flamboyant fashions, and were in the studio creating *Sgt. Pepper's Lonely Hearts Club Band.* In a little over a month on February 13th, they would release the single *Penny Lane* and *Strawberry Fields Forever.*

A generation was moving just as fast toward The Summer of Love that would include the Monterey International Pop Music Festival in June where over 200,000 people would watch performances from newer artists such as Jimi Hendrix, Jefferson Airplane, The Who, Janis Joplin and The Grateful Dead. Attendance at free concerts in London's Hyde Park and New York's Central Park could populate entire cities. On the horizon was Woodstock.

Stadium concerts would grow bigger and louder with stages as large as city blocks. Sound equipment, lighting and special effects would require fleets of semi-trucks and hundreds of road crew, assistants and advisors to move it all from one city to the next. Stadiums would regularly be turned into concert venues with major productions from a wide range of musical styles and a list of performers that continues to grow.

It all started when Sid Bernstein contacted Brian Epstein. It became reality on a small stage in the middle of New York's Shea Stadium with John, Paul, George and Ringo - and 55,600 witnesses.

Restoring The Television Special

Following their agreement, after *The Beatles At Shea Stadium* aired in the U.S., Clayco Films delivered all negatives and prints to Brian Epstein and destroyed the remaining copies and outtake footage. Unauthorized copies of the television special have circulated since the days of home video recorders, with the best advertised as "borrowed," "found" or even "stolen" from the ABC-TV vault. Soundtrack recordings, sometimes taken from reel-to-reel tape recorders with a microphone held up to a small television speaker in 1967, have also appeared on various bootleg vinyl albums, cassettes and CD's.

Over the years these poor quality reproductions have faded with age and subsequent copies of these same recordings. The Holy Grail for all dedicated Beatles fans would be the original film, which had been stored away and unseen by the public since they were given to Brian Epstein.

Then on October 7, 1988, two days before John Lennon would have turned forty eight years old, the unexpected happened. With the release of the Andrew Solt and David L. Wolper film *Imagine: John Lennon*, moviegoers saw for the first time on a big screen restored 35mm footage of the Beatles performing *Help!* at Shea Stadium. The dubbed-in audio was from the studio recording and enhanced by screaming fans, but the visual was in brilliant color and an obvious improvement over any bootleg "borrowed," "found" or even "stolen" from the ABC-TV vault.

Ron Furmanek

My buddy Andrew Solt produced that movie and I was one of the head research people. One of the things I did was make sure he was given a newly struck IP made from the camera negative for the footage used of *Help!* from the original 35mm film so we didn't lose any quality.

•

The restoration of *The Beatles At Shea Stadium* had started a few years earlier when Neil Aspinall, once the Beatles' personal assistant and now head of their company Apple Corp, hired Furmanek as their first archivist. They had the original negatives and film given to Epstein, who had died in 1967, but Aspinall wanted to know if there was any other footage or audio in existence.

Ron Furmanek

Around 1986-87, I was working for Apple and Neil Aspinall. My job was to go around the world and find whatever was missing or wasn't there in the first place. My main job was to hunt things down.

I discovered that Mr. M. Clay Adams was living about an hour from me in New Jersey and met with him. He was great. He just wanted to hear from Bob Precht and Neil, so both contacted him and he gave me everything he had from Shea Stadium.

Unfortunately, he had no film since he had recommended all the outtakes be destroyed six months after it aired. But the miracle of miracles was that he had the two stereo reels of the concert, all the original audio tape recordings. He had kept all the tapes and what he had was amazing. It was the original multi-track tapes.

He also had all of the work tapes from the mixing sessions. They had made several mixes of the live concert and studio re-recordings before coming up with the final master. He also had many reels of the mixed tapes and interviews conducted for the film.

I physically carried the tapes on the plane. I didn't ship them or put them in luggage. I also wouldn't let them go through security. I handed them to the airport security guy and said, "We can't put this through the x-ray because it's audio tape." Remember, this was back in 1986-87, so things were a lot different than they are today. But I physically carried those tapes on the plane, because they were gold. They're sitting there comfortably in the Apple vaults to this day.

Neil wanted me to do this and made sure I carried those tapes on the plane. I remember a friend of mine in Los Angeles had found the original master two inch video tape for another Beatles project which we gave to Neil, and he physically carried the tape on the plane back to the U.K. Neil was so protective of everything having to do with them and in my opinion really was the Fifth Beatle. He was truly the real heart and soul of Apple and the Beatles and was with them until the end.

When I was restoring the film I was looking for anything on Shea Stadium. The only footage they had was the original camera cut negative. There was nothing else at all. In fact Apple had no audio other than what was on the optical track film negatives. That's why it was so great to find the reels M. Clay had. Even if I had wanted to restore the film back to the original mono soundtrack like on the television version, at least he had the mono mix reels and that can still be done. I chose to re-mix it in stereo.

•

Seven years after *Imagine: John Lennon*, in November 1995, ABC-TV broadcast *The Beatles Anthology*. The documentary aired over three nights (six in the U.K.) and chronicled the beginning of the Beatles to their break-up. When the series focused on the Shea Stadium concert, it was Furmanek's restored version of the film with audio from the original television special mixed in stereo. The Beatles were shown performing *Twist and Shout*, *I Feel Fine*, *Baby's In Black*, *I'm Down* and *Help!*

Furmanek also used the original audio tapes from Clay Adams to remix into stereo the concert's lost songs, *She's A Woman* and the only lead vocal by Harrison, *Everybody's Trying To Be My Baby*. Though *She's A Woman* remains unreleased, *Everybody's Trying To Be My Baby* was heard by fans for the first time when it was included on *The Beatles Anthology 2*, but unfortunately it was not the stereo mix.

For unknown reasons, the *Anthology* version was mixed down from stereo to mono, which is also how the television special was broadcast almost thirty years earlier. The difference is obvious when compared to the much superior stereo version produced by Furmanek from Fine's original recording.

Ron Furmanek

I think the song is really hot sounding and still don't understand why they squashed it to mono. They didn't give us, meaning Bob Fine and myself, any credit for doing this.

Restoring the picture and the audio, especially, was a lot of work. Doing the audio alone was a bit of a nightmare. It took Mike Jarrett, who was my engineer at Abbey Road, and myself over a week to do.

I remember being invited to AIR Studios in London one evening to watch George Harrison during a recording session with Jools Holland and Joe Brown. I was there for about three hours hanging out and watching George sing the song *Between The Devil And The Deep Blue Sea* over and over, and I got to talk with him. I'll never forget it because I told him I was working on the Shea Stadium film and the screaming level on the audio was a mess. It was really tough to do.

And George said to me, "It was tougher doing it." That was great!

Working on the film was one of my favorite projects. We did it all digitally. I finished it around 1991 and restored the film to perfect quality for use in *The Beatles Anthology*.

They also issued some promotional clips when *Anthology* came out. They released *Dizzy Miss Lizzy* as the complete song for a promotional clip. If you can find the right version out there, it's in true stereo and sounds fantastic.

FINAL
WORDS

The Beatles At Shea Stadium

The concert at Shea Stadium has maintained a unique place in rock'n roll history. It wasn't the first stadium rock concert, since that honor will forever be held by Elvis Presley. And in 1972 Grand Funk Railroad broke the Beatles' record for fastest ticket sales when they sold-out Shea in only seventy two hours. Of course The Beatles' record might still be standing if only Sid Bernstein could have opened all the thousands of mail-in ticket requests sent to his post office box within that time limit.

The Beatles' record for largest stadium attendance was topped in 1973 when Led Zeppelin drew 58,600 fans at Florida's Tampa Stadium. The gross sales also bettered their highest payday, but not by much. Even with higher ticket prices and more seats, Led Zeppelin only grossed $5,000 more than the Beatles had eight years earlier. Currently the record for the largest crowd at a stadium rock concert occurred in Maracan Stadium in Rio de Janeiro, Brazil when both Paul McCartney (1990) and Tina Turner (1988) drew over 180,000 people.

Within a year after the Beatles' second concert at Shea Stadium on August 23, 1966 outdoor music festivals lasting days and including multiple headline performers became more newsworthy. The Monterey International Pop Music Festival is credited with kicking off The Summer of Love over three days in June, 1967. Two years later, Woodstock earned legendary status by attracting a "nation" of approximately 400,000 people. According to the *Guinness Book of World Records*, the largest attendance for a rock concert occurred in 1994 when 3.5 million turned out to see Rod Stewart at Copacabana Beach in Rio de Janeiro.

Nearly five decades have passed since the four Beatles ran to the stage in their Shea Jackets and Wells Fargo Badges. It's a defining moment in modern pop culture and also a remnant of an era of innocence. There was no trace of a marijuana haze over Shea Stadium and no warning announcements to be careful of bad drugs. There was no violence. Police were there to keep fans safe and make sure no one was hurt during the massive outpouring of excitement, emotions and energy.

In what would have been a fairytale come true for tens of thousands of girls who screamed, cried, wished, prayed and even fainted to make it happen, two young women at the concert were watching husbands. In 1969 Linda Eastman married Paul McCartney Barbara Bach married Ringo Starr.

Shea Stadium was demolished following the 2008 baseball season and the land is now a parking lot for the new ballpark, Citi Field. In July that year New Yorker Billy Joel performed the final two concerts at the stadium, *The Last Play at Shea*. On the final night he introduced Paul McCartney to close out the show with *I Saw Her Standing There* and *Let It Be*. And even though the songs had never been performed by The Beatles at Shea Stadium, it put a Fab Four exclamation point on the closing celebration.

Since August 15, 1965 the first generation of Beatles fans has matured. Time will do that. The youthful screams of Beatlemania were handed down to younger fans and younger artists. But for many who fit the description of teeny-bopper all those years ago, the feelings still live with memories of John, Paul, George and Ringo.

For the lucky ones who were there with the Beatles that night at Shea Stadium - whether it was backstage, onstage or in the stands - the memories remain special. There's nothing else that can really compare to what they experienced on August 15, 1965.

•

Cousin Bruce Morrow

The Beatles affected everything that we did. I never realized and neither did any of the "quote" geniuses including Sid or anybody else. We didn't realize the effect that these people were going to have to this day. That's what I learned. It was a very big lesson at Shea Stadium that things are not what they always seem and you don't go by the past. You're going to have to take a look at what's happening right now and with the Beatles it was very obvious that something different was happening.

When a group goes past the music it ain't just showbiz anymore. It becomes part of our lives. The Beatles had sociological significance on our lives. To this day they still do. That's what I learned.

Here's a story about what I mean. I have a very interesting photograph. I've shown it on *Good Morning America* several times. There are five or six kids at Shea Stadium and they're in absolute ecstasy. Their faces are frozen in time and really represent Beatlemania. When I got off the air the producer came over to me and said, "Hey, somebody on the phone wants to talk with you."

It turns out to be the daughter of one of those kids who was fifteen years old at the time. She was watching and saw her mom was one of those girls and asked if I could talk to her. I did and got a reunion where I brought all of those women in and we put them back together on *Good Morning America* about two months later. I still talk to them every once in awhile.

So that's my ongoing experience with Shea Stadium. It was terrific and probably the most energetic and exciting day of my career to date.

Steve Marinucci

You could easily say the Beatles notoriety was probably at its height at Shea Stadium because the concert got so much publicity. And then it was on television. Everybody watched it. Who hasn't seen that Shea Stadium film?

There had been a lot riding on their first appearances on *The Ed Sullivan Show*. Every first generation Beatles fan knows where they were on February 9, 1964. Basically, they were watching it. I know I was. But as notable as the *Sullivan* show is, the Shea show was huge. What Sid Bernstein did with that show was create a huge happening. It was the biggest thing anybody had seen at that point as far as rock concerts go. It was absolutely amazing. If all their shows had been like Shea, I think they may have kept going.

It changed the face of the entire concert industry. It didn't happen right away, which is kind of funny that it didn't. But a lot of what's going on today can be traced back to what happened that night. I mean a lot of the concerts then, and a lot of the Beatles' shows, were small time things. They weren't in stadiums, but were in smaller venues. But Shea Stadium was a huge place. Sid Bernstein told me that Brian Epstein was worried the Beatles wouldn't be able to sell it out. But they did and it changed everything.

Arthur Aaron

There were no posters for the Shea concert. But there are posters out there with the date August 15, 1965 and I'll tell you why. Because Sid and I went to a graphics studio in either 1999 or 2000 and we made up a poster that would have been. That was what Sid said the poster would've looked like if he'd had one made before the concert sold out. So that's what some people have.

After the Beatles broke up, John Lennon lived in The Dakota and Sid used to see him all the time. Sid got John and a friend from Liverpool tickets for a show at Carnegie Hall. It was sold-out so Sid's kids gave John their tickets. He and Sid were sitting next to each other.

At the end of intermission, John looked at him and said, "You know Sid, that concert in 1965 at Shea Stadium...I saw the top of the mountain on that unforgettable night."

Sid looked at him and said, "I know what you mean, John. I saw the top of the mountain, too."

Clay Cole

One thing the Beatles really changed was the way acts were presented. Up until then people like The Four Seasons or The Beach Boys, if they did a show... And by the way, they were never called concerts before The Beatles. They were a *personal appearance*. Concerts were for Maria Callas and Metropolitan Opera singers and Victor Borge, but not necessarily rock stars.

Beatles concerts demanded so many things. They demanded a first class sound system. They demanded security and so much lighting and specific sound things in the backline equipment. The American acts started to want parity. So The Four Seasons and The Beach Boys demanded a percentage of the house, first class sound, first class lighting and backline equipment and so on. So they were beginning to now earn five or six or seven thousand dollars a night, rather than five hundred like they used to. And they were being presented with good sound equipment. When you used to go back and entertain you were lucky if they had a PA system. Four guys had to sing through one microphone with no lighting and it was horrible.

The Beatles changed it all for the better for American entertainers. They began to really earn good money and have first class stage presentations. Yes, they did influence American groups.

Diane Gunther

I just feel so fortunate that I was at that performance. Even now if I see some younger person that has a Beatles shirt on, I will always go up to them and say, "Are you a Beatles fan?" If they say yes, I always tell them that I was at the Shea Stadium concert and every time they're like, "Oh my God, how wonderful that was!" It's like a proud thing to have been there. It's a big deal. It's an incredible big deal.

Nedra Talley-Ross

It changed the rock'n roll side of things to where it went up to a whole new level. If I look back at the sock hops, then at Murray the K's rock'n roll shows, and then going out in front of more than fifty thousand people... That had never happened before. There was a change in the wind, but there were so many changes going on at that point. It was the 60's and everything changed. What happened at Shea Stadium was that down the road you've got all these people doing major stadium shows. The Beatles opened the door to that.

I remember more of when The Ronettes performed with them the next year because I was not one to go to shows just to go to a show. It's like; if you work someplace you don't go there to sit. You know? So I saw the stadium side from my perspective when we were performing.

I saw then that you could not really show talent. I didn't feel like the Beatles could really show their talent because of the noise. And for the people watching the show, it was like *what do you get from it?* You get people shaking their head and their mouths are moving, but the screams were so deafening it was like they paid to just scream. They did not pay for a show. To me it was just pure screaming.

The next year we did the Beatle tour and the sound... We had never heard anything like that before. We were used to the whistles. The girls screamed for The Beatles and the boys yelled and whistled for The Ronettes. And there were boys who were just as excited about The Beatles, you know, but of course girls show their emotions much more -

even fainting. Any boy that was fainting at the concert, he has a problem.

I remember that night calling off my engagement to Scott for my mother's sake. *Give me another year and I'll be ready!* We've been married for over forty years and still in love.

Scott Ross

About ten years ago I was with Bill Wyman from The Rolling Stones. I stayed at his house and Ringo and his wife Barbara Bach came over. We were all out at dinner that night and it was the only other time I had any contact with him at all. And Ringo used to have a crush on Nedra. It was like a thing when they were out on tour. He was always hitting on her. So I reminded him of that and told him Nedra and I had been married, at that time over thirty years. So that was a conversation that was kind of interesting.

Peter Bennett

I wound up as The Beatles promotions manager when Brian Epstein died. Mick Jagger was close to John Lennon. So when I was with Murray the K at Forest Hills Stadium he was telling the guys – and Brian Epstein was there too – that I was the promotions manager for The Rolling Stones. And then Brian was telling me about Cilla Black and other artists he had that he wanted me to promote. But when Brian Epstein died, all of a sudden they were up in the air.

> "What happened out of that for all of us in the business is that we started thinking on a grander scale."
> - Ken Mansfield

If you want to know if the four Beatles were nice guys, yes they were nice guys. I liked them and I got along with them. They were four great guys and I enjoyed working with them for many years. And I did more than promote records with them. Personally I was with them and traveled with them and knew them as individuals.

We had a ball together. Ringo used to say, "Is John talking about me? Is he alright today?" Everybody was worried about what John Lennon was talking about. And Paul would say, "Is he talking about me?" And George would say the same thing. And John would say, "Did he say anything about me?" And things like that. So we had a game going around and it was funny. But with my hard work I managed to get their records on the top of the charts.

What I noticed with them was that they liked honesty and it was very hard for anyone to get their trust. They liked me a lot and they trusted me and I got them to do things that they never did, like interviews. I'm the one that set up the first interview with *Rolling Stone Magazine* for John and Yoko and I arranged and negotiated their week as being co-hosts for *The Mike Douglas Show*. I also got John and Yoko and later George Harrison to appear on *The Dick Cavett Show* on the ABC Network.

The Beatles changed the whole business around. They had a lot of heart. And I say right now there is no other group in the world today that's changing anything around. They come and go.

Pattie Noah

Since then, the Beatles and John have remained a constant focus. Very shortly after seeing them at Shea, we went to see the movie *Help!* in the theater. When I saw John sing *You've Got To Hide Your Love Away*, that was the precise moment I knew I wanted to be a musician. I got a 12-string guitar for Christmas that year and that was the first song I learned. Here we are more than four decades later and I'm now playing and singing in one of the few female Beatles tribute acts in the world, Luv Me Deux.

Ron Schneider

Shea Stadium and *The Ed Sullivan Show*... When you think about it, those were the two things that really changed it all. In The British Invasion, those were the battlefronts. When you look at pictures you can see the changes in culture by looking at the audiences. I mean prior to that the kids looked different than they did in 1965 and 1966. I always liked looking back at it with the Beatles coming in '64 and then seeing the rest of The British Invasion and all the changes that happened because of it.

Joan Murray

It was probably one of the highlights of my life. It was being a part of history and even at that time I knew it was a part of history. When they first hit America I was standing at the foot of the airplane with my little microphone. The reporters then weren't quite as bad as they are today and the Beatles were so nice. They would always take time for us. I always got a premier place for some reason and I wish I could find those tapes of me interviewing them when they were getting off the plane at the airport. I know they would be priceless.

When I lived in New York I had a lot of photographs of me and the Beatles; the Beatles publicity shots and all of that. I also had many other things and they were overrunning my apartment. And right across from my door was an incinerator. And do you know I put them all down the incinerator? I could kick myself. Kick me to the curb. I didn't know any better. Some I still have and some I gave to my nephew. But I still think they were fabulous. I feel The Beatles are forever.

Ken Mansfield

I think Shea Stadium was a moment where everyone went, *wait a minute...* You know. I don't think we really realized there could be music and rock'n roll on that level as far as a concert appearance. It was a new form of venue and just took everything to such a different level. What happened out of that for all of us in the business is that we started thinking on a grander scale. In every respect and not only concert appearances and the obvious revenue from something like this.

With The Beatles we started realizing just how big a powerhouse they were as an enterprise and a company with a brand. We saw there were all these things that an individual act could be and eventually we set up Apple (Corp). Here was a band that was strong enough to set up a multi-corporation. And I mean this was a major corporation with divisions. And what's interesting about

Ken Mansfield with The Beatles

it is Apple was the forerunner of a lot of what happened in business later on. A lot of people modeled companies after this concept.

Because The Beatles were so big and could draw that much at Shea Stadium, they realized they could just about do anything they wanted. With Apple we brought in the publishing, we brought in the record company, we brought in the management and we brought in all the aspects that other people were making money from. That was big and I think we all realized that now we can start painting on a bigger canvas. As far as record deals and the production companies, artist tours and just everything we did, it just cranked up. So I think that's my view on how Shea Stadium changed the music business.

Peter Altschuler

Murray never said anything to me about being disappointed at Shea Stadium. He may have talked to other people about it, but he just had this feeling that he got a little short-changed. Given the realism of the business and the pecking order of the people who wielded the power, he took what he could get and I think he was happy with that. Beyond that he didn't tend to focus too much on what had happened and just kept forging ahead and doing other things.

I'm not going to tell you Murray Kaufman was remarkable and head and shoulders above everybody else, but he definitely knew how to promote what he got a hold of. He knew how to promote himself and he had a great eye and ear for talent and did not owe anything to The Beatles beyond sort of a step up in recognition that he hadn't had outside of the New York market.

In fact, in 1965 he did a national television broadcast under the auspices of the Office of Economic Opportunity. Murray put together essentially an on location version of his Brooklyn Fox shows, which took him all over the country. That was broadcast over CBS which gave him national attention. And he still had that ability to spot talent and showcase them. At his final rock'n roll show, which was in Manhattan at the RKO 58th Street Theater in 1967, he brought The Who and Cream over for their first U.S. appearances.

When he died in 1982, I got letters from people as far away as Nebraska who had listened to him because WINS had a 50,000 watt transmitter. When the clouds were low that signal would literally bounce off the cloud layer and go as far as the Midwest. Kids listened to him.

I had lunch with Lance Freed, Alan Freed's son, and we talked about our respective fathers. He said, "Yeah, I pretty much say that my father gave birth to rock'n roll, but your father raised the kid."

I thought that was fairly accurate because if anybody helped make rock'n roll acceptable to an adult audience, I think Murray the K really did it. He had numerous appearances on all kinds of talk shows in which he defended the quality of the music, the business that produced that music, the talent behind that music, and the fact that it wasn't the same thing in the 60's as it had been in the 50's. It was actually sophisticated, mature and worth a listen.

George Orsino

I was asked in an interview if there was anything I had to say or any regrets. And I said I regret I didn't have more film. I regret that I wasn't a Beatle fan. If I was a Beatle fan I would have had a ton of film.

Michael Sergio

Fast forward to 1986 and at that point I'm a strapping young man. I'm a sky diving instructor jumping out of airplanes and doing all this other stuff like acting and television. A few years earlier, George Steinbrenner had invited my sky diving team to jump into Yankee Stadium. But it got weathered out and we couldn't do it.

In 1986 The New York Mets and Boston Red Sox are playing each other in The World Series and up in Boston they released all these balloons that said, "Go Sox!" And the media made such a big thing out of it. "Oh, look at what they're doing in Boston. Look how much they love their team. This is incredible, this is unbelievable!" And I'm thinking: *What? Wait... What was that?! The balloons? The balloons were incredible?*

It just riled me up and I said to myself, *you know what? Let me just jump into Shea Stadium for the Mets. Let's just do this thing.*

I went to a Woolworths, bought a sheet and spray painted, "Go Mets!" on it. I put into motion a whole bunch of stuff and then here I am, floating over Shea Stadium during Game Six of The World Series. The parachute is open, the banner is out and everything is good. I'm feeling good, you know?

I'm coming down and I'm very cautious about this. I'm in half brakes. I'm coming in over the lights right from dead center field and towards home plate. Then suddenly I hear, "Ahhhhhhh!" I'm hearing this roar and I'm like, *what's going on? Is there a play that I'm not seeing?*

I'm looking around and right about then I must be about three hundred feet over the stadium light extensions and I'm coming down. The umpire looks straight up at me, waves his hand and stops the game. In my head I go, *he stopped the game! This is great! I'm in! I've got no problems.* I'm descending and I say to myself, *okay, really take a good look at this.* I'm coming down

and I literally made myself turn my head right and left to look at the whole thing.

Again I hear this roar and now the crowd is on their feet. They're up and they're cheering and they're roaring and they're yelling and I'm focused. I'm bringing it down and the noise is hyper loud. Right at the very end I flair the parachute and my foot touches the grass. It was unbelievable and everybody was clapping and applauding. There was so much energy there. There was so much good vibe and it felt like a terrific thing to do for the team.

The only other time I heard yelling like that, and I'll tell you exactly, was when I was sitting in the bleachers watching The Beatles at Shea Stadium. The roar I heard in that stadium was like the roar I heard when The Beatles were playing. And the next time I heard that roar I was hanging under a parachute coming into the stadium during The World Series. That sounds a little pretentious, but the truth is that's what I heard.

The second I landed two security guards came and held onto my arm on either side. All three of us grabbed the parachute and they walked me to the dugout. As soon as I got through that door, I totally knew where I was inside the stadium.

I think the coolest thing that came out of all that was that one of the sports writers wrote, "In Boston, they send balloons. In New York, we send human sacrifices."

Debbie Stern

Almost five decades later the Beatles' Shea Stadium concert is more than just a memory; it actually defines who I am today. Unfortunately I use it relative to my advanced years as in, "Do you know anyone who has seen the Beatles live in concert – twice?" Yes, I made a return engagement for the 1966 concert. Or, "I bet you can't guess how old she is." (Since I look younger than my age – thank goodness). "Well, this will give you a clue; she's seen The Beatles live in concert."

Cindy Salvo

I was only eight years old and it's been something in my life that has come up a number of times because I was so young. I was sort of the only person from my own generation who can say they saw The Beatles at Shea Stadium because it's unusual for eight year olds to go to a concert, I think. And it was only because my dad was willing to take me. So when I tell people that, I always say, "Well, I'm probably making myself sound older than I am, but I saw The Beatles at Shea Stadium." It's a great memory.

Shaun Weiss

I still get chills when I think about it. It's like going back there and makes me think about how lucky I was being part of something. Now all these years later I honestly look back and think of it as being not a rock and roll journey, but a spiritual journey.

I look back at the progression of all the things that happened to me and you couldn't write a better script in Beatles history. I mean, how is it that on February 7th I walked into this *thing* I knew nothing about? Then I meet Mal Evans, go to *The Ed Sullivan Show*, Shea Stadium and eventually to England where I get to listen to Beatles songs being recorded and watch them play on the rooftop of Apple. I was also there when they walked across Abbey Road for the album cover. All that came from a trip to pick up my father and mother from vacation at the airport and the rest becomes a footnote in Beatles history.

I never imagined it to the extent that we got involved and when I talk about it I have to pinch myself. When I look at the pictures of me with the Beatles I have to say *are they superimposed?* It happened to me, but even I don't believe it sometimes.

I don't look at it as being a coincidence anymore or just being at the right place at the right time. I feel it was a spiritual journey and a spiritual growth with The Beatles. I got to talk with them and be around them. I got to eat with them. I was a fan first and a friend second. I guess it was all a planned stepping stone that very few people had and I feel very blessed that I have that. But I still get tongue-tied. All these memories come at me at one time. It's like my head starts seeing it and the vision of the Beatles walking down the hall at Shea Stadium is prevalent. It's right there. It's being in the dugout and peeking over the top and seeing the girls crying. It's there. For a Beatles fan I'm blessed.

I think that as an entity all four of them loved to perform. I don't think they got bored performing. I think they got bored with the fact that technology restricted them. When they got on stage everyone could feel the sincerity and the love that they had in their music. That's what lasts today; the love that the Beatles put into it. Everything was in their music and when you got in their presence, you got into their emotional presence too. It would just sweep you away.

Judith Kristen

What a time in history to be a teenager. That's all I can say. Do I mind having my next birthday? No. I really don't. I wouldn't trade it in to be ten, twenty, thirty, forty years younger and have missed the experiences I had because I was a Beatles fan. I've met wonderful people that I'm still friends with almost half a century later and I'm still meeting new people because of our love for The Beatles.

We didn't realize it then that Shea was the first huge rock'n roll show in a stadium ever. I mean none of us had a clue we were part of history. We just wanted to be part of that happening that came along with seeing The Beatles. It was just phenomenal.

As much as second and third generation fans love them, it's not as full an experience as we had. We could turn on television and watch them on *The Ed Sullivan Show* and were there when *A Hard Day's Night* came out. It was just a whole different ballgame. I'm not taking away from the second and third generation fans, but even they know that we've got the edge. When you mention attending the Shea Stadium concert it's like being at a hallowed place in rock'n roll history. It's like when I went to Woodstock. Now there are a hundred million people who say they were at Woodstock. But there were only so many of us, and there were only so many of us at Shea Stadium.

> **"Shea Stadium and The Ed Sullivan Show... When you think about it, those were the two things that changed it all." - Ron Schneider**

But it's more than that. It's like a kind of magic that stays with you. You look at those old Shea Stadium videos and it just takes you right back. It's more than just a memory in your head. It's soul-filled. It's beyond what most people can comprehend. I mean it's just imbedded in me for the rest of my life. It just is. I never could thank the four of them enough for the fun that they gave to me.

Michael Adams

I've got a whole bunch of stuff from the Shea Stadium concert. I have all the audio of them talking that my dad didn't use in the film. They were followed around by Larry Kane and he would leave his tape recorder in the hotel room and go do whatever he was doing. Then the Beatles would get on it and make their own tapes.

A lot is with them talking and they just couldn't use it all. It had nothing to do with the concert. Some of it was serious stuff. They were talking about race relations when we weren't. You know, Europeans saw it differently than we did. Also there's a lot with them joking around, which is like listening to Monty Python or something. There are hours and hours of this stuff and it's not like a press conference because they're just screwing around. So I ended up with all that stuff. I also have the *Beatles For Sale* and the British *Rubber Soul* albums that my dad brought back from England. *Beatles For Sale* had been autographed.

But there are some things I don't have, like my dad's still photos that he dropped off and never got back. And I had other autographs from when they first came over during the time of *The Ed Sullivan Show*. I met them and got an autographed picture. I was standing there right in front of them and they were passing it around. I stuck that on my wall at private school and went home for Easter Vacation. When I came back it was gone. You don't know what you've got... You just don't.

Russ Lease

I own Paul's Shea Stadium Jacket. I bought it at auction through Sotheby's in London in the mid 90's.

I went to the Hard Rock's facility in Orlando because they have the original jacket John wore on the cover of *Rubber Soul* I was flying down to take measurements and photographs so it can be part of our line here at R.W. Lease. But the icing on the cake was they also have Lennon's Shea Jacket and they had pulled it out for me to see. And I've seen Ringo's. Ringo's has bounced among a handful of collectors over the last fifteen or twenty years.

The only one we've never seen is George Harrison's. It's never come up for public auction and he never mentioned it in any interviews. Harrison was kind of known for saving a lot of that stuff. I guess we all sort of theorize that it's probably hanging in his wife Olivia's closet somewhere.

Lennon and McCartney used to wear them casually. You know if they were going out to dinner or something. In fact, there are a lot of photos. And I didn't realize this until I started researching all the clothing in preparation for doing patterns and all that, but like their Shea Jackets and other stage outfits, this stuff apparently just hung in their closets. If they needed a jacket, they just reached in, grabbed one and pulled it out.

I don't know how McCartney's got out of his possession. Lennon's I do know. Lennon at some point in 1966 was out clubbing in London with a group of people and was wearing his Shea Jacket to whatever club they were at. And the story is there were a few different couples who were part of this small entourage he was with. When they came out one of the women was cold and wasn't wearing a jacket that night. So Lennon, before he got into his limousine, took his jacket off, gave it to her and said, "Here, wear this. It'll keep you warm."

Supposedly within the next week or two somebody attempted to return it to him and he just said no, keep it. He didn't really care. He didn't need it and he wasn't caring of it, so it stayed in her possession for a long period of time. In fact, and this is all kind of sacrilegious to me that you would even touch a coat like that, the buttons were all taken off and moved over about two and a half inches. That's actually the

John Lennon's Shea Jacket

Inside sleeve of John's Shea Jacket

condition it is still in today. The buttons were all moved over because this woman was obviously much smaller than Lennon was. They moved the buttons over so when she buttoned it up it would fit a whole lot tighter. And it's very apparent the coat has been really worn significantly. It's really sad because the jacket is not in very good shape for being such an iconic piece. But the McCartney jacket is in very good shape for being as old as it is.

George Orsino

I had Russ Lease look for the pinhole from the Wells Fargo badge. I showed him a picture I took of Paul McCartney at Shea Stadium and he said, "I own that jacket. Do you want to see it?"

My son and I went up there and he took it out of the closet. It was in a plastic bag and he had rubber gloves on. He laid it on the bed and I said, "By the way, where's the pinhole?" He said, "What pinhole?" And I said, "Where the Well's Fargo badge was."

He's looking at me and I'm looking and I'm searching the jacket and there it is. And I said, "See? I just authenticated that jacket for you. That's the one." We both laughed and he always remembers that. I found the pinhole. It was there.

Maxine Ascher

I used to have this little ten year old girl that lived next door to me. Her parents worked and she used to come over a lot. I'd play Beatles music for her. I taught her their names and I taught her the songs. I'd say, "Listen to this song."

One day she came into my house, looked around and said, "Okay Max, how'bout we listen to *The White Album*." I was so happy. I made a fan. I passed along my love.

"When you mention attending the Shea Stadium concert it's like being at a hallowed place in rock'n roll history." - Judith Kristen

Eve Hoffman

Other than my memories, my most valued treasure from that night was the ticket stub I kept for years. I had shown it off to several friends

> **"It was being part of history and even at that time I knew it was a part of history."**
> **- Joan Murray**

and eventually it was not returned to me by one of them. How I wish I had it today.

Shaun Weiss

I know I'm off the track, but I once sat with George on Abbey Road steps at night. It was me, Mal and George who was eating this Indian dish. We're sitting outside and these two German kids walked up to him and asked for his autograph. Then one of them asked George a really straight question. "How do you come up with the songs you write?"

You know what? George couldn't answer him. They got their autographs and left. We're sitting there and George turns around and says to me and Mal, "It's all spiritual. What I put out is what comes into me. And it's from a higher being because I'm not smart enough to write this music." Then George got into telling us about growing up in Liverpool and how he had a hard time getting through school and that all of a sudden he's in the greatest band in the world and this music flows through him. He doesn't know why he wakes up and this music is in his head.

When you think about it, it says a lot. George felt that he was being touched by a higher power. The reality is if you just take their progression from 1962 to 1970, the main thing that still stands out today is the love and peace that they all projected. It was Paul by not eating meat, George by going a spiritual road, Ringo with his peace and love and happiness, and John with his simple love. That's all John wanted was love and peace. That's what the essence of their music was and that's what touches our hearts.

Judith Goodspeed

It was an event that I've been able to take with me through my whole life. When people say, "What's your claim to fame?" All my life I've been able to say, "I saw The Beatles in Shea Stadium when I was ten years old." It was an awesome experience. It's something I've remembered every day of my life and I love The Beatles.

The neatest part about all this is how it came full circle for me as an adult. When my father and I left for the concert that day, the other neighborhood kids didn't have tickets and it wasn't real easy for them to see me go. Then one of the neighborhood kids, somebody that I've loved my whole life, passed away back in 1993. A couple weeks after her funeral I found out she had left instructions. There was a post-it note on the back of a Shea Stadium poster she'd had framed and it said to have that poster sent to me. I've had it in my home ever since and I'm honored to have it. So I do finally have something to show that I was at that concert. It was beautiful.

Mary Troumouhis

The Beatles didn't have the video and audio technology that bands have today. It was all them. I feel very lucky to have been able to experience this time in music history. It has lasted a lifetime.

Cousin Bruce Morrow

Years after they split up John Lennon retired and went on to become a house-daddy where he lived over at The Dakota at Central Park. He was out of the business for about five years. We kept in touch and I called him one day and said I was doing this thing in Central Park for the Police Athletic League.

John was always a guy that cared about kids. He liked kids. He liked his audience and he loved kids. I said we're going to have around a hundred thousand people there and I'm sure they'd love to see him. He was like, "Bruce, you know I don't sing anymore. I'm out of it and haven't done anything in awhile."

I asked him to just come and make an appearance and say hello to New York. He loved New York. He thought about it and said, "Alright Coo'zin, I'll do it. But I'm not gonna sing." He was adamant about that and I said it was a deal. So I surrounded John Lennon with a lot of groups on that show including I think, Alice Cooper. It was a wild show.

About two days before the show he called and said, "Coo'zin, do you mind if I bring a friend?" I said sure and asked who it was and he said, "Ah, I'll surprise you." Well he showed up with Harry Nilsson.

One hundred thousand people together looked like an ocean. And I'll never forget this, because there's a photograph in one of my books. There's a picture of Lennon and myself with Nilsson on the stage and he said, "Coo'zin, I told you I'm not gonna sing. Why are all these people here?"

I said, "John, they know you're not going to sing because I said that on the air." And he had heard me say that because he used to listen. And he said, "Are you sure? I don't want to be embarrassed." And I said, "No, no. It's okay. They just want to share space."

Now Lennon never really understood that. He never understood about the power that he had. Lennon had a huge amount of power as a human being, as an advocate and as a poet. He came out on the stage and was quite nervous about this because he was afraid people were going to be very disappointed. He didn't want to disappoint the people because he really appreciated his audience. That's what I think about Lennon and I kept on assuring him, "John, they know you're here just to share space with them."

> **"That's all John wanted was love and peace. That's what the essence of their music was and that's what touches our hearts."**
> **- Shaun Weiss**

He never got it. And the day he died he never understood that. He really didn't understand how people wanted to be near him just to share the earth with him.

To this day they still have that power. The Beatles have that power sociologically. That's what it really is. It's more than just the music. It's the magic.

Acknowledgements

In case you were wondering, writing a book about The Beatles is a lot of fun. The entire process is full of memories and music, along with the occasional surprise of, "Hey, I didn't know that!" For those reasons alone, this has been a truly enjoyable experience.

But the real excitement of working on a project about the most influential group in the history of popular music is the doors it opens to new contacts and friendships. I want to thank all the contributors for taking time to share your valuable memories and photos. This book would not be complete without each and every one of you.

I'm sending a special thank you to Michael Adams for sharing with me the raw, unedited audio tapes of the Beatles' performance recorded by his father during that night at Shea Stadium. These were invaluable in granting me front row access to describe the actual sounds and excitement of Beatlemania generated both on stage and off.

Also special thanks to Ron Furmanek for your personal and technical insights into the television special about this concert. In case you couldn't hear it in my voice, every conversation included a "Hey, I didn't know that!" moment.

For helping in my efforts to play detective and locate contributors and fans through their personal friendships within the Beatles community, radio shout-outs, on-air interviews and networking, thanks go to Steve Marinucci, Charles Rosenay, Joe Johnson, Donnie G., Woody Lifton, Cha Chi Loprete, Terri Hemmert, Dennis Mitchell, Pat Matthews, Rob Leonard, Ken Michaels, Tony Traguardo, Mitch Axelrod and Louie at centerfieldmaz. I also want to thank Beatles insiders Tony Barrow and Tony Bramwell for your supportive emails. Cheers!

_____**VIP SHEA ROCKS THANK YOU!**_____

Philip Kamin, Ellen Sherman, Luna Borromeo, Ken Boser and Susan Ann Carroll, Christine Deavers, Gary Dunaier, Jan Eckley, Sally Fish, George W. Jackson Jr., Jeff Korn, Lisa A. Lijoi-Spielmann, Alan McKee and Douglas C. Schefft. You guys are so cool...

I'd also like to send a rock'n roll thanks to Beatle-pal Brian Luoma, Robbie Martin, Erica Sales, and my Beatle email buddy Mindy Scheel for your *Help!*

And finally thank you to Arlys, Debbie, Kevin, Paul, Blake, Brooke and Ambre. I wouldn't have a finished book without mentioning you. Oh wait, there's one more. Thanks to our dog Snickers for the hours of loyal friendship he provided snoozing on my office floor as I relived the magic and excitement of Beatlemania that went into this. You are all very special to me.

- Dave Schwensen

Quotes & Credits:

* - *New York, New York* by John Kander and Fred Ebb, 1977

(1) – *The Beatles Anthology* by The Beatles, Page 119

(2) - Ibid, Page 119

(3) – *Billboard*, April 4, 1964

(4) - www.scottymoore.net

(5) - *Ticket to Ride* by Larry Kane, Page 40

(6) - www.beatlesinterviews.org from audio of press conference

(7) - *John, Paul, George, Ringo & Me* by Tony Barrow, Pages 163-164

(8) - Ibid, Page 164

(9) – *The Beatles At Shea Stadium*. Sullivan, NEMS & Subafilms

(10) – Ibid

(11) – Ibid

(12) - *Tomorrow with Tom Snyder*, NBC Television, April 25, 1975

(13) - *Twist and Shout* by Phil Medley and Bert Russell (Berns), 1961

(14) - *The Royal Variety Show*, London, November 4, 1963

(15) - *She's A Woman* by John Lennon and Paul McCartney, 1964

(16) - *Dizzy Miss Lizzy* by Larry Williams, 1958

(17) - *Rolling Stone* Interview by Jann S. Wenner, 1971

(18) - *Ticket To Ride* by John Lennon and Paul McCartney 1965

(19) - John Lennon *Playboy* Interview, 1980

(20) - *The Beatles Anthology* by The Beatles, Page 187

(21) - *John, Paul, George, Ringo & Me* by Tony Barrow, Page 165

(22) - *Act Naturally* by John Russell and Voni Morrison 1963

(23) - *Rolling Stone* Interview by Jann S. Wenner, 1971

(24) - *The Beatles* by Bob Spitz, Page 510

(25) - *A Hard Day's Night* by John Lennon & Paul McCartney, 1964

(26) - *The Beatles Anthology* by The Beatles, Page 187

(27) - *I'm Down* by John Lennon and Paul McCartney, 1965

(28) - *The Beatles Anthology* by The Beatles, Page 187

(29) - *The Complete Beatles Chronicle* by Mark Lewisohn, Page 199

(30) - *John, Paul, George, Ringo & Me* by Tony Barrow, Page 166

(31) - Email from Tony Bramwell to author, 2010 - cheers Tony!

(32) - *Magical Mystery Tour* by Tony Bramwell, Page 164

Photo Credits

Pg 29 - Cousin Bruce Morrow, Bruce Morrow

Pg 29 - Clay Cole, the Ronettes & the Capris, Nedra Talley-Ross

Pg 30 - Murray the K, the Ronettes, Nedra Talley-Ross

Pg 39 - Epstein Letter, Ron Furmanek

Pg 45 - Posters, Author's Collection

Pg 47, 51, 52 - Letters, Author's Collection

Pg 62 - Joan Murray & autographs, Joan Murray

Pg 66 - Rockette rehearsal schedule, autograph, Author's Collection

Pg 74 - Shea Stadium postcard, Author's Collection

Pg 75 - Arrival Shea Stadium, George Orsino

Pg 79 - Concert ticket, Marc Catone

Pg 83 - Scott Ross, the Ronettes, Scott Ross & Nedra Talley-Ross

Pg 89 - Beatles dressing room, George Orsino

Pg 96 - Paul McCartney Shea Jacket, Russ Lease

Pg 97 - Wells Fargo Badge, Russ Lease

Pg 99 - Beatles preparing for stage, George Orsino

Pg 105 - 1965 Tour Program, Author's collection

Pg 119 - The Beatles, George Orsino

Pg 138 - Upper Deck Shea Stadium, Marc Catone

Pg 150 - The Beatles, George Orsino

Pg 173 - The Beatles, George Orsino

Pg 195-219 - Production notes & letters, Ron Furmanek

Pg 225 - M. Clay Adams letter, Michael Adams

Pg 232 - M. Clay Adams letter, Ron Furmanek

Pg 249 - Beatles Poster, Author's Collection

Pg 253 - Ken Mansfield & The Beatles, Ken Mansfield

Pg 256 - Michael Sergio, Author's Collection (autographed)

Pg 261 - John Lennon Shea Jacket, Russ Lease

All reasonable efforts have been made to identify proper credits. If there are any mistakes or omissions please accept my apologies and note these can be corrected in future editions.

Index

About The Author

 Dave Schwensen is an award-winning humor columnist, entertainment journalist and author. A nationally recognized comedy coach, his insider's knowledge of the comedy industry was earned as talent coordinator for the television show *A&E's An Evening at the Improv*, The Improv Comedy Clubs in Los Angeles and New York City, and as a talent consultant for many television programs, networks and film studios.

Dave is also the author of *The Beatles In Cleveland: Memories, Facts & Photos About The Notorious 1964 & 1966 Concerts.*

For information about workshops, books and live programs visit:
TheComedyBook.com
DavePresents.com
NorthShorePublishing.com
BeatlesSheaStadium.com
BeatlesInCleveland.com
BeatlesProgram.com

For a humorous look at your favorite classic rock songs follow:
TheClassicRocker.com

The Beatles In Cleveland
Memories, Facts & Photos About
The Notorious 1964 & 1966 Concerts

Hot on the success of their film *A Hard Day's Night*, the Beatles' 1964 North American tour filled auditoriums with screams of delight and excitement - and in some cases, full-blown hysteria. This was the setting for the Fab Four's concert in Cleveland, Ohio when fans stormed the stage and stopped the show. The next year, the group was banned from appearing in the city that is now home to The Rock'n Roll Hall of Fame.

In August 1966 The Beatles launched their final tour, but the innocence portrayed in *A Hard Day's Night* only two years earlier was missing. Controversy raging over John Lennon's remarks about religion and the group's massive popularity made safety more of a concern than ever before. A scheduling change helped lift the "Beatles Ban" and brought the group back to Cleveland for a show at Municipal Stadium. The results of Beatlemania were the same - but on a much larger scale.

Told through eyewitness accounts and never-before published photos, go behind the scenes, onstage and backstage for two of the wildest and out-of-control concerts in Beatles - and rock'n roll - history.

* Selected for The Rock'n Roll Hall of Fame & Museum Library & Archives

"Totally drew me into the whole experience and gave me new insight into something I thought I knew something about." - Ken Mansfield, Former U.S. Manager of The Beatles' Apple Records

"If you'd like to experience what it was like to participate in a Beatles concert, we can't recommend The Beatles In Cleveland strongly enough." - Bob Malik, host of *The Beatle Years*

"What a fun book!" - Joe Johnson, host of *Beatle Brunch*

Paperback & eBook, 192 pages / www.NorthShorePublishing.com

How To Be A Working Comic
An Insider's Business Guide To A Career In
Stand-Up Comedy: Revisited, Revised & Revamped

Here's the world of comedy in one supportive, informative and enjoyable package by an author with the expertise and experience aspiring comics will benefit from. *How To Be A Working Comic* tells it like it really is: To have a career and survive, you must have an understanding of the industry - and to be a success you must be fully prepared. Provides the information and more insider's advice than any other manual, explaining how to try out comedy material; get on-stage experience; market your act to talent bookers, agents and managers; go on the road; get on television and much, much more. Plus invaluable advice and career experience from many of today's top performers including: Drew Carey,
Jeff Foxworthy, Carrot Top, Tommy Smothers, Dom Irrera, Budd Friedman, Rhonda Shear, Jeff Dunham, The Amazing Johnathan, Rondell Sheridan and others. Foreword by Ray Romano.

"Schwensen certainly knows the ins and outs of making it in comedy. He has put his knowledge to work in *How to Be A Working Comic*, a book that shows aspiring comics everything - from how to hire an agent to how to handle road gigs." - Chicago Tribune

"The volume is full of proactive ideas and hands-on experience." - Back Stage, The Performing Arts Weekly

"A MUST have!" - The Comic Bible

"This instant industry classic is brimming with enough priceless tips on every aspect of comedy to help even the most clueless comedian write his own gags-to-riches story." - Spot Entertainment Magazine

"Might very well be the best manual ever written on the comedy business. An absolute must for anyone looking to work in comedy today." - Chucklemonkey

Paperback & eBook, 176 pages / www.NorthshorePublishing.com

Comedy FAQs And Answers
How The Stand-Up Biz REALLY Works

Here is the ultimate guide to surviving and thriving in the world of stand-up comedy. Some of the biggest comics in the business - including Lewis Black, Eddie Brill, Brett Butler, George Carlin, Margaret Cho, Mark Curry, Earthquake, Bill Engvall, Mike Epps, Jeff Foxworthy, Richard Jeni, Lisa Lampanelli, Kathleen Madigan, Brian Regan, Ray Romano, George Wallace, Weird Al Yankovic and many others - share the lessons they learned the hard way, while club owners, talent agents, managers, and publicists reveal what goes on behind the scenes and what it takes to succeed in the serious business of making people laugh. Written in an entertaining and informative style, *Comedy FAQs And Answers* is a series of thoughtful questions and answers that every aspiring comedian needs to know to launch a successful career.

"FOUR STARS (Highest Rating). This is the bible for everyone and anyone who ever wanted to know just what it takes to be a successful stand-up comic. (It takes more than just being funny, that's for darn sure!). Author Dave Schwensen covers it all. This book could have easily been titled *Everything You Always Wanted To Know About Stand-Up Comedy, But Didn't Know Who To Ask*." - Todd Schwartz, CBS

"A MUST: one of the best industry insider guides on the market." - *Bookwatch Monthly*

"No one has written a more comprehensive and interesting and illuminating book on the subject of stand-up comedy than our Dave Schwensen." - Budd Friedman, Improv Comedy Clubs

"One look at this table of contents and you'll know you've hit the comedy information jackpot. You'll consult this book again and again. I know I will." - *Laughing Matters*, Back Stage Newspaper

ISBN 1-58115-411-9, paperback, 207 pages
Allworth Press / Skyhorse Publishing, NYC

Comedy Workshop
Creating & Writing Comedy Material
For Comedians & Humorous Speakers

Comedy material can come from just about anywhere when you know how to look for it. Learn to take creative ideas and real life experiences onto the comedy stage and speaker's platform. The author of *How To Be A Working Comic* and *Comedy FAQs And Answers* returns with an innovative guidebook dedicated to creating and writing original comedy material.

Written in a conversational and easy to read manner similar to *Comedy FAQs And Answers*, Schwensen relies on nearly two decades of comedy workshop and coaching experiences to cover writing topics provided by aspiring and working comedians and humorous speakers.

Being original is a key element for success in the humor business. Following specific comedy writing formulas only succeeds in creating more copies of the same style. To stand out from the competition, this book urges writers to explore their personal creativity and individual sense of humor through shared techniques, tips and practiced advice. The final goal is simple - making audiences laugh.

5 STAR reviews from Amazon.com readers…

"This book gave me the guidance to put together my ideas into a set that I will use on stage. Easy to read and follow. Good job!" - aj111

"The book helped me to focus on what is most important in developing a stand-up act and humorous speaker presentation. I definitely learned a few things from the book." - Book Aficionada

"Invaluable instruction for the contemporary comics learning to hone their craft. It has easy application for the novice and refreshing tips for the vet." - Geminii

Paperback & eBook, 82 pages / www.NorthShorePublishing.com

Father's Days... And Nights

Humorous Tales from
The Frontlines of Fatherhood

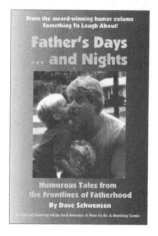

When asked about his children, every dad worth his weight in fatherhood has stories. The best ones are like the collection shared in this book: entertaining, funny and full of love. Author and humorist Dave Schwensen declares his life was never the same after becoming a father - and neither was his nervous system. Thanks to his wife Debutant Deb and their sons six year old Dangerous Paul and thirteen year old Chaos Kevin, the author accepted his diminished family role an instigator and observer and wrote about it every week in his award winning newspaper humor column, *Something To Laugh About.*

Father's Days... And Nights includes twenty of the author's favorite columns about parenthood from a father's point of view. With the emphasis on family humor, this book is perfect for every family member.

5 STAR reviews from Amazon.com readers...

"Great book for families. Reads like Cosby without the notoriety. Great humor on fatherhood and parenting." - Warren

"Parents will see themselves and their children. It is both funny and heartwarming." - Sarah M.

"Becoming a dad changes everything. It definitely takes a sense of humor to deal with all the insanity and suddenly becoming 'uncool.' This funny book will remind you you're not alone." - epreston

"Funny and not just for dads!" - The Booker

Paperback & eBook, 98 pages / www.NorthShorePublishing.com

Made in the USA
Middletown, DE
10 November 2015